*Straight from the Heart*

# Straight from the Heart

## Gender, Intimacy, and the
## Cultural Production of *Shōjo Manga*

**Jennifer S. Prough**

University of Hawai'i Press
Honolulu

**Library of Congress Cataloging-in-Publication Data**

Prough, Jennifer Sally, 1968–
Straight from the heart : gender, intimacy, and the cultural
production of shojo manga / Jennifer Prough.
    p. cm.
Includes bibliographical references and index.
ISBN 978-0-8248-3457-9 (hardcover : alk. paper) —
ISBN 978-0-8248-3528-6 (softcover : alk. paper)
    1. Comic books, strips, etc.—Japan—History and criticism.
2. Girls—Books and reading—Japan—History—20th century.
3. Girls in popular culture—Japan—History—20th century.
4. Women in the book industries and trade—Japan—History—
20th century.  I. Title.
PN6790.J3P76 2011
741.5'95209—dc22

                                        2010022658

Designed by Josie Herr

Printed by Integrated Book Technology, Inc.

*I dedicate this book to my parents:*

Betty and Russell Prough
&
Pat and George Richter

# CONTENTS

# ACKNOWLEDGMENTS

People to whom I owe debts of gratitude are too numerous to count. First and foremost, thanks to Anne Allison, Kären Wigen, Leo Ching, Charlie Piot, Ralph Litzinger, and Orin Starn at Duke for their guidance, patience, and support throughout this arduous process. Thanks to the Monbu-kagakusho for the financial support for a year and a half in Japan, and to the Asian Pacific Studies Center and the Center for International Studies at Duke, Northeast Asia Council, and Valparaiso University for a variety of smaller grants that funded various aspects of this research. I am also grateful to Yoshimi Shunya for space to affiliate at Tokyo University and the intellectual stimulation of his seminar. I thank Azami Toshio, Miyamoto Hirohito, Natsume Fusanosuke, Maruyama Akira, Yamamoto Junya, and everyone in the Mangashi Kenkyūkai for invaluable conversation and assistance in understanding the world of manga studies. I thank all those who gave me their time and insight at Shogakukan, Shueisha, Hakusensha, and Kodansha. Finally, I am grateful for all my colleagues, former and current, at Valparaiso University (and in Christ College in particular) for their support and guidance in the process of publishing this research.

I thank Sophie Houdart, Kris Chapman, Shimizu Katsunobu, Yoshida Kyoko, and Iijima Eriko in particular for their friendship, enthusiasm, and inspiration throughout my fieldwork. I am indebted to Katherine Lambert Pennington, Melissa Checker, and Noell Wilson for reading and helping shape the earliest drafts of this manuscript. At Valparaiso University, research assistants Jenna Throw, Chiaki Ishihara, Jenna Johnson, Brittany Partin, Brittany Byers, and Kaori Naka provided much needed help pulling loose ends together along the way. Those who read and reviewed this manuscript provided invaluable help honing the ideas herein, especially Jan Bardsley and Laura Miller. Thank you. And I thank Pamela Kelley and the folks at the University of Hawai'i Press for their composure and guidance throughout the publishing process, which has been quite a mystery to me.

Eternal thanks to my family on both sides, the Proughs and the Richters, who provided unwavering support and interest in my research and the fruits of my labor. Emmett Aaron Prough Richter was born in the middle of this project. His presence helped keep this all in perspective, and it is impossible to imagine my life without his laughter. At last, Andy, my most ardent supporter, partner, and proofreader who has been a part of this project from the beginning: Thank you.

# CHAPTER ONE

# The Heart of the Matter

Gender, Intimacy, and Consumption in the
Production of *Shōjo Manga*

> When I grew up, in the countryside, there weren't as many
> dramas and things like there are now and manga really was the
> most important thing for the girls in my school; it provided us
> with a *waku waku* [thrilling or exciting] life. We passed manga
> back and forth and talked about it; it was fun and important to
> us, so I really wanted to provide that same kind of *waku waku*
> feeling to others, particularly girls outside of Tokyo.
> —Interview with Sōda Naoko, 2001

On a sunny afternoon in the spring of 2001, in a conference room on an
upper floor of a Tokyo office building, Sōda Naoko and I discussed the
ins and outs of editing *shōjo manga,* from deadline details, to shopping
for survey prizes, to brainstorming with artists on a new story.[1] Much of
the two years that I spent in Tokyo researching the *shōjo manga* industry
was organized around such encounters, across tables scattered with colorful
*shōjo manga* magazines.

*Shōjo manga* is manga for girls. This is apparent through the abundance
of pastel and glitter, hearts and stars, and doe-eyed cuties that populate the
pages of most *shōjo manga* magazines; it also peppered many of my conversations with editors, artists, and scholars about the history, aesthetics, and
production of *shōjo manga* magazines in Japan. In fact, in the manga industry, titles, magazines, and even publishing house divisions are all organized
by gender. Thus, gender is at the heart of *shōjo manga*. Discussions about
the genre overflowed with adjectives describing what girls dream about,
highlighting concepts of emotion, intimacy, and community—*doki doki
mono* (things that make your heart race). Suda Junichiro, a young editor
working his way up the corporate ladder, commented to me, "*Shōjo manga*
is not just entertainment; it is less game, toy, and media mix oriented than
*shōnen manga* [boys' manga]. For girls, *shōjo manga* is not entertainment
and escape, but love and exploring the range of human relationships and

1

emotions." Veteran editor Yamaguchi Akira similarly mused, "They [girls] like to think about people's hearts. Girls that age [fourth through sixth grade] like to read about human relations, boys and girls, and friendship. They are trying to understand their own abilities and gain confidence in relationships. For them we write stories about their hopes and dreams, things that are important to them." *Ningen kankei* (human relations) was one of the key terms editors, artists, and scholars used to describe the themes in *shōjo manga* to me, along with friendship (*yūjō*), love, and romance (*ren'ai*). Following their lead, I use the term *ningen kankei* to frame the notions of interior life, friendship, family relations, and romance that dominate the pages of *shōjo manga*.

This notion of *ningen kankei* brings together two of the defining features of this book—anthropology and *shōjo* sensibilities. Translated as human relations, *ningen kankei* is defined as (1) person-to-person association or interaction within society; (2) relations between individuals including a correspondence of emotions; and (3) the number one workplace complaint (Shinmura 1998). Here we encounter emotion and intimacy in the very definition of human relations, as it is about people relating in groups. As the study of humankind, anthropology is fundamentally concerned with the ways that people relate to each other within society. Thus, in this ethnographic account of the *shōjo manga* industry, I attend to the relations between people, within the workplace itself, within the pages of *shōjo manga* magazines, and within *shōjo manga* stories.

As the epigraph that opens this chapter highlights, I begin with the voices of the creators of *shōjo manga*—editors and artists. Sōda's personal narrative exemplifies the relationships that frame this ethnography of the industry. By focusing on the human relations (*ningen kankei*) at work in the production of manga at multiple levels (text, magazines, personnel, and industry), I examine the concrete ways that *shōjo manga* reflects, refracts, and fabricates constructions of gender, consumption, and intimacy. Through an analysis of the extra-manga content of *shōjo manga* magazines, such as readers' pages and artists' contests, as well as representations of gender and sexuality in *shōjo manga* at the turn of the millennium, I argue that it is precisely through gendered content and narratives of human relations that girls are fashioned into their role as consumers. In fact, in the new millennium the very vision of consuming schoolgirls has become paradigmatic of relations of production in contemporary Japan, beyond the pages of *shōjo manga*. Turning to the site of production, I use the concept of "affective labor" to complicate the binary between producers and consumers inherent in much of media theory. I posit that editors and artists who grew up reading manga approach the products they create, the wider medium, and their readers (both real and imagined) through a more intimate lens, melding conceptions of human relations and labor along gendered lines. This is in part a function of the way that culture industries work in today's media-saturated and media-savvy late capitalism.

The manga culture industry has become the backbone of contemporary popular culture in Japan, supplying stories for television, movies, video games, and even novels, art, and theater. Within this, *shōjo manga* is a subgenre, but one that has been seminal to both manga itself and to girls' culture throughout the postwar era. This book examines the *shōjo manga* industry as a site of cultural storytelling, illuminating the ways that issues of mass media and gender, production, and consumption are entailed in the process of creating *shōjo manga*.

## What Girls Like: The Mediation of *Ningen Kankei*

This ethnography of the *shōjo manga* industry is framed around the notion of "what girls like," a phrase that editors and artists used consistently to discuss what *shōjo manga* is and how it is produced. While it may seem simple on the surface, this notion is the glue that holds fast the structures of economics, creativity, authenticity, and ideology within the *shōjo manga* industry. At the most basic level, editors and artists used "what girls like" to describe *shōjo manga* as a genre—always in relation to *shōnen manga* (boys' comics). Here it is descriptive of content choices reliant on gender stereotypes such as "girls like plots driven by human relations and romance while boys like adventure and violence" or "girls want stories filled with the interiority, intimacy, and emotions while boys want fast-paced action." In statements such as these that filled my interviews, gender was at the fore, articulated as dichotomies of preference.

In the realm of economics, editors used "what girls like" to indicate the often mysterious qualities of what the readers will buy, what stories they like, and what will keep them coming back for more—set up as a kind of bottom line. *Shōjo manga* is, after all, contingent on girls' purchasing power. Accordingly, there are a variety of ways that editors and artists elicit readers' feedback in attempts to determine "what girls like" and thus what will sell. Moreover, editors and artists also used this notion as the qualifier for the turn to all women artists, and young ones in particular, under the rubric that those who are recent graduates from girlhood can better intuit the *fushigi* (mysterious) things that girls like. Finally, this phrase was also lobbied as praise or critique for young editors who "know what girls like" or "don't know the hearts of young girls," as witnessed by the popularity (sales) of the manga they oversee. Thus, editors use the phrase "what girls like" as a descriptor of *shōjo manga* and the essence of both its content and economic variables.

Yet there is something inherently productive, not just descriptive, about this notion of "what girls like." As a major culture industry, the *shōjo manga* business produces stories and images for girls that reverberate throughout *shōjo* culture. Networked with candy companies and toy manufacturers, as well as animation and video game companies, the manga industry underwrites girls' commercial culture. Whether couched as gendered preference, economic necessity, or questions of authenticity, the *shōjo manga* industry takes part in producing "what girls like" in conversation with wider social and economic trends and concerns. This notion underscores the discursive nature of manga production. In the Foucauldian sense, *shōjo manga* can be understood as a system of texts that describe and circumscribe their subjects, girls, but not without the input from girls themselves (Foucault 1978, 1979). As I argue here, editors and artists in the mainstream manga publishing industry do pay attention to what readers want and will buy; in fact, many I spoke with genuinely considered readers to be an important part of the process of making manga, perhaps precisely because schoolgirls loom large as cultural consumers in contemporary Japan. However, through the stylized content of *shōjo manga* stories (focused on love, friendship, and a fun life) as well as the mechanisms that encourage girls to interact with manga magazines (readers' pages, survey prizes, and artists' contests), "what girls like" is itself constructed. Thus, the *shōjo manga* industry is both contingent on and constructive of notions of "what girls like," and the discourse is polyvalent—constructing the content within manga stories and non-manga items in the magazines, while shaping the bottom-line economics of manga publishing, as well as the relationships between readers, artists, and editors.

Finally, *ningen kankei* was always a part of the answer to "what girls like" in my conversations with editors, artists, and scholars. Indeed, human relations make up the bulk of the story content in manga, providing girls with stories about friendship, love, and romance. It also suffuses the non-manga magazine content as girls are encouraged to join the fabricated community of the *shōjo manga* world through contests and readers' pages, and even have the chance to become a manga artist. But *ningen kankei* can also be seen in the relationships between the various constituencies involved in the production of *shōjo manga*—the readers, artists, and editors. Thus, I argue throughout this book that the human relations involved in the production of *shōjo manga* as a corporate enterprise speak to the affective nature of relations of production today.

## Affective Production and Consumption in *Shōjo Manga*

Contemporary theories of capitalism characterize the current age in terms of sentimentality. In terminology such as "care capital" (Scholte 2005), "affective labor" (Hardt and Negri 2000), "affective economies" (Jenkins 2006), and "emotional branding" (Gobé 2001), academics and culture industry gurus alike are linking identity and human relations to the processes of production and consumption. What each of these terms posits is a new relationship between our labor, our consumption, and our selves. This focus on sentiment brings constructions of intimacy and identity firmly into the realm of production and consumption.

These discussions of emotive economies all entail at some level a discussion of media and its role in creating and marketing sentiment. Theorists Michael Hardt and Antonio Negri argue that immaterial labor is becoming the norm, outpacing the more material labor of factory work in contemporary capitalism, and affective labor is one face of immaterial labor. Affective labor, in this instance, involves the creation and management of affect, emotional labor, and interpersonal service work, which is on the rise in the global empire (2000, 289–294; 2004, 107–115). Health care and service positions that require not the physical production of items but the production of such immaterial goods as care and interpersonal relationships typify this domain. In this sense, affective labor is corporeal and emotional in practice, even as its products are both immaterial (social relations and services) and material (domestic chores and even child care).[2] Hardt and Negri write, "What is really essential to it [affective labor] are the creation and manipulation of affect" (2000, 293). The entertainment industry is one main site of the development of affective labor as it creates and manipulates affect across various media. This book on the production of *shōjo manga* provides a case study of affective labor serving to clarify the way that affect is created, manipulated, and experienced by those who produce it.

By focusing on accounts of human relations within the production of *shōjo manga* I aim to demonstrate how that industry creates and manipulates affect through manga content, magazine content, and relations of production. Affective labor is particularly useful in analyzing the relationships between the various people involved in the creation of *shōjo manga*. Over the course of my research, discussions of the turn to all female artists in the early 1970s were couched in affective terms—young women artists are closer to girls themselves. Similarly, younger editors who grew up reading manga expressed a strong investment in the text that they produced, citing the role that manga played in their own lives, as Sōda's comments that begin this chapter attest. In each of these cases, the creation and manipulation of affect is apparent on several levels, in the texts themselves and in the social relationships negotiated around such texts—between readers, artists, and editors. Furthermore, gender is critical to the production of *shōjo manga*. Like the content discussed above, manga production is structured by gender at every turn; the magazines and titles are organized by gender and age, but more important, the *shōjo manga* industry is structured by a gendered division of labor, where the corporate editors are primarily men and the artists are all young women. In my research, gendered notions of consumption, typified by "what girls want" and *ningen kankei,* were at the heart of the matter, shaping not only the stories and magazines, but even the industry personnel and editor/artist relations. Thus, the *shōjo manga* industry proves an apt place to examine the affective labor that occurs in the culture industries more generally, because of the importance of affect in the stories themselves, but also in relations of production, and between production and consumption.

Finally, thinking about affective labor in the production of *shōjo manga* brings us to the relationship between production and consumption more broadly. One of the most significant changes in global capitalism today is an increasing reliance on consumption. Indeed, Hardt and Negri begin their discussion of immaterial labor by outlining a shift in modes of production from a Fordist production model, where production was at the fore, to a Toyota production model, where consumption drives production (2000, 289–290). Similarly, Daniel Miller argues that we are moving from a time when manufacturers made goods and then looked for ever expanding markets to one where retailers, and increasingly consumers themselves, tell manufacturers what to produce (1995, 1997). From discussions of the Wal-Mart effect to theories about fan involvement in media production, scholars and cultural pundits alike are retheorizing the relationship between production and consumption (Fishman 2006; Jenkins 2002, 2006).

If theorists of contemporary capitalism are right that consumers are no longer simply the end point of production, detailed analysis of the ways in which consumption is entailed in and coterminous with production today

becomes a provocative inquiry. This is particularly true of the culture industries where the distinction between producers and consumers is inherently
blurred. Precisely because many who seek jobs in the culture industry grew
up deeply invested in the very media they now create, they are both consumers and producers. Furthermore, many who work in mass media have
a different relationship to the consumers of the texts they produce than
other kinds of production. This is the flipside of the argument of Henry
Jenkins and others, which holds that fan subcultures and Web communities
are active producers of the media that they love; that is, through fan fiction,
cosplay,[3] and the like, devoted consumers become producers (Cassell and
Jenkins 1998; Jenkins 1992, 2006). Most discussions of the relationship
between production and consumption focus on the ways that through this
participatory culture consumers shape processes of production. In this book
I take this argument about consumers as producers into the realm of mainstream production by focusing on the stories of the editors and artists who
create manga to theorize the ways that media producers think about and
engage with consumers.

Within the manga world, the story of a child—boy or girl—who grew
up reading manga, spent his or her spare time and allowance reading and
drawing manga, and made this passion his or her career as an artist is told
time and again. My research in the *shōjo manga* industry examines the ways
in which this narrative, which collapses the distance between production
and consumption, impacted the editors and artists I interviewed and their
understanding of the texts they create. In each of the chapters that follow I
examine a specific site where consumption is entailed in the production of
*shōjo manga*. Here production and consumption themselves are intimate
rather than estranged. Thus, this book interrogates the ways that *ningen
kankei* are mediated in the production of *shōjo manga,* focusing on the
relationships between readers, artists, and editors, as well as between each
of these interlocutors and the texts themselves.

## *Mokuji* (Table of Contents): Defining *Shōjo* and Manga

There is no clearly apt English translation for the term *shōjo*. It is most
frequently used to mean little girl or young girl. But neither captures the
essence of what the category has meant since its emergence in the Meiji era.
Coined originally for unmarried women, *shōjo* signified the stage between
being a girl child and an adult woman. Jennifer Robertson defines *shōjo*
in its origination as a "not-quite-female" female, to highlight the liminal

quality of this social category (1998, 64–65). In line with this betwixt-and-between space, what keeps the *shōjo* from being a woman is her sexual inexperience (Robertson 1998, 65; Treat 1996a, 281). Hence *shōjo* is typically associated with innocence, virginity, and cuteness—girlishness, in essence—even though she may surpass preadolescence.

As with any social category, the parameters and meanings of *shōjo* have changed throughout the century following her birth. In the late nineteenth and early twentieth centuries, at the peak of modernization, the newly prominent middle and upper classes began to send their daughters to school for refinement, rather than employ them in domestic work (Horikiri 1991, 108–110; Takahashi 2008, 115–117; Treat 1996a, 280). Thus, *shōjo* emerged as a social category that defined a stage between female childhood and adulthood. Yet it was not confined to wealthy schoolgirls. The new young working women in the urban service industry, the *moga*, were also referred to as *shōjo* (Robertson 1998, 65). Hence *shōjo* was at some level a tale of female adolescence and pre-womanhood, from puberty to marriage.

As social life changed over the course of the twentieth century, expectations and experiences of girls before marriage changed. By the 1970s and 1980s girls were attending college before marrying. Today, *shōjo* has come to signify grade- and middle-school girls in general usage. In the late 1980s and 1990s women began postponing marriage later and later in order to remain working, causing much ado about plummeting birthrates. As this pattern became more widespread, the term *shōjo* became common in reference to girls up to adolescence, while the term *gyaru* (from the English "gal") became the choice of young women in their teens and early twenties. Thus, as the gap between the end of childhood and marriage has widened, the social stage typically covered by *shōjo* has receded. As a social category *shōjo* has retained its innocent, cute, and presexual connotations, while *gyaru* insinuates street-smart sophistication and sexual experience (Robertson 1998, 65). Here, female sexuality is no longer contained within marriage, if indeed it ever really was.

In the 1990s there was some slippage between the two categories of *shōjo* and *gyaru*, embodied in the term *kogyaru*.[4] *Kogyaru* (*kogal* in English translation), refers to a fashion trend that hit the streets of Tokyo in the 1990s. *Kogyaru* can be seen as a new category of sexualized *shōjo*—retaining little-girl cuteness but with a sexy edge. In some sense *kogyaru* are the liminal, fascinating, and threatening counterparts to the *moga* of the 1920s.

The progression from *shōjo* to *gyaru* to *onna* marks both life-stage progressions in twenty-first-century Japan as well as lifestyle progressions inextricably intertwined with consumption. While women have been a substantial marketing category throughout the twentieth century, with the increasing affluence of the late 1970s and early 1980s the category of "teens" in Japan emerged as a consumer market (White 1993, 1–48). At this time, *shōjo* became a considerable marketing category, and by the late 1980s and 1990s young girls had become the emissaries of rampant consumerism.

In fact, for cultural theorists like Ōtsuka Eiji and Horikiri Naoto, *shōjo* came to signify all of the failings of Japanese culture in the 1980s and 1990s. Ōtsuka writes, "Our existence consists solely of the distribution and consumption of 'things' brought to us from elsewhere, 'things' with which we play. Nor are these 'things' actually tangible, but are instead only signs without any direct utility in life. . . . What name are we to give this life of ours today?—The name is *shōjo*" (1989b, 18; cited in Treat 1995, 282). Furthermore, for Ōtsuka, the turn from a production-based economy in the 1960s to a consumption-based economy by the 1980s is directly related to trends in *shōjo manga* and the character marketing of Sanrio (Hello Kitty et al.). He writes,

> Girls who read *Ribon* [one of the leading *shōjo manga* magazines] learned from the magazine's supplements (*furoku*) that "things" were not only useful, but could be cute as well. Then they went out into consumer society as consumers with the "girls" drawn by Mutsu Ako as role models. In the late 1980s some of them who pursued financial technology careers and remained unmarried were referred to as selfish *Hanako-san*s, but their home remained within the ambiance of *Ribon*. Or, rather, they represent grown-up *Maruko-chan*s who make their way in consumer society, taking their cues from the ambiance in which Mutsu Ako's "girls" exist. (1991a, 100)

Ōtsuka parallels the tenor of manga with that of the age. In the 1970s boys' manga, with its dreams of competition and success, was all the rage and Japan was still highly productive, but in the 1980s girls' manga, with its cute characters, took up the mantle and the streets became filled with consuming *shōjo manga* characters (Ōtsuka 1991a, 96; 1995, 59–66).

Horikiri takes this sentiment a step further when he proclaims that even Japanese men have become *shōjo*, losing their productive capacity along with themselves through rampant consumption. He writes, "The '*shōjo*,' that new human species born of modern commodification, has today commodified everything and everyone" (1991, 115; Robertson 1998, 158; Treat

1993, 363). At some level these male theorists are simply providing more recent articulations of debates about the dangers of female consumers and the feminization of consumption. This is an old story: women are the consummate consumers and as such represent the problems inherent in social change. In this incarnation, the change is from a Fordist production economy to one reliant on consumption and service adorned with the glitz and glamour of luxury goods. What is important about this theorization of the *shōjo* is that in the 1990s she not only represented contemporary social ills and consumption itself (particularly through the *enjo kōsai* and parasite singles phenomena),[5] but she also became the symbol for the feminization and infantilization of postmodern Japan. It is within this context, wherein schoolgirls are billed as the quintessential consumers, if not mascots for new economic models (with all of the attendant hopes and fears), that I situate this study of the *shōjo manga* industry.

## DEFINING MANGA

In Japanese the term "manga" (written 漫画、まんが, or マンガ) refers to comics.[6] Manga literally means "various pictures" and came to be associated with the expressive medium that combines words and images to tell a story—comics—in the early twentieth century (Miyamoto 2001; 2002, 40–43; Shimizu 1991). Manga are marketed to consumers differentiated by gender and age, from early childhood through adulthood. As a mass medium like television or film, manga span the gamut, ranging from historical romance to futuristic fantasy; baseball to mah-jongg; businessmen to superheroes; and erotica to business tips. Manga encompass a wide range of formats, from one-frame political satire, to four-frame humorous comics (not unlike newspaper funnies in the United States), to longer two-to-three page gag manga, to dramatic short stories, and even to multivolume novelized stories. Manga, in Japanese, encompasses all of these forms, yet by far the most common referent for the term "manga" is the latter. These narrative manga are first released as thirty-to-forty-page serialized episodes in monthly or weekly magazines that run three hundred to four hundred pages; if a story proves popular it is then compiled into books. If the popularity of a series continues, it may be re-released in color format or special editions.

My research focused on the monthly *shōjo manga* magazines that are filled with serialized manga. *Shōjo manga* magazines are categorized by age and then genre. The first tier of magazines covered in this study includes *Ribon* (Shueisha), *Nakayoshi* (Kodansha), *Ciao* (Shogakukan), and *Hana to yume* (Hakusensha), which aim at the youngest readers, around fifth year in grade school.[7] Magazines for the next generation, *Margaret* (Shuei-sha), *Shōjo friend* (Kodansha), *Shōjo comic* (Shogakukan), and *Lala* (Haku-sensha), are aimed at junior high girls. Finally, magazines such as *Cookie* (Shueisha), *Dessert* (Kodansha), *Bessatsu shōjo comic* (Shogakukan), and *Shōjo comic cheese!* (Shogakukan) aim at high school or college girls.[8] Throughout this text I use the term "manga magazine" to refer to the maga-zines, "manga" to refer to the overall medium, and "manga books" to refer to the recompiled books.

As one of the main crafters of stories for girls, the *shōjo manga* industry is part and parcel of discussions of *shōjo*. In this realm the term *shōjo* retains more of its original breadth. After all, magazines for girls, from which mod-ern manga magazines evolved, began as the *shōjo* herself was emerging at the turn of the nineteenth century (Yonezawa 1980).[9] *Shōjo manga* as a category refers to manga for girls ranging from grade school through high school. Manga for women, *rediisu manga* (ladies' manga), caters to work-ing women and young mothers and also falls within the purview of the *shōjo manga* division in the publishing houses. In recent years *shōjo manga* publishers have begun to create a liminal genre for older readers—typically college age. Shueisha's *Chorus*, with the tagline of "*Shōjo manga* also grows up," is a pertinent example of this trend, advertising itself as *shōjo manga* for post-*shōjo* readers (Ogi 2003, 792; Spies 2003). *Flowers* (Shogakukan), *Chorus* (Shueisha), *BE LOVE*, and *Kiss* (Kodansha) are all marketed as *shōjo manga* rather than ladies' manga and cater to young women who are still interested in the drama and romance of *shōjo manga* rather than the more realist style of most ladies' manga. Even though the lines are blurry at times, I use the publishers' own categories to shape my analysis. Thus, my research focused on *shōjo manga* as the publishing houses defined it, rang-ing from grade-school magazines to those aimed at high school students, and it is in that sense that I use the term throughout this book.

### *Oshirase no Peiji* (Information Pages): This Industry, This Study

The manga industry is not a specialty industry. Most manga come from a division within a major publishing house.[10] There are approximately 4,200 publishing houses in Japan of various shapes and sizes, most of which are located in Tokyo. However, within this diversity, the top five publishers make up between 40 to 50 percent of the sales of new books (Shuppan Nenpō 2005, Shuppan News Company 1997). In the manga business today there are five main publishing conglomerates—Kodansha, Shogakukan,

Shueisha, Hakusensha, and Akita—all of which are located in Tokyo.[11] Of these, Kodansha, Shogakukan, and Shueisha have been the top publishing houses throughout the postwar era and thus are frequently referred to as the "publishing big three." Furthermore, these three companies produce much of the manga each year (Shuppan Nenpō 2005). Thus, publishing is big business in Japan, and manga is an integral part of the publishing industry.

The first time you enter a Japanese bookstore, there are two things that stand out: the prominence of manga and the significance of publishing houses. In Japanese bookstores the shelf space devoted to manga can rival the literature section in scope, and the aisles of brightly colored books can be overwhelming to navigate for the uninitiated. This is in addition to the plethora of manga specialty shops and *manga kissa* (cafés where you can read manga for an hourly charge), which pepper the streets of cities and towns throughout Japan. The second thing that is striking as you first try to find a book is the fact that books are not organized simply by genre and author name but by genre, *publisher*, and then author. To an American trying to buy her first Japanese novel this is confusing at best. This simple organizational detail, however, speaks volumes about the positioning of the publishing industry in Japan. Publishers are a part of the way books are categorized, and this is especially true of manga. Manga are always organized by gender/age genre (*shōnen, shōjo, seinen*) and then publisher, magazine series, and artist, reflecting levels of loyalty and control cultivated by the publishing industry. It is within this mainstream manga industry that this research is located.

## SHŌJO MANGA FIELDWORK

During two years of fieldwork (2000–2002, 2007) in Tokyo, I conducted research on the production of *shōjo manga* within the top four *shōjo manga* publishing houses—Kodansha, Shogakukan, Shueisha, and Hakusensha. My study culminated in over seventy interviews with a wide range of publishing industry personnel, artists, and scholars.[12] Within this vast mass medium I concentrated my research on the production of manga aimed at girls between the ages of five and eighteen. Each of the four publishing houses I worked with organizes their manga divisions and products into categories by gender and age, providing a relatively stable and easily identifiable genre of girls' manga composed of roughly fifteen monthly and bimonthly magazines on which I focused my research.[13] The structure and parameters of the making of manga texts themselves are the same in all manga divisions, which enables me to draw links beyond the parameters of *shōjo manga*. Moreover, the industry has placed an emphasis on *ningen kankei*, intimacy, and community through its magazines that enhances the aspects of culture industry production I examine in this book.

When we hear the word "manga" most of us think of a pictorial narrative story written by an artist/author, whether of pulp or literary quality. This image obscures the fact that for the last fifty years virtually all manga have originated in a manga magazine. Even the longest-running multivolume manga make their debut in thirty- to forty-page segments in a manga magazine. If the title isn't popular, it is discontinued. If a title proves popular, it can continue for years. In such a case, the thirty- to forty-page serials are regularly compiled into books (*tankōbon*), and these are the novelized manga most of us are familiar with.

When I set out to study the mainstream *shōjo manga* industry I knew that almost all manga began in magazines and that I would be researching in the publishing industry in Tokyo. But what I did not realize at the time was the role that manga magazines, as such, would take in my research. I found that the creation of manga is as much about the production of magazines as the writing of narrative stories. Both in Japan and the United States, research on comic books has treated them primarily like novels, examining content, form, and particular artists. Indeed, manga is a literary genre in Japan and to study it as such is appropriate. However, such an approach leads to assumptions about coherency of narrative and authorial intention that are not necessarily born out in research on the production of manga. In fact, editors have almost equal, and sometimes greater, control over the narrative flow of the text as artists do. Of course, this perspective differs for editors and artists; nonetheless, the arc of the story is affected by the whims of market as well as the rhythms of the magazines' production business. Examining manga from the perspective of its production in the magazine system allows for a discussion of the ways that the push and pull of the manga culture industry itself shapes the form and content of manga as a genre.

Furthermore, manga magazines themselves do not make any money; in fact, most are perpetually in the red. In manga lore, there was a period around 1985 when *Shōnen jump* (the long-standing champion boys' manga magazine) was at its peak, that it actually was in the black, however briefly.[14] Other than this instance, the magazines exist to sample manga and to evaluate what will sell more books, character goods, anime, and so on. Thus, while manga books are still the main product—where the money is made, how artists become famous, and what publishers are known for—their format is determined by the magazine system. Today there are approximately three hundred manga magazines on the shelves, many of which are published by the publishing houses covered in this study (Shuppan Nenpō 2007). Thus, this book focuses on the production of the weekly and monthly magazines in which almost all *shōjo manga* originate as a way to look at how manga are created.

I arrived in Tokyo in the fall of 2000 with hopes of a small job or research position with one of the *shōjo manga* publishing divisions, a plan that didn't come to fruition. In the introduction to her sociological study of men's manga entitled *Adult Manga*, Sharon Kinsella writes of her research experience at Kodansha in the early 1990s: "I do not believe that it would be possible to enter the manga industry and the amateur manga world again today in quite the way that circumstances made it possible to access them in the early 1990s. The culture industries as a whole are notorious for their secretive tendencies. The manga industry has shown the same reticence exhibited by the culture industries in general, about providing interviews and information about its internal affairs" (Kinsella 2000, 15). As I slowly gained introduction to various heads of manga divisions at the main publishers, I was told time and again, "In the early 1990s we would have loved to have an anthropologist study our manga divisions, but now, with economic hard times, we can't afford such luxuries." Whether this was typical Japanese polite refusal or an honest account, it points to the prescience of Kinsella's prediction. However, each of my initial meetings led to a network of interviews throughout a wide variety of levels within the *shōjo manga* division, giving me the scope that grounds this book. While there were a few exceptions and serendipitous end-run encounters, for the most part my interviews were driven by *kone* (connections). In the beginning I was frequently frustrated by misconceptions—of anthropology on the part of my contacts and of *kone* by myself—as I tried to gain access to those at the lowest end of the hierarchy. Most of those I met were inclined to introduce me to the head of the division who is the face of the division to the outside, someone with a wide range of experience in the industry and the division itself—the "Division Chief."[15] Thus, typically my connections started at the top levels and each interview would introduce me to two or three editors further down in rank. At the end of each interview I would explain that my project involved understanding the production of *shōjo manga* from a wide variety of perspectives, and asked if there were other editors and artists that the interviewee could introduce me to. Through this *kone* network I was able to interview several editors from each of the main magazines that this study covers.

Artists, however, were another matter entirely. They are notoriously busy and sheltered from public exposure by the publishing house that employs them. As such, artists were much harder to gain access to, a residual fret of my fieldwork (another point in common with Kinsella's experience) (Kinsella 2000, 15–16). However, after two years of attempts I was able to converse with a small sampling of artists in the final months of my field research. With a few exceptions, these interviews were arranged by an editor and were held in conjunction with a meeting with their editor, making them guarded and within the industrial parameters. While candid interviews and the inside scoop are always preferable, this "canning" (*kanzume*) of artists by the publishing houses they work for is a part of the way *shōjo manga* are made and managed and a part of editor-artist relations. Thus, my own fieldwork frustrations reflect this production system.

## *TAISHŪ BUNKA JINRUIGAKU* (POPULAR CULTURE ANTHROPOLOGY)

As an American cultural anthropologist studying the manga industry, I was both intriguing and confusing to many whom I interviewed. Just a decade or so earlier my interest in manga as a foreigner would have been surprising in and of itself. However, the recent popularity of manga overseas was widely known and discussed in Japan at the turn of the millennium (Amano and Sumiyama 2002, Hosogaya 2002, Iwabuchi 2001, Kakinuma and Kobayashi 2001, Kyotani 1998, Natsume 2001, Okada 1997, Ōtsuka 1998). My status as a foreign researcher affected my research in two readily apparent ways. On the one hand, as more than one Japanese manga scholar was quick to point out, the manga industry is fairly closed, and most researchers are not granted the range of access I was able to gain (even as it felt restricted to me). Furthermore, the publishing houses were just beginning to think about taking Western markets seriously, and some interviews were mutual; I asked about *shōjo manga* and then was asked about the American market, American girls' comics, and whether and what *shōjo manga* might sell.

My role as a cultural anthropologist was more puzzling to many industry folk I encountered. The discipline of anthropology (*jinruigaku*) or cultural anthropology (*bunka jinruigaku*) in Japan has remained relatively traditional, focusing its attention on indigenous peoples near and far. Thus, my presence as an American cultural anthropologist studying the manga industry in Tokyo was a bit of an anomaly. Usually, at the beginning of an interview, after exchanging business cards and during preliminary small talk, the interviewee would express some confusion about what interest the production of manga would have for an anthropologist. I explained that while traditionally anthropologists studied village life in indigenous communities, anthropologists today use these same methodological tools and questions to explore the numerous facets of urban society as well. Usually, the interview simply proceeded from there. However, in a few instances this explanation really struck a chord with the person I was talking with. In one poignant example, while we were discussing changes during his tenure in the industry, Miyamoto Kotarō mused, "In the early postwar years, [Japanese] culture and tradition were transmitted in movies and the traditional arts, but now manga and anime are where the spirit and culture of Japan are reflected the strongest." He paused, then continued, "That is why a cultural anthropologist would be looking at them!" In another case, as Udagawa Toshiya and I were formalizing the parameters of my research and what resources the publishing house would be able to provide me with, he replied, "I understand, as an anthropologist you want to speak to various people throughout the company about what they do, how they think about their work, and how they relate to one another. So you would like me to introduce you to editors from seasoned old [male] editors to young new female editors, so you can understand what it is like to work here, and how the various parts fit in relation to each other—readers, editors, and artists." Thus began my research on the making of *shōjo manga,* shaped as it was by my own positioning as an American anthropologist affiliated with the University of Tokyo, the Heisei recession and publishers' fears of falling profits, the glimmering of hope for a vast foreign market, and the vagaries of "what girls like" in Japan in the new millennium.

### *Dokusha Peiji* (Readers' Pages): Situating This Project

Precisely because of my own interdisciplinary background, this research is informed by and addresses issues of importance to cultural anthropology, Japanese studies, gender studies, and manga studies. Prior to the 1990s both anthropologists and Japanese-studies scholars tended to relegate popular culture to the realm of the modern and/or Western. Frequently denounced or ignored altogether, popular culture was sometimes seen as a threat to traditional objects of study—whether religion, traditional arts, or patterns of exchange; kabuki, Bushido, or woodblock prints. Yet by the 1990s scholarship on popular culture blossomed in both anthropology and Japanese studies as scholars increasingly addressed the importance of mass culture in everyday life, taking popular culture and social engagement with it as a serious realm of inquiry.

In the past decade media anthropology has come into its own as a sub-field of cultural anthropology, as evidenced by the publication of three substantial edited volumes on the field in recent years (Askew and Wilk 2002; Ginsburg, Abu-Lughod, and Larkin 2002; Rothenbuhler and Coman 2005). Mass media is, at once, an industry (as this study highlights) and a collection of texts and commodities that become a part of our everyday lives. As the study of humankind, anthropology seeks a view of the world from the ground up, rooted in the everyday perceptions and meanings of the culture being studied. Thus, anthropological inquiries into popular culture have tended towards discussions of the various uses that media are put to and the meanings people make of media in the context of their everyday lives—from television (Abu-Lughod 2000, 1997; Das 1995; Rofel 1994), to film (Jackson 2001, Mankekar 1999), to art (Marcus and Myers 1995), to advertising (Davila 2002, Miller 1997), and to activism (Ginsburg 1991, 2002; Turner 2002).

Because of a long-standing commitment to study "out of the way" places, work on indigenous and minority populations has shaped the discipline of cultural anthropology in important ways. Yet research on corporate culture has remained a subfield of anthropology. The notion of studying corporate or institutional culture, or "studying up," was first introduced in order to pursue questions of power and institutional structural effects on everyday life (Nader 1972). While several studies have followed this call throughout the years,[16] only a few have turned such research to corporations that emanate outside of the West, many of which focus on Japan (Allison 2006, Hamabata 1990, Ibata-Arens 2005, Kondo 1990, Miller 1997, Roberts 1994). To look at corporate culture in the *shōjo manga* industry is to continue this call to "study up," yet by focusing on the culture industry this corporate study examines the affective labor involved in the creation of stories for girls, tracking human relations along multiple axes.

Within the field of Japanese studies there is a long-standing tradition of theorizing both work and leisure. Throughout Japan's rise to economic prominence in the postwar era scholars have sought to contextualize and characterize working lives in Japan through important studies of corporate life big and small (Allison 1994, Brinton 1993, Gordon 1998, Hamabata 1990, Kawashima 1995, Kinsella 2000, Kondo 1990, Lo 1990, Moeran 1996, Ogasawara 1998, Plath and Coleman 1983, Roberts 1994, Robertson 1998, Vogel 1963). Similarly, scholars have also paid consistent attention to ways that Japanese workers supplement their working lives with leisure activities such as hostess clubs, mass entertainment, sports, theater, and the like (Allison 1994; Linhart and Fruhstuck 1998; Napier 2005, 2007; Plath 1964; Raz 1999; Robertson 1998; Spielvogel 2003).

Again, with the 1990s as a turning point, amid discussions of postmodernity and the rise of cultural studies, Japanese studies began to critically engage with popular culture, as witnessed by the array of edited volumes on Japanese popular culture available (Craig 2000; Lent 1995, 1999; Lunning 2006, 2008; MacWilliams 2008; Martinez 1998; Moeran 2001; Skov and Moeran 1995; Treat 1996b; Tobin 2004). Interdisciplinary in scope, these volumes provide analysis of diverse topics such as shopping, popular fiction, manga, anime, toys, magazines, and music, seeking to understand the complexities of life and leisure in contemporary Japan. In fact, research on Japanese popular culture and mass media has blossomed in fields such as history (Partner 1999, Sato 2003), sociology (Kinsella 2000, White 1993), literature and film (Frederick 2006; Napier 2005; Seaman 2004; Shamoon 2008a, 2008b), and cultural studies (Gottlieb and McLelland 2003; Iwabuchi 2002, 2004b; Miller 2006; Miller and Bardsley 2005; Mitsui and Hosokawa 1998; Moeran 2001; Napier 2005). Here too anthropologists of Japan have contributed to our overall understanding of media experiences. In particular, Moeran (1996) applies classic ethnographic approaches to an advertising agency, illuminating the process of creating desires. Ian Condry (2006), Christine Yano (2002), and Carolyn Stevens (2008) each discuss the production and consumption of popular music in contemporary Japan. Jennifer Robertson's work on Takarazuka (1998) and Bill Kelly's edited volume (2004) both address the realm of fandom as acts of both production and defiance. Anne Allison (2006, 1996) and Susan Napier's research on manga, anime, and children's toys (2005) address issues of production and consumption in contemporary popular media. Finally, Sharon Kinsella's study (2000) of the men's manga industry based on fieldwork at Kodansha in the early 1990s weaves together the story of postwar manga's ascendancy as a mass medium. By focusing on the production of shōjo manga, this book joins scholarly conversations about culture industries as particular nodes that integrate profit and play, work and leisure through the products they create.

## GENDER STUDIES

This research also adds to discussions of the relationship between girls and popular culture that makes up a major theme in gender studies, especially within the emerging subfield of girls' studies. Focusing on girls' exposure to and engagement with media from Barbie to video games, these scholars discuss the ways that girls are shaped by popular culture and the ways that they actively craft their own uses and meanings from mass media (Cassell and Jenkins 1998, Driscoll 2002, Douglas 1994, Gray 1992, Mazzarella and Pecora 1999, Nash 2006, Rand 1995). Research on magazines, a main component of girls' media, has primarily analyzed the construction of girlhood through fashion magazines as well as girls' own understandings of these magazines (Currie 1999, Driscoll 2002, McRobbie 1991, Pinsent and Knight 1998). In particular, girls' magazines blur the lines between entertainment, information, and advertisement as product placement frequently dovetails with informational articles, all the while providing consumer entertainment (Currie 1999). Manga magazines are both similar to and different from fashion magazines in Japan. While manga magazines do not directly sell fashion, through ads and information the characters and stories therein are all modeling lifestyles for contemporary *shōjo*.

Girls' studies is likewise a burgeoning field within Japanese studies as well. Within research on gender in Japan, several scholars have laid the groundwork for an analysis of contemporary *shōjo manga,* through both historical and contemporary analyses of Japanese women's magazines (Frederick 2006, Miller 2006, Miller and Bardsley 2005, Sato 2003, Skov and Moeran 1995). Building from these literary analyses of girls and magazines in Japan, this study tracks gender relations in *shōjo manga* at multiple levels. Manga and magazines for girls are gendered in content that is both shaped around and helps shape notions of "what girls want," issues that will be particularly salient in chapters 3 and 5; but the relations of production in the *shōjo manga* industry are also gendered—where almost all editors are men and artists women, an issue I analyze in chapter 4.

## MANGA STUDIES

Given its mass presence and appeal, there has been considerable discussion of manga by both scholars and the intellectual popular media in Japan. Besides the plethora of manga filling Japanese bookstores, there is a wide range of literature on manga, most written from outside academic circles by "free scholars."[17] This group, loosely defined, is perhaps best epitomized by the Nihon Manga Gakkai (Japan Society for Studies in Cartoon and Comics) founded in the summer of 2001. I quote the Gakkai Statement of Purpose, given on July 29, 2001, at length below.

In the Japan of today, manga is not merely a type of entertainment, but a form of communication, a media with a unique style different from language or film that has penetrated into a wide spectrum of society. Through the influence of such phenomenon as the rapidly growing popularity of its export overseas, awareness of the cultural and social importance of manga has only recently at last begun rising to higher levels. . . . What has manga meant to us in the past, what is it to us now, what will it become in the future? The goal [of the Japan Society for Studies in Cartoon and Comics] is to create a forum for people who have posed this question to themselves that they might enrich their ways of thinking through the mutual sharing of ideas. Receiving the participation of numerous persons with connections to manga, or to affairs related to manga, we would like to undertake this project, which is also an experimental attempt to redefine the very nature of academism as well. (Nihon Manga Gakkai 2001).[18]

The establishment of the Gakkai is prescient in that it brings together free scholars, journalists, academics, and a few ambitious industry personnel (artists and publishers) to carve out a discipline of "manga studies." This speaks both to the growth in the quantity and quality of research on manga in recent decades and to the prominence that manga has acquired as a part of the landscape of postwar Japan.

The body of manga scholarship that the Nihon Manga Gakkai helps to solidify falls primarily into three categories: *hyōron* (criticism), *rekishi* (history), and *shakaigaku* (sociology). There are several important English-language overviews of manga scholarship, most notably "A Guide to Books on Japanese Manga," which was produced in part by the Manga Gakkai and provides brief reviews of important manga scholarship in both Japanese and English (Hosogaya 2002). Similarly, Sharon Kinsella (2000, 97–101) and Jaqueline Berndt (2008) have succinctly depicted this body of scholarship. Thus, my focus here will be on the segments of manga scholarship that my own research directly speaks to: social analysis and gender.

There has long been a strain of manga scholarship in Japan that addresses manga from a sociological perspective. Much of this literature chronicles the effects, either deleterious or beneficial, of manga on Japanese society more generally (Matsuzawa 1979; Miyadai, Ishihara, and Ōtsuka 1993; Miyadai 1994; Miyahara and Ogino 2001; Okada 1997; Ōtsuka 1995, 1989b, 1991b, 1994). Ōtsuka Eiji, Miyadai Shinji, and Okada Toshio are particularly well known for their ethnographic research on manga and manga subcultures.

Not surprisingly, literature on *shōjo manga* comprises a subset of the works on manga studies. Much of the literature on *shōjo manga* has focused on the "golden years" of the 1970s and on the group of young women artists that debuted at the time (Takahashi and Yonezawa 1991a, 1991b; Yamada 1998; Yonezawa 1980). Sociological accounts of *shōjo manga* with a distinct gender focus make up much of the rest of the literature (Eiri 1994; Miyadai, Ishihara, and Ōtsuka 1993; Nanba 2001; Nimiya 1997; Yokomori 1999). By far the most prominent name in the study of *shōjo manga* is Fujimoto Yukari, whose work utilizes a personal feminist perspective to chart the changes in themes in *shōjo manga* throughout the postwar era within the context of women's roles in society more generally (1998, 2000). This book adds to this focus on sociological questions in *shōjo manga* by providing an analysis of cultural production and gender relations from inside the Japanese culture industry.

In the English publishing world, the categories of academic and popular are more clearly divided. Yet due to manga's recent global popularity, both realms have increased exponentially in that past decade. In the realm of popular accounts, most focus on what manga is and its history (Amano 2004; Gravett 2004; Lehmann 2005; Patten 2004; Schodt 1983, 1996). A review of academic writing on manga in English shows that scholars tend to highlight aspects that are different from Western comic traditions, namely women's comics and/or adult comics. Following wider social concerns, feminists have been particularly concerned with the representation of girls and women in Japanese manga. These texts outline the general parameters of *shōjo manga* as a genre (Ito 2003, Takahashi 2008, Toku 2008, Tsurumi 1997) or analyze the gendered social relations in Japanese manga through textual analysis (Behr 2003, Grigsby 1999, Ledden and Ledden 1987, Matsui 1993, Napier 1998).

Similarly, academic research on manga outside of Japan has more often than not focused on adult content, and sex in particular (Allison 1996; Buckley 1991; Ito 2002; Jones 2002, 2004; Ogi 2003; Orbaugh 2003a; Shamoon 2004; Shigematsu 1999; Shiokawa 1999; Spies 2003; Thorn 2004; Welker 2006). These analyses of the representation of sex in manga are split between a focus on manga for men and manga for women; that is, feminist analyses of sex in manga are not relegated only to pornography in men's manga, but have also focused on representations of sex in ladies' manga. In addition, much of the current research on *shōjo manga* published in English has focused on the *shōnen ai* (boys' love) subgenre and its contemporary counterpart, *yaoi* (Buckley 1991; Matsui 1993; McLelland 2000; Mizoguchi 2003; Nagaike 2003; Shamoon 2008a, 2008b; Shigematsu 1999; Thorn

2004; Welker 2006). My research at the site of *shōjo manga* production fits firmly within these collegial concerns, but my focus on the mainstream *shōjo manga* industry shifts to a discussion of everyday fare rather than focusing on the particular subgenres of the media.

Thus, in conversation with media anthropology, Japanese studies, gender studies, and manga studies, my research interrogates issues of gender, production and consumption, intimacy and human relations in the *shōjo manga* industry from within the publishing houses and the pages of manga magazines.

## *Tsuzuku* (To Be Continued) . . . : The Chapters That Follow

*Shōjo manga* is about *ningen kankei* (human relations), and that is what this book is also about. By focusing on the human relations involved in the production of manga at multiple levels (text, magazines, personnel, and industry), each of the following chapters weaves together issues of production and consumption, human relations, gender, and intimacy within the *shōjo manga* world.

Situating the *shōjo manga* industry firmly within the context of the publishing industry in postwar Japan, chapter 2 traces the history of the genre, outlining major shifts in format, industry, and content. Synthesizing much of the research in Japan on the history of manga, this chapter places the development of *shōjo manga* in the postwar era in the context of economic and social shifts. While grounding the ethnographic chapters firmly within postwar social history, chapter 2 pays particular attention to the ways that the manga publishing industry developed in relation to the proliferation of the mass media (publishing boom, magazines, television, and new media). The second half of the chapter outlines the history of the postwar development of *shōjo manga,* focusing on thematic trends and aesthetic stylings that not only characterize the genre but have come to influence other types of manga and girls' media more generally.

In order to capture and retain readers loyal to the magazine and its sibling publications, *shōjo manga* magazines are more than a collection of manga episodes. Chapter 3 delves into the pages of a *shōjo manga* magazine, analyzing the components that surround manga. I argue that in these magazines girls are raised to be both consumers and readers, readers are raised to be artists who will create manga for the next generation of readers, and the construction of community within the pages of the magazines facilitates this process. The use of readers' pages, surveys, contests, and prizes geared towards piquing the interests of readers (and honing an understanding of those interests) generates an atmosphere wherein readers are encouraged to participate in the creation of *shōjo manga* magazines and, by extension, *shōjo manga* itself. The pièce de résistance of such community fabrication is the Manga School system where interested readers have the opportunity to become manga artists. Through a notion of fabricated community, this chapter examines the interchanges between the various actors involved in *shōjo manga* magazines—editors, artists, and readers—culminating in the cultivation of artists from readers.

Stepping back from the in-depth look at *shōjo manga* magazines, chapter 4 examines the human relations involved in the creation of *shōjo manga*. Beginning with the extant history of manga, the chapter focuses on the relationships of editors and artists within the *shōjo manga* industry, paying attention to gender and generation in particular. The first half of the chapter discusses the gendered division of labor within the industry, where editors are primarily older men and artists are young women. The second half looks at the lives and desires of younger editors, examining the ways that they think about their role in the production of *shōjo manga*. Thus, chapter 4 provides a case study of affective labor, arguing that the intersection of gender and generation in the organization of the *shōjo manga* industry is another instance of the convergence of production and consumption.

In Chapter 5 I delve into the pages of *shōjo manga* itself. This chapter analyzes the relationship between *shōjo manga* and representations of girls' sexuality that dominated the national landscape of the 1990s. Through the frame of one *shōjo manga* called "Gals!" I examine the ways that the wider discourses about girls' sexuality reverberated in the *shōjo manga* magazines and how this echo resounded back into girls' culture itself. This chapter explicitly puts the push and pull in notions of "what girls want" in conversation with wider societal trends and anxieties and explores the role that editors see themselves playing in the production of representations of girls' sexuality.

In the epilogue I turn to the international popularity of manga, bringing the issues of gender and intimacy, production and consumption that frame this book out to the global level. Through a discussion of the ways that the *shōjo manga* industry has changed since I conducted my research, embracing new media and foreign markets, I ask, How is *shōjo manga* understood in the global market? And how do global markets affect the relations of production and consumption examined throughout this book? Bringing the book full circle, the final chapter zooms out to examine *shōjo manga* in global context.

With this road map to theory, context, and method laid out, let's turn now to gender, intimacy, and consumption in the production of *shōjo manga*.

# Descent and Alliance in the Shōjo Manga *Family Tree*

## A Postwar History

> Publishers cannot rid the world of evil and wrongdoing, but they can instill healthy values that help steer society in the right direction. We believe the publisher's role is to sow seeds that bear intellectual fruit and enhance the quality of people's lives everywhere.
> —Shogakukan Corporate Philosophy [1]

> After the Pacific War ended, someone who looked at the advertisements which suddenly overflowed throughout the towns would be struck with admiration, saying "The atmosphere which we breathe consists of oxygen, nitrogen, and commercials," but thinking about the situation today I think he would say, "The atmosphere which we breathe consists of oxygen, nitrogen, and manga," would he not?
> —Maruyama Akira, *Tokiwasō jitsuroku*
> (The real story of Tokiwasō), 6

As the two quotes above imply, the publishing industry and the manga industry within it have played a significant role in the shaping of postwar Japan. Indeed, as Shogakukan's corporate philosophy suggests, the media can shape the way that values are understood, and in Japan manga is a primary form of media. For many of the scholars, editors, and artists I spoke with, manga's history was coterminous with postwar history, as Maruyama suggests above. By examining the ways that the development of the *shōjo manga* industry was in conversation with wider economic and cultural trends, this chapter provides a deeper context for the three ethnographic chapters that follow. [2]

Given the popularity of manga internationally in recent years, there are a variety of histories of manga available in English, and I do not wish to duplicate that work. [3] In telling the history of *shōjo manga* this chapter is divided into two parts. In the first half of the chapter I focus on the development of mass media in postwar Japan and manga's role therein, paying particular attention to economic, technological, and cultural transformations. In the second part I focus in on the development of *shōjo manga* style and content in dialogue with shifting notions of gender in the postwar period.[4] I begin with a sketch of the four publishing houses where my research was conducted in order to situate this history firmly within this industry.

## *Oyagaisha* (Parent Company) Origins

In the world of publishing in Japan, Kodansha and Shogakukan are often discussed as rival "families," located across the river from one another in neighboring regions of central Tokyo. Publishing giants in the prewar era, particularly in the children's genre, they and their offspring have all but dominated the postwar manga industry. It is with this notion of family, and kinship in particular, that I frame this history of the *shōjo manga* industry. In fact, there are familial ties between three of the publishers I cover in this book—Shogakukan begat Shueisha and Shueisha begat Hakusensha. Furthermore, editors, artists, and scholars frequently used kinship terminology such as "parent" and "child" companies (*oyagaisha* and *kogaisha*) in discussions about *shōjo manga* production. Finally, manga magazines divided by age are referred to in the industry as sibling magazines, and by the terms "older sister" and "younger sister" magazines (*oneesan* and *imōto zasshi*).

In the context of Japan this application of kinship terminology is not particularly surprising, as kinship is an important framing category overall. The *ie* (household or lineage) system hierarchically links generations together, from long-dead ancestors to future progeny. These extended families typically included a main house lorded over by the eldest son, and branch houses consisted of the remaining sons and their families. Based roughly on the model of nineteenth-century samurai families, the *ie* system tied family and business together. Japanese anthropologist Nakane Chie argues that the *ie* system is organized by relationships of an economic enterprise, rather than one based on intimacy of blood or sexual relations (1970). This model of social structure has been used to represent a wide range of relationships, from those of the emperor and his Japanese subjects to the workings of the business world (Hendry 1987, 22–24).

Likewise, corporate terminology frequently echoes older familial tropes (Hendry 1987, 22–26), as can be seen in the manga industry terminology. Yet in the case of *shōjo manga*, the use of kinship terms lends a tone of familiarity to discussions of industry, production, and consumption. The intimacy of family relationships between parents and their children and between siblings resonates particularly with the human relations represented in *shōjo manga* stories. Furthermore, concepts such as *oneesan* (older sister) and *imōto* (younger sister) magazines are polyvalent. On the one hand, these terms indicate the relationship between magazines within the publishing house family—they are sisters within the parent company, related hierarchically. At the same time, sibling terminology indicates the intended readers of the magazines and their relations to each other. Terms like *oneesan* and *imōto* indicate publishers' hope that older sisters will introduce their younger sisters to its magazines and siblings will grow with them, moving up to the next magazine in the lineup. Thus, kinship terms organize magazines within the industry in a familiar cast, but also organize readers in attempts to keep them from straying to other publishing family magazines.

While this history will focus on the postwar production of *shōjo manga*, I want to outline briefly the emergence of the four publishing houses on which this study focuses—Kodansha, Shogakukan, Shueisha, and Hakusensha.[5] In the early twentieth century, mass consumer society burgeoned in the cities in Japan and mass media flourished. Meanwhile, new railways made it easier for newspapers and magazines to reach the remote countryside. By this time Meiji education reforms had substantially increased literacy rates in several ways: both written and spoken dialects were standardized and the education system itself was codified so that children throughout the land had a set curriculum. Furthermore, the adoption of a colloquial written language through the use of *furigana*[6] to indicate the pronunciation of the kanji (Chinese characters) increased the readability of newspapers, books, and magazines.[7] Directly linking the education system and the magazine industry, the Ministry of Education encouraged the emerging publishing industry to focus on popular education (*taishū kyōiku*) in order to supplement the newly established school system in the early 1920s (Sudō 1999, 66). In this atmosphere of increased interest in reading bolstered by state promotion of the links between publishing and education, the publishing industry exploded onto the scene. Between 1918 and 1932 the number of magazine titles increased from 3,123 to 11,118 (Kasza 1988, 28). And it is in this nascent magazine business that many of today's large publishing houses got their start.

Kodansha and Shogakukan were founded in 1909 and 1922 respectively, in response to the Ministry of Education's focus on popular education. But the question of how to educate *and* entertain was still open to debate (Sudō 1999, 66). Kodansha's focus was on magazines, and it was the

1911 establishment of *Kōdan kurabu* (Story club) that brought it initial success. *Kōdan club* was a monthly children's magazine featuring a collection of traditional tales (*kōdan*). Before entering the publishing world, Kodansha's patriarch, Noma Seiji, worked as an educator in elementary and junior high schools and sought to encourage the growth of moral character from within the pages of his magazines as well. As one of the early boys' division editors recounts, "He [Noma] created *Kōdan club,* keeping in mind the idea of making popular *kōdan* [traditional oral narratives] and *naniwabushi* [heartwarming lyrical poetry from Osaka] into texts which make the virtues that are important to the Japanese easy to understand, while making them fun, interesting, and attainable to ordinary people" (Sudō 1999, 65). Such magazines embodied the integration of moral education and entertainment by retelling folk tales in the new guise of modern, mass-produced entertainment magazines (Katō 1968, 117; Sudō 1999, 72–73).

Kodansha is perhaps best remembered from the prewar era for its seminal children's magazines, *Shōnen kurabu* (Boy's club) and *Shōjo kurabu* (Girl's club), founded in 1914 and 1922 respectively (Takahashi and Akiyama 1986, 78). *Shōnen club* was the bestselling children's magazine in the 1930s, selling 720,000 copies a month during the Taishō and early Shōwa years. These sibling magazines are considered some of the precursors to the contemporary manga magazines, and their influence was strongly felt in the children's magazine genre throughout World War II and the early postwar years. Kodansha remains one of the largest publishing houses in Japan today, and one of the top manga producers in postwar Japan.

Shogakukan likewise focused on children's magazines that were educational and entertaining. Yet unlike Kodansha's more moral and traditional notion of education, Shogakukan's magazines paralleled the modern school system itself. Shogakukan's charter magazines consist of a series of children's educational magazines organized by school year: *Shōgaku 1 nensei* (First-grade student), *Shōgaku 2 nensei* (Second-grade student), all the way through the *Shōgaku 6 nensei* (Sixth-grade student). Still popular today, the *gakunenshi* (school-year magazines) introduce vocabulary and kanji as students learn them in school, but in the context of stories, articles, learning pages, games, and even manga. The number of serious articles and learning pages included in these magazines increases as readers progress in school and move up the magazine ladder. This escalator-style magazine system—with children progressing to the next magazine as seamlessly as they do in school—still dominates much of the children's magazine industry.

While Shogakukan diversified significantly in the century that followed, education with an entertainment angle is still their primary focus. In 1925 Shogakukan established a division devoted to entertainment magazines (supplemental to the educational magazine mentioned above). But a year later the division moved down the street (literally a block north) and Shueisha, a publishing company concentrating on entertainment magazines, was born. Today Shueisha is one of Japan's largest magazine publishers, and children's magazines are where it got its start. With titles along the lines of its parent company, Shueisha established six children's magazines in their first official year of business: *Danshi yōtien* (Kindergarten boys), *Joshi yōtien* (Kindergarten girls), *Shōgaku ninen dansei* (Second-grade boys), *Shōgaku ninen josei* (Second-grade girls), *Shōnendan* (Boys' group), and *Shōkōjo* (Girl citizens). Shueisha remained a relatively small publisher before World War II. However, it established its legacy in the 1960s with the turn to all-manga magazines. Today their sibling magazines *Shōnen jump* (Boys' jump) and *Ribon* (Ribbon) are long-running leaders in the children's manga magazine genre. And it was out of their top tier *shōjo manga* division that the final publishing house I am focusing on emerged—Hakusensha.

A part of the Shogakukan "family," Hakusensha branched out of Shueisha's *shōjo manga* division to become an independent publisher in 1973. Just five months later it released its first *shōjo manga* magazine for grade-school girls entitled *Hana to yume* (Flowers and friends). A year later Hakusensha released its second magazine called *Lala,* aimed at a slightly older audience of middle- to high-school girls. While their products have expanded over the past thirty years, 70 percent of their inventory is still *shōjo manga;* the rest is composed of *shōnen* (boys) *manga* and fashion and movie magazines. Hakusensha has remained significantly smaller than the three publishing houses outlined above, but it is focused almost exclusively on *shōjo manga,* making it an apt publisher to include in this research.

With the prewar origins of the publishing houses this study focuses on as a grounding, I turn to the postwar history of the *shōjo manga* industry. In the section that follows, I focus on the development of the manga industry in relation to technological advances and social concerns in the postwar, as well as the ways that these changes affected the genre of manga magazines.

## Part 1: The Postwar Development of Manga Print Culture

During World War II the paper and material shortage, along with rigid censorship strictures, all but choked the publishers out of existence. Many publishing houses closed and the few that remained had to consolidate their magazines. For example, in 1942 Shogakukan merged all eleven of its children's magazines into one (Shogakukan 2006). By the end of the war, the only remaining girls' magazine was Kodansha's *Shōjo club*. And the July 1945 issue of *Shōnen club*, released only a month before the bombing of Hiroshima, was a scant 32 pages (a fifth of its usual 150 pages) and included only text because one color of ink was all that was available (Schodt 1983, 51).

After the war, the first *Shōjo club* appeared without skipping a beat, a combined issue for August and September of 1945 consisting of thirty-six monochrome pages on recycled paper (Maruyama 2001). For the publishing industry, in some ways the early occupation years were not much different than the war years. Not only did it take time for paper, materials, and human labor to return to ample supply in Tokyo, but the city lay in ruins and much had to be rebuilt. Furthermore, the occupation forces led by General Douglas MacArthur instituted the Civil Censorship Detachment, which rivaled the strictures of the wartime regime. Nevertheless, the print industry was one of the first commercial sectors to recover after the war. Because books and magazines could be started with minimal labor power and materials and could be purchased or rented cheaply, providing light entertainment in the harsh conditions of the early postwar era, publishing companies proliferated. In the first two years of the occupation around four hundred magazines surfaced (in addition to the forty-one that had continued throughout the war), some that were new and some that were prewar titles reestablished (Dower 1999, 182; Shuppan News Company 1997, 4–5). Likewise, in August 1945 there were around three hundred publishing houses in Japan, but by the end of the Allied occupation (1952) there were close to two thousand (Dower 1999, 181; Shuppan News Company 1997, 4).

Children's magazines were a large part of this publishing explosion. A plethora of newly established children's magazines vied for the upper hand in the children's entertainment market. New magazines competed with those from the prewar, oftentimes reissued with a facelift to fit the new times and minimize censorship (Takahashi and Yamamoto 1987, 18–19). For example, in December 1946 Kodansha changed the "club" in *Shōnen club* and *Shōjo club* from the kanji (倶楽部) to katakana (クラブ), the syllabary used for foreign loan words. Like their prewar kin these magazines were *sōgō zasshi* (general magazines) containing a mixture of short stories, serialized illustrated novels, manga, informative articles, and essays, as well as entertainment articles on stars and heroes. In fact, manga made up only around 20 percent of magazine content.

Many consider these early postwar children's magazines to have captured the consciousness of the first postwar generation (Takahashi and Yamamoto 1987). Despite lingering difficulties, there was a sense that the shackles of wartime had been broken and that the new age must be crafted. As manga scholar Yamamoto Akira reminisces, "On August 15th [1945] we children were all bewildered. It was not that we didn't understand 'we lost the war.' But we could not imagine what 'peaceful everyday life, without war' could possibly be like. Back then children in the second year of middle school had been born the year that the Manchurian Incident occurred, Showa 6 [1931]. That is, in 1945 the children in elementary school and junior high had no experience of the days in which peace = no war" (Takahashi and Yamamoto 1987, 4). He goes on to write that while parents and teachers worried about what would happen to these children, from the children's perspective the future was bright. Air raids, work service, and mandatory Young Citizens Association meetings were no more; instead the U.S. Army arrived with jeeps, candy, and gum (Takahashi and Yamamoto 1987, 4–5; Takahashi and Yonezawa 1996a, 4–5). It was the hope and excitement of this genera-tion of children that the newly launched and relaunched magazines sought to capitalize on with their entertaining adventures, dramas, and comedies. Boys played out adventures through the stories and manga of magazines such as *Shōnen club, Shōnen, Shōnen king,* and *Shōnen sekai* (Boys' world). Likewise, girls lived vicariously through the short stories, manga, and movie stars featured in the girls' magazines of the time, such as *Shōjo club, Shōjo, Shōjo no tomo* (Girls' friend), *Shōjo book,* and the like. In the most roman-tic of manga lore this generation would continue to shape manga print cul-ture throughout the postwar era as both consumers and producers.

MEDIA MIX IN THE 1950S

In these early years the genre of manga was being crafted across several media: the general children's magazines (where it was only one component) as well as cheap books for rent and sale. However, by the end of the 1960s manga had become primarily the domain of the mainstream publishing industry. Throughout this era of consolidation, manga itself would not only gain new prominence and visual style, but it also would become a funda-mental foundation of the publishing industry as well.

The end of the occupation years saw the first tier of the age proliferation that would characterize the magazine industry throughout the post-war, adding *oneesan* and *imōto* (older and younger sister) and *oniisan* and *otōto* (older and young brother) magazines to the lineup. Borrowing from Shogakukan's *gakunenshi* segmentation by age, these new magazines added a level of specialization according to children's different interests and abilities to the realm of the general entertainment magazines (Takahashi and Yamamoto 1987, 18–21). But these *sōgō zasshi* were just one way that children read the manga stories they loved.

*Akahon,* literally "red books," in reference to the gaudy red ink that was used on the cover, were cheap manga books that began in the 1930s but flourished in the early postwar period. Produced in Osaka's wholesale toy district, *akahon* were sold in toy and candy stores. They ranged in price from ten to ninety yen, depending on the quality, and thus were within the range of what children could afford (Shimizu 1999, 85; Yonezawa 1980, 16). While *akahon* was essentially a cheap pulp genre, many artists who would become renowned in the ensuing decades first published their works within the pages of these red books, including Tezuka Osamu (Takahashi and Yonezawa 1996a, 9; Yonezawa 1980, 17–18). *Akahon*'s production and sales peaked around 1949, although they could still be found for close to a decade later. As people began to have more money, the glossy, colorful magazines and books had greater appeal (Yonezawa 1980, 18).

By the end of the 1950s *akahon* had all but died out and the artists were absorbed into either the *kashihon* (rental books) or mainstream magazine industry. As the name implies, *kashihon* could be rented from small book rental stalls and shops wherein children could rent a book for ten yen a day. These rental shops cropped up throughout the streets of cities and towns in the 1950s, precursors to the manga cafés (*manga kissaten*) that populate urban streets today. Like *akahon, kashihon* was a popular, cheap entertainment genre that catered primarily to urban youth seeking some relief from the harsh conditions of everyday life. *Kashihon* were roughly 150-page, hardcover books printed on newsprint paper, a step up from *akahon* (Schodt 1983, 66). While *kashihon* consisted of manga, illustrated story books, and magazines, manga made up an increasing percentage of their inventory. Many renowned manga artists, such as Chiba Tetsuya, Mizuki Shigeru, and Shirato Sanpei, got their start pumping out titles for little pay in this burgeoning industry. Yet in the early 1960s the lure of the lucrative mainstream magazines siphoned off many of the best and the brightest of the *kashihon* world, and by 1964 *kashihon* too would disappear (Shimizu 1999, 89; Takahashi and Yamamoto 1987, 82–84).

However, while manga boomed in the 1950s, there were some growing pains, namely the bad-book elimination campaign (*akusho tsuihō*). The rapid proliferation of manga and the emergence of children's consumer culture catalyzed a moral panic surrounding juvenile literature. More of a contagious fervor than a unified movement, the manga world and *akahon* in particular were caught in the middle of a range of attempts to monitor the quality of children's reading materials. The first shots were fired in an April 1949 issue of the *Asahi weekly* that criticized "children's *akahon*" as the worst influence on children (Takahashi and Yamamoto 1987, 21). Manga were banned from school premises, and some groups even staged public book burnings in protest (Maruyama 1999, 101; Sugiyama 1998, 35). Many editors and artists were called in to testify in front of groups with names like Protecting Children (*Kodomo wo Mamoru*), and In Consideration of Children's Culture (*Kodomo no Bunka wo Kanngaeru*), where they were made to account for their actions. The industry and its artists all maintained that while certainly not all manga was artistically sophisticated or educational, it was a wide-ranging medium and should be compared to other such genres, not simply dismissed (Maruyama 1999, 99–100).

In the end the fire died out, but this episode had important implications for the development of manga print culture. On the one hand, it helped consolidate the mainstream industry's position by ensuring the demise of *akahon*, many of whose artists turned eventually to the mainstream publishers. It also encouraged the mainstream industry to be more proactive at policing the boundaries of what was appropriate for children in order to "instill healthy values that help steer society in the right direction," as Shogakukan's corporate philosophy, cited at the beginning of this chapter, states. Thus, the mainstream manga industry took on the mantle of social regulators as they consolidated the manga production industry.

## THE ADVENT OF STORY-MANGA

During this period of growth and consolidation into the massive mainstream industry that dominates manga print culture today, manga as a genre itself began to change. Many herald Tezuka Osamu as the figurehead of manga's early postwar history. Tezuka's public life began just two years after the end of World War II with the publication of *Shintakarajima* (New treasure island), cowritten with Sakai Shichima. *Shintakarajima* was an instant success, quickly becoming a best seller, and sealing Tezuka's success as well (Shimotsuki 1998, 68–74; Takahashi and Yonezawa 1997, 5–6). The book told a tale of grand adventure and employed visual effects never before seen in a manga. In *Shintakarajima* Tezuka introduced cinematic techniques, giving his written text and pictures the speed and flow of film through an elaborate use of sound effects, narrative style, mood cues, and a lavish spread of frames to portray one scene from various perspectives. Finally, Tezuka added his own touch to the characters of his manga, the quintessential big, expressive eyes.[8]

In the early 1950s Tezuka moved to Tokyo in order to began serializing manga for the big-league publishers, starting with his second hit "Junguru taitei" (Jungle emperor) in *Manga shōnen,* and "Atomu taishi" (Ambassador atom)—which would later become "Tetsuwan atomu" (Mighty atom)—in *Shōnen* (Schodt 1983, 63; Maruyama 1999, 90). But Tezuka wrote for both boys' and girls' magazines. His "Ribon no kishi" (Ribbon knight)[9] was serialized in *Shōjo club* from 1953 through 1958 and was also a big success (Maruyama 1999, 12; Takahashi and Yonezawa 1991a, 6). As I will discuss later, "Ribon no kishi" influenced the development of *shōjo manga* as well.

Tezuka's innovations were indeed influential; he is arguably the most famous manga artist in Japan, even posthumously.[10] In fact, he is frequently credited with creating the genre of story-manga, long serialized comics that have been the core of postwar manga. Yet as Jacqueline Berndt persuasively argues, he was not alone (2008, 301–302).[11] Tezuka was just one of a generation of artists who had grown up reading the children's magazines and manga of the 1930s and watching films and were beginning to put them all together and create the genre we know today as story-manga (Shimizu 1999, 66; Ueda 2001).

The narrative style of story-manga took its cues from the longer manga stories that emerged in the 1930s, linking shorter manga formats and the dynamic narrative styles of novels (Schodt 1983, 51; Shimizu 1999, 88). Before story-manga, manga tended to be episodic, with each seven- to ten-page installment forming a complete escapade. Story-manga, in contrast, are serialized narrative manga, some concluding in only a few episodes and others running for ten years and tens of volumes. Influenced by theater, film, and television, story-manga utilize a wide range of visual techniques such as bird's-eye views, close-ups, and long shots, while the frames themselves are more dynamic, freely stretching to suit the need of the scene (Maruyama 1999, 93). Yet story-manga's innovation was more than just in form, but also pervaded its content. No longer was manga solely the domain of comedy and laughter; now a broader range of emotions was beginning to be expressed, and manga could be (and are) romantic, moving, frightening, epic, or historical.[12]

Story-manga is important to this history of *shōjo manga* not simply because it came to dominate the postwar genre, but because it fused narrative techniques of film and novels into a new visual format that could be produced cheaply, read quickly, and discarded easily. Through its blending of visual panache, heartfelt drama, and fast-action pacing, story-manga was the original media mix, and whose narrative style has become the main story weaver of twenty-first-century Japan.

## *BIJUARUKA* (VISUAL RENOVATION) IN THE 1960S

As national recovery became more than a distant dream, the vision of the bright new future came into focus for the growing middle mass and their growing disposable income. According to historian Simon Partner, the advent of television in the late 1950s fueled this dream through depictions of the bright life on screen in your own home (1999, 173). This visual renovation, and indeed televisual technology itself, encouraged several transformations in the print industry, namely an increased focus on visualization through more images, more color, and an acceleration of publication pace. Magazines depicted the bright life through a turn to a more visual style visible in the glossy covers, increasing use of color throughout, as well as increased quantity. Throughout the print media images of this new life came into full color as a *bijuaruka* (visual renovation) ensued.

The visual renovation had resounding effects on the burgeoning manga industry and the genre itself. Within the genre of children's magazines this new visual style prompted larger magazines with colorful, glossy covers that seemed decadent at first. Now in the larger B5 size, there was an increase in overall pages (to between 250 and 350 pages), and in the number of color pages within (Shimizu 1999, 78; Yonezawa 1980, 34–36). New magazines were released at a rapid pace, including Shueisha's *Ribon* and Kodansha's *Nakayoshi* (Best friends), which would compete to produce some of the postwar era's most quintessential *shōjo manga*. A fundamental part of this visual turn was an increase in the amount of manga in the children's general magazines. In addition to more space generally, manga also increasingly included more color pages. Initially, only the first page of the few top stories was in multiple colors, but by the end of the 1950s a few of the lead manga (which rotated position month to month) were printed in colored monotone ink instead of the standard black and white. Thus, in a very practical way, the increase in page numbers and the rising popularity of manga led to a boom for the development of the genre.

Moreover, in response to the draw of television and its weekly schedule, the late 1950s saw the incarnation of weekly magazines across genres from adults to kids and from news to entertainment (Takahashi and Yonezawa 1996b, 4–6). The new weekly format was not simply an effort to sell more manga quantitatively, but was formulated to compete with the weekly serialized television shows. Maruyama considers the turn to a weekly format to be part of the publisher's "television offensive." He writes, "We wondered if it was going to be the fate of the children's magazines to disappear from this world, having been crushed by television. No, it can't be, there must be some way out. All brains were put to use and all ideas considered. One of the answers was the change to weekly magazines. The tempo of life was transformed into weekly units because of television, so the idea was to keep pace with them" (1999, 209). Thus, the weekly magazines were an attempt on the part of publishers to counter the draw that television had on children and to reorganize themselves to fit the new weekly lifestyle timetable spawned by television.

In March 1959 Kodansha launched *Shūkan shōnen magajin* (Weekly *shōnen* magazine) followed just one week later by Shogakukan's *Shūkan shōnen sandee* (Weekly *shōnen* Sunday). These two magazines became the frontrunners of the boys' manga magazine boom, and during their first decade they each sold between 1.5 to 2 million copies a week (Shimizu 1999, 93–95). Girls' weeklies lagged slightly behind. In 1962 Kodansha discontinued its flagship *shōjo manga* magazine, *Shōjo club,* replacing it with a weekly girls' magazine called *Shūkan shōjo furendo* (Weekly *shōjo* friend) (Maruyama 1999, 209). In 1963 Shueisha launched a weekly older-sister magazine for *Ribon, Shūkan Maagaretto* (Weekly Margaret, replacing *Shōjo book*), and Shogakukan followed suit a few years later, introducing the *Shūkan shōjo comikku* (Weekly *shōjo* comic) in 1965. These magazines would soon become stars in the *shōjo manga* magazine galaxy. The weeklies dominated the children's magazine and manga scene throughout the 1960s (Maruyama 1999, 196; Takahashi and Yonezawa 1991a, 8–9; 1991b, 6). The development of weekly magazines proved a successful tactic for the mainstream publishing houses—Kodansha, Shogakukan, and Shueisha— whose weekly magazines solidified their position at the top of the postwar manga market, further consolidating their dominance in the manga publishing world (Takahashi and Yamamoto 1987, 152).

The visual renovation in manga was not only fueled by affluence and changing technology, but also by demographics. The baby-boom generation became the first of the postwar child-consumers, and both general magazines and manga again played a role in this transformation. As several of the editors I interviewed recounted their youth, they commented on the joy of receiving magazines as a gift from their parents. Manga artist Satonaka Machiko recalled her mother's decision to buy her one magazine of her choice each month beginning in her first year of grade school. Relishing the choice, Machiko scoured the colorful covers to find the best one that month (Sugiyama 1998, 28). The poignancy with which this generation recalls receiving magazines from their parents is striking, pointing to the newness of such a luxury, which these magazines symbolized at the time. Moreover, magazines were among the first items, along with candy, that children purchased with their own pocket money (Maruyama 1986, 2001). Frequently, these magazines were their first entry into consumer life. From this era on, manga would take an increasingly active role in this process, as I discuss in chapter 3.

## MANGA SCHOOL SYSTEM

The *bijuaruka* quickened the pace of manga in two major ways: through the increase in manga content in the children's magazines and through the acceleration of weekly production. The attendant boost in the manga production rate was nearly fourfold, putting extra pressure on artists to work virtually nonstop. In tales of this time, one of the main jobs of an editor was to keep tabs on the artists to make sure they met their deadlines. Maruyama recalls meeting Tezuka in 1954 when he was assigned "Tezuka duty" (*Tezukaban*) for *Shōjo club:* that day he camped out in Tezuka's apartment with editors from several other magazines all pushing Tezuka to finish their stories (Maruyama 1999, 10–20). As this story attests, competition between the various publishing houses heated up in the race for more artists, new and entertaining manga, and greater sales. Consequently, from the early 1960s on, a system of exclusive contracts was established, guaranteeing that an artist would work with only one publisher for the duration of the contract (Maruyama 1999, 196). Clearly a positive turn for the publishing industry itself, this was a double-edged sword for the artists. They now had a level of job security and a more secure rate of pay, but they also lost a large measure of control and independence (Maruyama 1999, 96). At the same time, manga artists began to gain more credit for their work, their names were now prominently displayed, and artist name recognition became as much of a selling point as the colorful pages themselves, at least for the top tier (Maruyama 1999, 91).

With the speed up to weekly cycles, the children's magazines were in such dire need of new artists that they created a new method of finding them—the Manga School system. *Manga shōnen* was the first magazine to solicit and publish reader contributions of manga (Maruyama 1999, 91–92; Schodt 1983, 66–67).[13] But Kodansha took these contribution pages a step further in the winter of 1964, launching the Kodansha Shōnen Shōjo Shinjin Manga Shō (Kodansha Boys and Girls Newcomer Manga Award). The following spring it was announced that Satonaka Machiko had won the first Kodansha Boys and Girls Newcomer Manga Award at the age of sixteen, and her story, "Pia no shōzō" (A portrait of Pia) ran in the February and March issues of *Shōjo friend* (1965).[14] By the end of the 1960s all of the major children's magazines carried these contests, which, by then, included prize money and the chance to be published for the top winners. Under various names such as Manga Gakuen (Manga Campus) or Manga Sukūru (Manga School), this system is the primary way that new artists are found today, particularly in the *shōjo* divisions. The development of the Manga School system is particularly important to the *shōjo manga* world because it creates a production/consumption feedback loop wherein artists are culled from the readers (see chapter 3). Thus, through the development of the Manga School system, by the early 1970s most of the artists writing for *shōjo manga* were women, a point I will return to shortly.

In the end, the visual renovation wrought by competition from the new media of the time, television, served to energize the manga industry. The quickened pace of the children's magazines along with glossy covers and more colorful pages highlighted the vibrant drama of manga stories. Accordingly, the weekly magazines increased the percentage of manga stories in their pages, which enhanced the pace of production and even the stories themselves. Additionally, the weekly format allowed for the further development of serialized manga. Now you could find out what was happening to your favorite characters even faster, fueling the appeal of manga stories. This increase in both the pace and volume of production required a dramatic increase in manga artists, prompting the creation of the Manga School system. Quickly almost all *shōjo manga* artists were found through the magazines themselves, further consolidating the position of the mainstream manga industry.

## ALL MANGA ALL THE TIME: THE 1970S AND 1980S

By the end of the 1960s the big publishing houses had won out consolidating their markets and methods. In fact, they would dominate the children's entertainment market until video games and cell phones began to take hold in the 1990s. Furthermore, in the 1970s a new generation of artists who had grown up reading postwar manga wowed audiences, both new and old, with their inspirational stories. In the 1970s and 1980s manga soared to new heights of circulation and saturation, culminating in the turn to all-manga magazine formats.

In 1968 Shueisha released a new boys' magazine called *Shūkan shōnen jump* (Weekly *shōnen* jump). *Shōnen jump* was created in order to compete with the weekly boy's magazines *Shūkan shōnen Sunday* (Shogakukan) and *Shūkan shōnen magazine* (Kodansha), which first appeared a decade earlier. But *Shōnen jump* had a hook—it was all manga—and it was an immediate success. Its popularity is attributed to its all-manga format, a focus on new artists, and a three-word theme fitting of the era—friendship, hard work, and success (Nagatani 1995, 44–45), all of which would come to character-ize mainstream manga.

By mid-decade many of the children's general magazines had turned to the new all-manga format. No longer were short stories or articles about sports or pop idols included.[15] Even in their new all-manga format these magazines averaged 250 pages and were released weekly or monthly, which still holds true today. Children's general magazines are still popular, but the main titles I have been outlining switched to all-manga formats. Accord-ingly, a range of new all-manga *shōjo* magazines were released, including Shogakukan's *Ciao* and *Bessatsu shōjo comikku* (Special edition *shōjo* comic), and Shueisha's *Bu-ke* (Bouquet). Not only were manga popular, thus sustaining the switch to all-manga magazines, but the change itself was further indication of manga's popularity and presence. In this era manga became the main story weavers, creating stories in text and image that would nourish other forms of mass media, anime, television dramas, movies, video games, and the like. In the words of manga editor and scholar Yamamoto Junya, "By the early 1980s manga had become a part of Japanese culture with its own set of representations, criticism, and was a standard part of popular culture." Thus, this change in format and focus signals the role that manga had within the large publishing houses, as well as more broadly throughout Japanese society.

The 1980s started with a global recession that followed the oil crises of the 1970s. However, the publishing industry was hit later than other high-end production industries, heralding proclamations that "the publish-ing industry is strong even in recession," a trend that would be repeated in the 1990s. By 1976 the jinx of this initial arrogance hit, and the late 1970s and early 1980s saw a publishing recession (Shuppan News Company 1997, 67–69). In order to ward off a potential downturn, the manga industry began to tailor individual magazines to particular groups of readers' tastes (Takahashi and Yonezawa 1991b, 112). Rather than searching for megahits with wide appeal, companies looked to more specialized markets, or "micro-masses," using the notion of individualization and choice in their marketing campaigns (Ivy 1993, 254). Along with their flagship magazines, discussed above, the main manga publishers added a range of specialty magazines to their lineup to cater to a wider range of interests such as horror, mystery, love story, historical fiction, fantasy magazines, and the like (Takahashi and Yonezawa 1991b, 112). In these ways the mainstream publishers sought to widen their readership by creating niche markets of readers to satisfy with specifically focused magazines. While diversification and specialization occurred throughout the manga world, perhaps the biggest change in the manga market in the 1980s was the addition and solidification of adult manga. During this period, as the industry began to acknowledge that the original readership base had grown up, manga magazines aimed at adults rapidly expanded. In this era we see the advent of *rediisu komikkusu* (ladies' comics) and a surge in *seinen manga* (young men's manga), as well as manga for older men. In manga for both young men and women, an increase in adult themes, like working in a company as a *sarariiman*[16] or office lady (OL), as well as more explicit depictions of sexuality, made up the difference between these new genres and the existing fare. This is not to suggest that adult titles replaced the standard fair of children's manga, but that adults became a newly evolved audience. In fact, in the next two decades manga for adults would continue to expand the range of what stories can be told in the comic medium.

## "MANGA WILL SAVE US": PUBLISHING IN THE LOST DECADE

The end of the 1980s brought with it the close of several epochs. Emperor Shōwa died on January 7, 1989, at the age of eighty-seven, bringing the Shōwa period to an end. A month later, on February 8, the father of modern manga and anime, Tezuka Osamu, died at the age of sixty. Finally, by the early 1990s it was clear that the economic bubble that had sustained Japanese economic expansion through the 1970s and 1980s had collapsed, leaving Japan in a recession that continues today.

Continuing the mystique and charm that manga had held for the publishing industry throughout the postwar, the visibility and prevalence of manga was often perceived as the factor that held things together and kept the publishing industry not only afloat, but also growing during the early stages of the recession. The post-bubble recession did not fully hit the publishing industry until the mid- to late 1990s, five years after the GNP itself was affected. While both magazines and manga remained in a growth pattern, it was manga that was heralded as the savior of the industry. Until 1995, that is. In 1996, the *Annual Indices of Publishing* declared, "Until recently comics were considered 'a delicious market,' because they were so popular that they sold in spite of themselves. But since the recession has dragged on, readers have begun to purchase only their choice titles and bulk purchases have decreased" (Shuppan Nenpō 1996, 246). As this quote suggests, the recession did have a seemingly inevitable effect on even the behemoth manga industry. In 1995 magazines sales, which make up 86 percent of the manga market, dropped, leading to the first decline in manga sales in decades (-0.5 percent) (Shuppan Nenpō 1996, 245). Tables 2.1 and 2.2 show the fluctuation in manga sales year by year since 1995, highlighting that the publishing industry overall has seen a relatively steady decline since the mid-1990s. However, throughout the recession manga's percentage of total publishing sales has remained steady at 22 percent of sales and 37–39 percent in volume (see table 2.2).

Editors and scholars I spoke with attributed the decrease in manga sales

Table 2.1.   Changes in Manga Sales, 1995–2006 (from Shuppan Nenpō 2007, 217)

| Year | Total sales of manga books (billion yen) | % change | Total sales of manga magazines (billion yen) | % change |
|---|---|---|---|---|
| 1995 | 251 | - 0.5 | 336 | + 1 |
| 1996 | 254 | + 1.1 | 331 | - 1.3 |
| 1997 | 242 | - 4.5 | 328 | - 1.0 |
| 1998 | 247 | + 2.1 | 321 | - 2.2 |
| 1999 | 230 | - 6.9 | 304 | - 5.2 |
| 2000 | 237 | + 3.0 | 286 | - 5.9 |
| 2001 | 248 | + 4.6 | 284 | - 0.8 |
| 2002 | 248 | + 0.1 | 275 | - 3.1 |
| 2003 | 256 | + 2.7 | 261 | - 5.0 |
| 2004 | 250 | - 2.0 | 255 | - 2.4 |
| 2005 | 260 | +4.2 | 242 | -5.0 |
| 2006 | 253 | -2.7 | 227 | -5.9 |

Table 2.2.   Manga Sales as a Percentage of Total Publishing Sales,
1995–2006 (from Shuppan Nenpō 2007, 217, 225)

| Year | Total manga sales (billion yen) | Manga % of total publishing sales (billion yen) | Manga % of total publishing sales volumes |
|------|------|------|------|
| 1995 | 586 | 22.6 | 39.3 |
| 1996 | 585 | 22.0 | 38.5 |
| 1997 | 570 | 21.6 | 36.7 |
| 1998 | 568 | 22.3 | 37.4 |
| 1999 | 534 | 21.8 | 36.8 |
| 2000 | 523 | 21.8 | 37 |
| 2001 | 532 | 22.9 | 38.2 |
| 2002 | 523 | 22.6 | 38.1 |
| 2003 | 516 | 23.3 | 37.8 |
| 2004 | 505 | 22.5 | 37.2 |
| 2005 | 502 | 22.8 | 37.4 |
| 2006 | 481 | 22.4 | 36.7 |

not only to the recession, but also to new media trends. Beginning with the *famicon* (Nintendo Family Computer, marketed internationally as the Nintendo Entertainment System) boom in the mid-1980s, video games have captured some of the manga audience. Until the late 1980s manga still had the edge on games because of their portable format and the propensity for long commutes in urban Japan. However, the invention of handheld games cut into manga's commute status, particularly with *shōnen manga*'s audience. For the most part, *shōjo manga* was not affected by handheld video games, but today cell phones are seen as a major competitor for the its readership. Several editors theorized that communication with friends on cell phones has stolen away many girls who would otherwise have been reading manga. For both boys and girls, access to the Web via cell phones in the new millennium is perceived as another potential cut into the manga market. While there is no real quantifiable proof that new media are the cause of the decline in manga sales, they are primary pastimes for urban youth in Japan today. Thus, new technology has joined manga in the mix of Japanese youth culture.

Finally, it is important to remember that while the manga industry competes with other media such as video games and anime, it also is one of the main sources for stories in these industries. If a manga title proves popular, it is quickly serialized into an anime, its character goods saturate the market, and frequently a feature film and video game are made as well. Publishing houses retain tight control over the character and story rights to their manga, and the media mix that follows in the wake of popular manga is a large part of manga's profit margin. This "image alliance," as Saya Shiraishi has termed this lucrative cross-marketing network, is also a part of manga's relationship to new media (1997, 235), a point to which I will return in the conclusion of this book.

Economics aside, the 1990s began on shaky footing for the manga industry when it was linked to the 1989 conviction of Miyazaki Tsutomu, who was arrested for the mutilation and murder of four young girls. His room was found crammed with manga and anime, sending up red flags for the medium. Both the press and his defense case argued that Miyazaki's complete absorption in the worlds of manga and anime, particularly of the *roricon* (Lolita complex) genre,[17] led to his disconnect from reality (Kinsella 2000, 126–130; Treat 1993, 154–155). In much of the discourse that ensued, the violent and perverse worlds of manga and anime were held responsible for the creation of such a monster. However, like the moral panic of the 1950s, mainstream manga itself emerged relatively unscathed. Instead, the niche market of fan-based amateur manga, anime, video games, and their subcultures, including the Comikket (Comic Market, a biannual amateur marketplace), took the heat (Kinsella 2000, 126–130; Ōtsuka 1989a).

The world of amateur manga, known as *dōjinshi,* started in 1975 with the creation of the Comic Market as a place to foster creative expression (not controlled by the mainstream publishing industry). According to the late Yonezawa Yoshihiro, one of the founders of the Comic Market, it was modeled after the science fiction conventions in the United States in the 1970s as a space to gather, distribute, and discuss amateur manga. With the increasing availability of copy shops in the early 1980s, followed by computer technology in the 1990s, *dōjinshi* circles (groups of artists who publish amateur manga together) and circulation grew wildly. The primary place to get *dōjinshi* is still the conventions, but today it can be purchased on a wide range of Web pages as well as at specialty manga bookshops.

Today most *dōjinshi,* although not all, are parodies of popular mainstream manga titles. Many of these parodies are comical and serve to poke fun at as well as celebrate the heroes of the mainstream manga. In Japan this genre is known as *yaoi,* a compound that stands for *yama nashi, ochi nashi, imi nashi* (no climax, no resolution, no meaning), referring to the fact that the stories do not purport to be full narratives but rather excerpts (Thorn 2004, 171–172; Toku 2008, 28–29). Beginning in the 1980s *yaoi* became synonymous with depictions of homoerotic romances between lead male characters written by amateur women artists (Mizoguchi 2003; Nagaike 2003; Orbaugh 2003b; Toku 2008, 28).[18]

For the most part the mainstream manga industry and the world of *dōjinshi* have remained relatively separate. As several editors I spoke with explained, they ask their artists not to publish *dōjinshi* because the publishing house has no control over the rights, images, or profits. But all admitted that some do publish *dōjinshi*. Daniel H. Pink discusses the relationship between the manga industry and *dōjinshi* from the perspective of comic markets, arguing that publishers don't prosecute copyright infringement on the part of *dōjinshi* circles because interest in parody also fuels commercial manga sales (2007). This was corroborated by the editors I talked to who, rather than looking at it as a creative feeder for manga artists or a terrible misuse of their creative content, mostly ignored *dōjinshi*. Indeed, moving from the freedom of expression of the amateur comic markets, driven by fan desires, to the structure of mainstream publishing would be a difficult transition, since editors have a significant role in the shaping of manga, as I discuss in chapter 4. The most successful link between *dōjinshi* and the mainstream industry is the internationally popular CLAMP, which is a group of five women manga artists who got their start as a *dōjinshi* circle in 1989 and have gained both national and international acclaim. What is most striking about CLAMP is that they are some of the first artists to break down the gender and age barriers found in the manga industry. "Card Captor Sakura" was published in *Nakayoshi* (Kodansha) and was aimed at young girls (although its audience ranged widely), while "X" appeared in *Asuka* (Kadokawa), a fantasy *shōjo manga* for teens, at the same time. A few years later "Chobits" appeared in *Young Magazine* (Kodansha), a young men's manga magazine, and has a pointedly *roricon* theme. Thus, CLAMP are the poster children for the new trends in crossover manga, yet they are still the exception to the rule as most artists, especially for *shōjo manga,* are cultivated from the ranks of readers of mainstream magazines.

With new media and *dōjinshi* receiving a surfeit of attention and the recession holding strong, publishing houses have tried to compete through adding more mixed media content into their magazines. The magazines are still all manga, but the manga within is now tied into other popular culture phenomena like fashion, music, and even video games. For example, during my time in Tokyo, two of the *imōto* (younger sister) manga magazines, *Ciao*

(Shogakukan) and *Nakayoshi* (Kodansha), ran manga based on popular girl bands mini moni and Morning Musume, respectively. Likewise, according to the *Annual Indices of Publishing* reports in 2001, manga and magazines that include *furoku* (goodies tucked into the front page of a manga magazine) such as *keitai* (mobile phone) straps and mouse pads with characters on them were on the rise (Shuppan Nenpō 2001, 224). Thus, links between manga and other popular media were further strengthened in this era as the manga world increasingly felt pressure from new media.[19] In this section I have outlined the history of manga within the mainstream publishing industry in relation to wider trends in mass culture throughout the postwar period. Tracing the development of the mainstream manga publishing industry's role in the creation of manga magazines, I have highlighted the ways that the genre of manga itself developed in form and style through visual renovation and diversification. Thus, the process of media competition and consolidation, renovation, and reformulation has made the manga industry what it is today. I turn now to a more focused account of *shōjo manga*'s own history in order to understand the particulars of girls' manga in postwar Japan, paying attention to gender as a shifting social category.

## Part 2: *Shōjo Manga:* Growing Up in the Postwar Era

In the final section of this chapter I turn directly to *shōjo manga* itself. The aim is not to provide an exhaustive account of the history of *shōjo manga* but rather, as with the above, to point to particularly salient moments in the genre's postwar history, events that shaped the genre in fundamental ways in terms of creation, content, and construction.[20] Here we see the effects of both the industry changes discussed above as well as shifting notions of gender threaded throughout the history of this genre of girls' entertainment.

It was in the 1950s and 1960s that the distinctive genres of *shōjo* and *shōnen manga* really began to take shape, and to some extent we are just now seeing signs of this dichotomy breaking down.[21] Harkening back to their roots in the nexus between educational and entertaining magazines, for many publishers the puzzle of the early postwar era was how to raise a new generation of children. Thus, the early postwar manga characters and stories spoke directly to what ideal characteristics boys and girls should have. This narrative is the flip side of "what girls want," which editors use to characterize manga today. In this period, for girls, the air of equality that followed the equal rights clause in the constitution held great appeal, and the slogan "anything boys can do girls can do as well" was widely popular

(Sugiyama 1998, 19, 31). Manga scholar Yonezawa Yoshihiro sums up this turn: "As suggested by the symbolic phrase, 'in the postwar, women and socks got strong,' the western notion of women's rights ushered in a new image of girls—the '*otenba*' [tomboy]. At the same time both boys and girls required certain 'vitality,' and perhaps the graceful-Japanese-woman type was no longer essential" (1980, 20). *Shōjo manga* artists took this theme of tomboys and promoted it themselves.

Tezuka Osamu's "Ribon no kishi" (1953), discussed above, is considered the first epic adventure for girls. It is set in a mythical country in medieval times and stars an *otenba*. The story starts with a creation myth in which Sapphire (the heroine) is born with both a boy's and a girl's heart. We see in the opening pages that she loves girl things—dresses, dolls, flowers—and feels strongly that she is a girl, but she also loves and excels at swordplay (Tezuka 1953–1956). As both boy and girl, Sapphire was able to do things that proper Japanese girls had not been allowed to do before (like sword fight). This curious and mischievous *otenba* speaks to Yonezawa's speculation that "the graceful-Japanese-woman type was no longer essential in the postwar," but for a girl to fight and travel off on escapades of her own, she had to be part boy. While most artists didn't take it as far as Tezuka did, lead characters like Anmitsu Hime, Fuichin, and even Sazaesan were all girls in stronger roles than had been appropriate before this time.[22] The baby-boom girls embraced the *genki* (vital, fun loving) characters that populated the pages of girls' magazines in both stories and manga (Nakamura and Horie 2001; Takahashi and Yonezawa 1991a, 6). The new, strong, vital, and adventuresome *otenba* helped shape the *shōjo* characters that would continue to entertain readers for the rest of the century.

In this early period almost all of the manga artists were men, and this held true in the *shōjo manga* realm. Many of the men who would become famous artists got their start writing *shōjo manga* in the 1950s and 1960s. As the mainstream manga industry consolidated their hold on manga production, they also augmented the bifurcation of boys' and girls' manga. In particular, the turn to weekly magazines and with it the emergence of the Manga School system changed the shape of the *shōjo manga* industry by cultivating female artists. Prior to the 1960s the few female manga artist pioneers started out as assistants for their manga artist husbands, brothers, or friends. Once they learned the ropes and it became clear that they had interesting ideas, they were allowed to try their hand at writing manga on their own. These women would prove to reinvigorate the industry. Octogenarian Ueda Toshiko recalled her early artist days over tea at the Yayoi

Bijutsukan coffee shop: "Before the war, people thought only men could write manga, but when I started Fuichin [1956] I would get three bags of mail a day, so things changed quickly for women in society in those days" (Ueda 2001). For Ueda the tenor of equality that pervaded the early postwar years made the emergence of female manga artists possible.

Veteran editor Maruyama Akira, who worked with Ueda and other now-famous artists in the early postwar years, recalled this time as well. "At first only men drew manga. But when women artists started, you know Ueda Toshiko, Hasegawa Machiko, Maki Miyako, and the like, it was clear right away that girls were really drawn to the manga of women writers. Looking at the work I couldn't tell how it was different, but something was transmitted. By the time I left [early 1960s] most of the male authors were doing boys' stuff and almost all artists for *shōjo manga* were women. That's still true today." Likewise, Manga artist Takemiya Keiko attributes her early success to the fact that she was a woman and close to the readers' age (2002, 126). This notion that women make the best artists of *shōjo manga* is something that infused many of the conversations about manga that I was a part of and/or privy to. It was highlighted time and again in recounting the history of the genre, but more than that, it was assumed in discussions of who artists and editors are. As the quote from Maruyama alludes to, there is a feeling throughout the *shōjo manga* industry that women artists are closer to understanding the hearts and experiences of female readers. After all, who better to know what girls will like than a girl![23] By the early 1970s most of the artists writing for *shōjo manga* were women, a trend that still holds true.

## THE *SHŌJO MANGA* GOLDEN YEARS

The 1970s were the golden years for manga, *shōjo* and *shōnen* alike. However, it was in this period in particular that *shōjo manga* made its mark on the genre as a whole and developed several characteristics that define the genre today. The young artists who were cultivated through the Manga School system are responsible for the expansion and innovations of manga as a genre in this period. The industry itself was expanding, but it was the creativity and the ability to tap into what readers wanted that the new cohort of artists successfully harnessed (Takahashi and Yonezawa 1991b, 6; Yonezawa 1980, 176; 2002).

There was one loosely knit group of new *shōjo manga* artists that has received substantial popular and scholarly attention: the *24 nengumi* (24 cohort), in reference to the year in which they were all born—Shōwa 24

(1949). The *24 nengumi* is generally thought to include Hagio Motō, Take-miya Keiko, Ikeda Riyoko, Ōshima Yumiko, Yamato Waki, Kihara Toshie, and Yamagishi Ryōko.[24] These renowned artists honed the genre through an expansion of content, enrichment of the characters, and renovation of layout. While the advent of story-manga expanded manga stories to a nov-elesque narrative form, the *24 nengumi* added a literary quality of drama to what had been primarily a comedic medium. Their stories embraced wide-ranging humanistic concerns dealing with human relations and historical events, although comic relief still often played a role in the drama. In explor-ing the diversity of human relations, these young artists delved deep into the psyche of their characters, revealing the interior life reflected in the pages of their manga (Shamoon 2008b, 145–146; Takahashi 2008, 130–135).

The settings at this time ranged from historical periods to the future and focused on exotic places from Europe to fantastical settings. Hagio Motō's "Toma no shinzō" (Thomas' heart), Ikeda Riyoko's "Berusaiyu no bara" (The rose of Versailles), and Takemiya Keiko's "Kaze to ki no uta" (Poetry of the wind and trees) are well-cited examples of this moving literary style (Hagio 1972–1974; Ikeda 1972–1973; Takemiya 1976). All three are set in Europe past and present and explore matters of the heart in grand and dramatic style. Indeed, themes of love triangles, unrequited love, tragedy, and comedy have remained a critical component of *shōjo manga,* coming almost to define the genre.

Along with the literary expansion, exotic settings, and esoteric themes, *shōjo manga* also underwent a process of transformation, resulting in a new style of visualization. Rather than the more action/dialogue-based plot construction of the standard *shōnen manga,* these artists began to experi-ment with how to express emotion, inner thoughts and feelings, memories and musings—the stuff of *ningen kankei* (human relations). There were two main ways that these women artists played with methods of visualization based on their focus on interiority: experimenting with the style of char-acters' eyes and the use of frames (Takemiya 2002, 126). Moreover, both of these innovations—big eyes and an unorthodox use of frames—have become icons of Japanese manga internationally.

While large, round eyes were a part of story-manga dating back to Tezu-ka's innovations and the influence of Disney, *shōjo manga* artists at this time intensified the size and potency of eyes. In an iconic medium like manga, the eyes and mouths of characters are the most expressive, and comic artists everywhere have utilized these features to animate their characters. But the artists in the *24 nengumi* enlarged the eyes of their characters even further in order to complement and enhance their focus on human relations and innermost emotions. Indeed, the usefulness of eyes for expression is usually attributed to the fact that they are the window to the soul (Takahashi 2008, 124). As several artists explained to me, the larger the eyes and more various the techniques of drawing them, the wider the range of emotional states they can show, highlighting and utilizing the iconic nature of the comic book style to its utmost. It is not that every *shōjo manga* artist at the time and since has used this highly expressive iconic representation of eyes, but it has become the trademark of the genre.

Similarly, these new artists experimented with the frames that characterize the comic book genre. Rather than the linear march of boxed-in frames that characterizes comic books generally, *shōjo manga* are now renowned for their pastiche of frames. As one veteran editor described this turn to me, "When women increasingly started writing *shōjo manga*, the straight boxes with a lot of white background just didn't work with the heartfelt style of their manga. The flowing montage form felt more natural, and quickly became the norm." Utilizing overlapping and cascading panels, fade-outs, close-ups, and panels that fall off the page edge, the pictures in *shōjo manga* often flow from one to another (see figure 2.1). These artists took Tezuka's initial cinematic innovations a step further by adding interspersed layers and views to his use of close-ups and cutaways organized neatly in rows. As manga scholar Mizuki Takahashi argues, the use of montage frames draws the reader further into the text than traditional comics, taking engagement to a new level (2008, 134). Finally, in order to express inner thoughts and memories along with the main dialogue, different styles of font and text were experimented with, moving beyond word bubbles, to express a wider range of thoughts and feelings. Artists' use of montage in frames and text widened the scope of what manga could portray and is an important legacy of *shōjo manga* in the 1970s.

According to editor turned educator Yamamoto Junya, the novel mode of expression of manga that flourished in the *shōjo manga* of the 1970s was in part in response to the new visual age dominated by television. In both TV and movies you can play with the camera, and manga allows a kind of play with framing, view angle, and overall effect, along with the mixing of words and images that surpass the moving image media. This level of flexibility is a part of what helped keep *shōjo manga* competitive in the televisual age. In these ways the genre of manga itself developed new modes of expression through the experimentation of the *shōjo manga* artists in the 1970s. Importantly, the focus on interiority and montage layout would

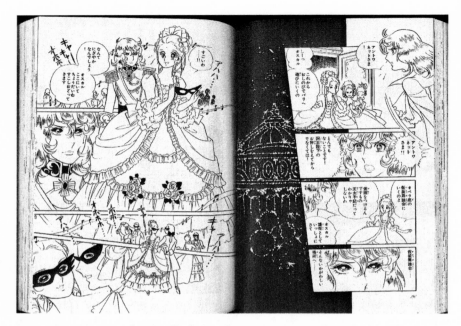

Figure 2.1. Montage frames. Ikeda Riyoko, "Berusaiyu no bara," 190–191. (Berusaiyu no Bara © Ikeda Riyoko Production.) [*Note:* Japanese is read from right to left. Accordingly, manga are read from the upper right to left, top to bottom.]

come to influence other genres of manga; even in the most mainstream *shōnen manga* frames are looser and eyes even sometimes approximate the cuties that suffuse *shōjo manga*.

Finally, it is important to note that the innovations identified here all came from artists working for the three main publishers we have been following throughout this history (Kodansha, Shogakukan, Shueisha), and it was in this era that Hakusensha started as a publishing house devoted to *shōjo manga*. The widespread popularity brought about by the *24 nengumi* and their new style further consolidated the positioning of these publishers in the world of *shōjo manga* for the years to come (Nanba 2001, 197).

## Cute and Sexy Collide

If you chart the trends in settings in *shōjo manga* across the postwar era, an interesting pattern emerges: alternation between the exotic and everyday, the national, international, and intergalactic. In the early postwar years,

up through the golden years and *24 nengumi,* the trend wa
settings, projecting notions of the good life with foreign de
volleyball, European flavor, or futuristic fantasy. As Japan :
from the devastation of World War II, gaining economic stature and regain
ing international respect, fantasies in *shōjo manga* were frequently set in
other, glamorous, and exotic locales. However, in the 1980s, the decade
of "Japan as Number One," as well as the maturing of consumer society,
fantasy returned home.[25] Japan itself became glamorous and even exotic,
as witnessed by the "Discover Japan" and then "Exotic Japan" campaign
sponsored by the Japan National Railway (Ivy 1995, 29–65). This shift
reflects national confidence levels. Just as Japan was gaining international
prominence (these were the bubble years) and the nation was looking both
inward and outward with pride, *shōjo manga* turned from the fantastic,
exotic fairy tales and foreign locales to everyday life in Japan.[26]

Love comedies, particularly those set in a quintessential Japanese high
school called *gakuen rabu-kome* (school love comedies), became a mainstay
of both boys' and girls' manga at this time. These everyday home and school
dramas featuring precocious young innocents have remained a part of the
genre and can still be found in the magazines aimed at the youngest girls
(*Ribon, Nakayoshi, Ciao*). Within the school love comedy genre, a new style
of *shōjo manga* took root, instigated by Shueisha's flagship *shōjo manga*
magazine *Ribon—otomechikku* (*otome* refers to a virgin, maiden, or innocent young girl and *chikku* makes it an adjective). The *otomechikku* stories
are known for their innocent schoolgirl characters, but also for dramatic
themes of human relations, unrequited love, family strength and tensions,
and the trials of friendship. In the words of one editor, "Girls' manga has
remained from the heart." They are quintessential contemporary *monogatari* (narrative stories), *bildungsroman*s about growing up as a preteen or
teenage girl in Japan today.

The *otomechikku* trend coincided with the rise of cute culture in Japan.
We are all familiar with the likes of Hello Kitty and Pikachu, character
goods whose adorability captured the hearts of consumers worldwide.
Manga/anime has played a large role in this trend through the proliferation of cute characters with big eyes that have become icons in their own
right, permeating popular culture and beyond in their ubiquity. While neither Hello Kitty nor Pikachu comes directly from the realm of *shōjo manga,*
the cuteness that they represent is very much in line with *shōjo manga* in
this era. Cultural critic and manga artist Ōtsuka Eiji argues that the link
between *shōjo manga* and the cult of cuteness was directly cultivated by the

girls who grew up reading it in the 1970s and who led the consumer boom as women in the 1980s (1995, passim). Thus, with the *otomechikku* trend the *kawaiisa* (cuteness) that had always permeated *shōjo manga* became fully solidified as a part of girls' culture and extended into popular culture more generally. By the end of the 1980s a wide range of household items and even appliances could be found adorned with cute characters, and major companies from banks to airlines all have adopted a cute mascot to adorn their products and properties. *Kawaiisa* is virtually unavoidable on the streets of urban Japan today and has its roots, at least in part, in *shōjo manga* of the 1980s.

As discussed above, the 1980s was the era when manga was said to have really grown up. That is, the confluence of market diversification along with a generation of people who had grown up reading manga led to the emergence of adult manga, and ladies' manga (*rediisu manga*) in particular. Within the world of *shōjo manga* we have seen the development of *imōto* and *oneesan* magazines catering to different ages of girls, and ladies' manga was another step in the ladder—manga for young women. One factor in the creation of this new genre was artists' interest in moving out of the grade school and middle school genre to write about things closer to their own interests as women (Morizona 2002). The first mainstream generation of women artists who grew up with *shōjo manga* now wanted to write about more adult themes: adult love, women's position in society, marriage, and motherhood (Jones 2002, 6; Takahashi and Yonezawa 1991b, 112). The first ladies' comic magazine to be released was Kodansha's *BE LOVE*, which hit the newsstands in 1980, followed shortly by a host of others. Moving on from school romances, these stories catered to young women working in offices, newlyweds, and new moms in magazines with titles like *Judy* (Shogakukan), *You* (Shueisha), *Young You* (Shueisha), *Office You* (Shueisha), *Feel Young* (Kodansha), and the like. These new themes opened up a whole new market for manga for women (Shuppan News Company 1997, 78–95). These magazines were started within the *shōjo manga* division as a step up the magazine ladder; in some publishing houses they are still under the divisional heading of *shōjo manga* even if the genre is considered separate in theme and content.

The development of ladies' manga in the 1980s received the most popular and critical attention at home and abroad. Ladies' manga can be sexually explicit, and controversial topics like rape and S/M are frequent fare in some genres of ladies' comics. However, as Gretchen Jones points out, currently there are two types of ladies' manga, those produced in the mainstream industry, which make up the bulk of the genre (as I discuss here), and those that focus on sexually explicit short stories (2005, 7).[27] Still, the development of ladies' manga in the 1980s forced the *shōjo manga* industry, where these manga got their start, to think about representations of sex in *shōjo manga.*

In the *shōjo manga* of the 1950s and 1960s sex scenes were not even insinuated, and kissing scenes were rare. Such proclivities were strictly taboo. However, in the 1970s the first kissing scenes and "bed scenes"[28] were gradually introduced in the magazines aimed at older teens. By today's standards these scenes were extremely discreet, not depicting anything explicit. However, these earliest bed scenes, another innovation of the 24 *nengumi,* are striking primarily for two related reasons. Firstly, the protagonists are boys rather than girls, virtually unheard of in *shōjo manga* before this time. Secondly, the love stories that encapsulate these *bishōnen* (beautiful boys) are with other *bishōnen,* not girls.

The *bishōnen* can best be described as beautifully androgynous. James Welker sums him up artfully: "This beautiful boy is visually and psychically neither male nor female; his romantic and erotic interests are directed at other beautiful boys, but his tastes are not exclusively homosexual; he lives and loves outside the heteropatriarchal world inhabited by his readers. He seems a queer character indeed" (Welker 2006, 842). To be sure, it is often hard for the uninitiated to identify these beautiful boys as male characters—their hair is typically long and flowing, their waists narrow, and their eyes big in *shōjo manga* style. In the 1970s stories of the twists and turns of tortured love between beautiful boys—*shōnen ai* (boys' love), as this genre came to be known—became all the rage in *shōjo manga* through the work of the 24 *nengumi.*

As the wealth of analysis of *shōnen ai* attests, many have wondered why the conservative realm of *shōjo manga* came to include this clearly subversive trend. On the one hand, these early *shōnen ai* stories were initially set in otherly places, typically historical Europe, and frequently in a boys' boarding school. Their exotic locale enabled a level of distance from the realities of Japanese girls' lives and thus was not perceived as threatening to the social order of the time (Shamoon 2008a, 6–7). On the other hand, these tales were the first to depict active sexuality in *shōjo manga,* and it was between two boys. As several scholars have pointed out, by crafting homoerotic love stories artists were able to evade the gendered power relations inherent in heterosexual couples (Matsui 1993; McLelland 2000b; Shamoon 2008a, 5–7; Toku 2008, 27). By using male characters (or gender-neutral characters) in these earliest representations of sexuality, the artists were not seen as proscribing sexual activity for their young readers, and yet it is precisely the visual femininity of these beautiful boys that allowed for identification on the part of readers (Fujimoto 1998, 45–62; Welker 2006, 852). Yet no matter who the actors or what the setting, the drama of emotions, attachments, and inner feelings remained the focus in *shōnen ai manga.*[29]

By the 1980s *shōnen ai* had almost entirely moved out of the mainstream manga magazines and into specialty magazines. *June* (established in 1978) is the magazine that is today most associated with *shōnen ai,* and it kept the genre alive throughout the ensuing years. Outside of mainstream publication, the *shōnen ai* genre thrives in *dōjinshi,* discussed above. Even though it is rare to have a *shōnen ai* romance in the mainstream *shōjo manga* magazines today, the *bishōnen* appears from time to time with his long hair, narrow waist, and gentle soul. He has become a *shōjo manga* classic type.

By the time *shōnen ai* moved out of the mainstream magazines, kissing scenes had become commonplace and the act of sex itself had even been shown, although it was still comparatively mild in the mainstream *shōjo manga* magazines. *Shōjo manga* scholar Fujimoto Yukari speculates that the popularity of television love-story dramas (*ren'ai dorama*), which increasingly depicted love scenes at this time, had an influence on the emerging genre of ladies' comics. However, the introduction of sexual content to *shōjo manga* was gradual. According to Fujimoto, from about the mid-1980s the levels of sexual activity in *shōjo manga,* which included A = kissing, B = petting, and C = sex, had all been breached. Beyond the tame bed scenes previously shown, the never before shown "C" was increasingly depicted in *shōjo manga.* "By the 1990s it [sex] was pretty common; a line had been crossed and *shōjo manga*'s virginity had been lost," Fujimoto quipped (2002). What is important here is the way in which the turn to more adult titles and micromarketing in the 1980s did lead to an increase in representations of sexual themes and sex itself in the genre of *shōjo manga,* a point I will return to in chapter 5.

By the turn of the millennium the *shōjo manga* industry sought to compete with new media by further diversifying their line; this time they added another level directly between *shōjo manga* and ladies' comics. In the 1990s publishers found that women were considered a harder market for manga because girls generally move on to fashion-oriented magazines or other women's magazines by the end of high school. In an attempt to keep young women interested in manga the mainstream publishers added a new range of magazines influenced by both *shōjo manga* and by women's magazines, thus focusing on fashion and fun in everyday settings. Aimed at high teens (end of high school and college age), these magazines keep a distinctly *shōjo manga* cute style and focus on dramatic love stories but add in more adult themes, including sexuality. They vary in theme and intensity; Kodansha's *Kiss* (1992), Shueisha's *Chorus* (1994) and *Cookie* (2000), and Shogaku-kan's renewal of *Bessatsu shōjo comic*—now called *Betsucomi* (2002)—all have a strong sense of fashion and a focus on love stories that clearly are in conversation with the trendy dramas that were popular on television in the 1990s as well.[30] However, these stories are still older-sister versions of *shōjo manga,* with love stories at the fore, not entirely unlike that of Harlequin romance novels, a genre that this generation of artists was familiar with (Takahashi and Yonezawa 1991b, 112).

Thus, in the 1980s the world of *shōjo manga* took two major turns, one cute and one sexy. On the one hand, *shōjo manga* had finally grown up with this first postwar generation, resulting in ladies' manga. The new mature themes in manga written by and for women added sexual situations to the dramatic love stories that have always been a part of *shōjo manga*. The sexual content that had been added to mainstream *shōjo manga* in the 1970s moved to specialty magazines (in the case of *shōnen ai*) or ladies' comics. On the other hand, stories within the mainstream *shōjo manga* magazines moved away from the exotic and historical dramatic style of the 1970s and to stories set in everyday Japan. The exotic themes that had exemplified the dramatic stories of the 24 *nengumi* were replaced by saccharine-sweet characters, which were amplified onto the national stage through the profusion of character goods. In the 1990s the two fields of cute and sexy were (re)united in the realm of *otaku* culture and the amateur manga market, a turn that would also reverberate through the mainstream *shōjo manga* world, as I will discuss in chapter 5.

## Conclusion

In this chapter I have traced the relations of descent and alliance in the *shōjo manga* family tree first through an account of the development of the manga magazine industry from children's general magazines through the peak of all manga magazines, and through the content of *shōjo manga* itself. This social history has focused on the ways in which the *shōjo manga* industry developed in relation to the burgeoning mass media industry. Manga has become the main story weaver for Japan, supplying kids and adults with tales that fuel imaginations, filling publishing house (and partners') coffers, and even participating in the construction of postwar history. But this chapter has also trained its eye on the subgenre of *shōjo manga* in particular, laying the groundwork for the three ethnographic chapters that follow. Now we turn to examine the ways that gender, intimacy, and consumption are articulated in the production of *shōjo manga*—the magazines, the industry itself, and *shōjo manga*.

# CHAPTER THREE

# Raising Readers, Rearing Artists

## Fabricating Community in *Shōjo Manga* Magazines

> In [our magazine] there are also what we call "Readers' Pages,"
> lots of them, actually. We aim at creating a magazine that
> readers will participate in. For example, we think about themes
> and fashion trends and what the readers like and dream about.
> We also have an advice column, and a corner to highlight what
> readers are interested in, in their own words. . . . Information
> about manga artists is also really popular. Recently, in this
> magazine we distributed a survey asking our readers what they
> want to be in the future. The number-one answer was a *tarento,*
> or actress. They dream of being actresses. But the number-
> two answer was a manga artist. They are really interested in
> manga artists, what a manga artist's life is like or what kind of
> apartment do they live in, etc.
> —Interview with Saejima Tomomi, April 2002

Amid the stacks of manga (both printed and drafts), character goods, and
the typical hustle and bustle of the manga office in the late afternoon, Saejima Tomomi and I discussed her experiences as an editor at a *shōjo manga*
magazine. Saejima's animated description of the magazine she edits highlights several of the issues I will examine in this chapter: the focus on readers' desires (for stories and goods), the link between readers and artists, and
ultimately the construction of a sense of community through the magazine
pages.

In discussing *shōjo manga* magazines, many of the editors I spoke with
used active verbs to describe the relations between readers and the magazines themselves, particularly *sanka shite kure* (to participate or be involved
in) [1] and *sodateru* (to bring up or to raise). *Sanka shite kure* was used mainly
in reference to the youngest *shōjo manga* magazines, which are created as
a space where girls can actively interact or participate, rather than simply
a text to be read and then discarded. In the case of *sodateru,* the term was
polyvalent: editors used it to refer to the magazines raising readers (creating a market of girls who can and will buy manga) and raising artists from

among its readers, but it was also used to refer to readers training the artists and editors through participation in magazine events and ultimately their purchasing power. *Sanka shite kure* and *sodateru* bespeak a more intimate (even parental, in the latter case) and dynamic relationship between the producers and consumers of *shōjo manga* magazines. And it is the geometry between these two verbs within the context of *shōjo manga* magazines that I interrogate in this chapter.

This chapter is less about *shōjo manga* narratives themselves and more about the format of the manga magazines within which they are situated and showcased. Based on a combination of ethnographic material and content analysis, I focus on several magazine events that editors claim encourage participation in their magazines—*furoku* (supplements), *zenin sābisu* (mail order service), and *ankēto kenshō* (survey prizes), readers' pages, and the Manga School system.[2] As always, selling more manga is the bottom line of production, and these pages contribute directly to sales by encouraging readers to buy their own copies of the magazines. Furthermore, several of these pages involve acquiring consumer items, feeding into the wider culture of character marketing that drives mass media in contemporary Japan. Thus, participation (*sanka shite kure*) here raises (*sodateru*) consumers as well as readers loyal to a particular publishing house brand of *shōjo manga*. But these pages also provide readers with ways to interact with the magazines—sharing their thoughts, experiences, and manga talents with likeminded readers. According to editors, these pages encourage girls to "stay inside" the manga magazine longer, a habit that reverberates in girls' manga reading habits more generally. It is here that readers' feedback and desires are put into conversation with each other and with artists, creating an intimacy between producers and consumers structured by editors. Yet this community is fabricated at least in part to further the overall magazine goals—more sales. Thus, while participation instigates magazine purchases and draws readers into a magazine and hopefully a publishing house's magazine system, boosting the bottom line, it also creates consumers, raises readers, and rears artists.

Many of the features analyzed in this chapter are not particular to manga magazines but rather have roots in the prewar women's and children's magazines and counterparts in contemporary fashion magazines as well.[3] Focusing on these magazine events in the context of manga magazines highlights two important points: on the one hand, the production of manga is the production of manga magazines, a genre that is firmly situated within a wider publishing context, as highlighted in chapter 2, and yet, compared to other women's magazines, manga magazines have comparably little non-manga content, almost all of which comprises features that encourage further participation on the part of the reader. Surprisingly, there are very few ads in most manga magazines and those that are included are for other manga magazines and books produced by the same publishing house, and thus serve to promote manga purchases. The participatory features are similarly linked to manga but also serve to articulate the reader into the dual role of consumer of manga and more, and of producer of manga in highly mediated ways.

In the end, the participatory features threaded throughout *shōjo manga* magazines construct an imagined community. Throughout this chapter I use the term "fabricating community" to highlight the active construction of this tenuous group on the part of magazine editors and the importance that editors placed on this sense of participation. This notion of fabricating communities is reliant on Benedict Anderson's concept of imagined communities. Anderson coined the phrase "imagined communities" to discuss the particulars of the modern nation wherein a national community is imagined as finite by citizens who will never all meet face to face, as sovereign by governments fostering national identities, and as a community through shared culture across great disparities. For Anderson these imagined communities were stimulated, in part, by the advent of mass mediation, particularly newspapers (1983, 6–7). The community fabrication of *shōjo manga* magazines by editors likewise provides a sense of connection and affinity among disparately located girls, and I use the term "fabricating" to capture both the sense of the imaginary and of the materiality of such communities. In fact, the process of fabricating community within the pages of *shōjo manga* magazines is productive of its very participants—consumers, readers, and artists—while at the same time relying on their participation.

## More than Meets the Eye: Inside the *Shōjo Manga* Magazine

To understand the notion of community fabricated within *shōjo manga* magazines, we first need to look closely at the magazines themselves. The manga magazines aimed at the youngest readers, in this case *Ribon* (Shueisha), *Nakayoshi* (Kodansha), *Ciao* (Shogakukan), and *Hana to yume* (Hakusensha), are the flagship magazines for the manga divisions. Even when these *imōto* (younger sister) magazines, as they are called, are not the top sellers they occupy a special place in the magazine hierarchy, for new readers are created primarily through them. *Imōto* magazines are the gateway to *shōjo manga* for the majority of readers, and the welcome they receive is lavish. Significant resources are channeled into these youngest magazines in the hopes that if readers are captured they will stay loyal to the publishing house (in their manga purchases and beyond) as they grow. Many of the elements I analyze in this chapter also appear in the *oneesan* (older sister) magazines and in boys' manga magazines. However, because this sense of participation is most strongly cultivated in the *imōto* (younger sister) *shōjo* magazines, that is where I focus this discussion.

*Ribon, Nakayoshi, Ciao,* and *Hana to yume* are all aimed at grade-school girls.[4] According to editors at each of these magazines, readers range in age, but the biggest share are in fifth grade. Unlike their older sister magazines, these youngest magazines have the task of teaching readers about manga and manga magazines. It is here that publishers reel in readers. As it was explained to me many times, in order to capture the attention of busy young minds these magazines are composed of what is known as "media mix" (or mixed media). Roughly 85 percent of their content is manga, but it is supplemented by a range of games, prizes, information, and "tie-ins" to toys, anime, and video games. As editor Takigawa Masahiro explained it,

> Our magazine is less about selling manga than other manga magazines. We also have the supplements, mail order goods, a model contest, anime links, which all make it a little wider than other manga magazines. For example, [boys' manga magazine title] is all about selling comics—they produce books really quickly and this is key to their mission—but ours is different. Our focus is on more than manga books, which we also produce, but the links to character goods, marketing, and other things are stronger for our magazine.

Saejima made a similar point.

> These magazines are the first manga magazines read by children. Of course, there are picture books and other kinds of books for kids, but this is their first *manga* magazine. They enter here. So there are more than just manga; there are also games, toys, presents, [character] goods, manga, information on popular bands, and the like. Also, since we want everyone to participate in our magazines, we have contests and make pages for and about readers. So there are various things involved in these initial magazines.

As Takigawa and Saejima allude, these magazines are a cross between the genre of children's general magazines and manga magazines, initiating new readers into the world of manga.

It is important to note that the raison d'etre of all manga magazines is to sample manga and to evaluate what will sell more books, character goods, anime, and so on, and the participatory pages help achieve this goal. In order to initially gain new readers the editors at the *imōto* magazines are more proactive about creating TV anime from their popular titles. Typically each of these *imōto* magazines has at least one TV anime running at any given time, and two or three is not uncommon. Discussing a recent hit, Saejima elucidated this process.

> The manga is really good. We [the artist and herself] were happy that we had made such a great manga so we approached an anime company. I never would have thought I would be doing that. So we made the anime and then toys as well. So, of course, we contacted a toy company and a candy company, too. And now we are going to release a game. And after the game we will make a video and then the music that goes with it. So, we don't just make manga, it becomes so much more. That is the kind of work I do.

Alongside anime come contracts with the cornerstone of children's commercial culture, toy manufacturers and then candy manufacturers. The manga magazines and character goods are advertised during the anime, and likewise the toys and anime are promoted in the magazines. Thus, manga is at the heart of the character-marketing system for much of children's media in Japan today.[5] While the manga magazines for older audiences include character goods and some anime links, the media mix is far less pronounced. If they branch out of manga it is more likely to be in the realm of fashion magazines and TV dramas.

The community fabricated through *shōjo manga* magazines is particularly felt in the *imōto* magazines and in the way that gendered "reading cultures" have evolved in postwar Japan. The notion of differential reading cultures came up in many of my conversations, both formal and informal, as people (from editors, to artists, to scholars, to neighbors and acquaintances) sought to explain *shōjo manga* to me. More than commenting on the content of manga itself, many impromptu accounts were gendered and entailed a discussion of how boys and girls read and interact differently with manga magazines. As Nakagawa Jirō, a middle-aged editor for one of the *imōto* magazines, explained, "Girls interact with the magazine more; they read it from cover to cover at this age. So all of the magazine, the readers' pages and other things, need to provide a fun experience for them. Like [video] games for boys, these are group entertainment for girls." Here we glimpse how the various elements of *shōjo manga* magazines are created to provide "a fun experience" and place for girls to interact in order to boost magazine sales and, more importantly, the sales of manga books and character goods.

To understand the participatory features in *shōjo manga* magazines, let's start at the very beginning (or end, in the case of manga magazines)—the table of contents. Figure 3.1 is a sample  from *Ribon* May 2002 (*Ribon* 2002a). On the left, each of the main *rensai manga* (serial manga) that make up the bulk of the magazine's 484 pages is listed, with title, author, page number, and character image. Below the serial manga is a section called "*Sensei kara hitokoto*" (Words from the artists). Each artist has a little rendering of themselves and imparts a tidbit about themselves, like, "Hello. I have been working very hard on my first serial manga!" or "I love sweet potatoes. I want to eat a grilled sweet potato now!" In the upper right corner there is a big layout highlighting a new serial manga called "Puzzle Nine." Below that is a section called the "Frontispiece *kenshō*" (Frontispiece prizes), which lists prize items advertised in the front color pages, along with their corresponding explanation pages found in the back of the magazine. Next is the "*Oshirase*" (Advertisements) section, which lists ads for other manga magazines, manga books, and anime, followed by "*Yomimono*" (Reading materials), which includes readers' pages, the Manga School, and a few other non-manga articles. "*Fanshi gyagu*" (Fancy gags), the next section in this example, lists the short, funny manga (two to four pages each) that are sprinkled throughout the magazine; and the final section lists the supplements that come inserted in the magazine cover. When taken as a whole, the materials that make up these manga magazines delineate a dialogue between the producers and consumers, fabricated by editors through tacking back and forth between manga, readers' interests, and artist information. In the analysis that follows I focus my attention on the main non-manga components of these *imōto* magazines: supplements, mail order goods, survey prizes, readers' pages, and the Manga School, in order to reveal the ways in which participation in the magazines creates consumers, raises readers, and rears artists.

## CREATING CONSUMERS: PRIZES, SUPPLEMENTS, AND CHARACTER GOODS IN *SHŌJO MANGA* MAGAZINES

Analysis of *shōjo manga* may provide a glimpse of the heartfelt desires of young girls, the anxieties of contemporary society, and perhaps even the

Figure 3.1. Table of contents, *Ribon*, May 2002, 484.
(Courtesy of Shueisha)

zeitgeist of the age, but making manga and selling manga magazines is at base a business matter. Nowhere is the linkage between manga as consumables more evident than in the supplements, mail order goods, and survey prizes. In these magazine events, young manga readers are becoming consumers, articulated into the nexus of character marketing and accumulation, as they learn to read and enjoy manga.

**Supplements (*Furoku*)**

The *imōto manga* magazines have long been one of the first things that children buy with their own pocket money and, according to several of the editors I interviewed, supplements are a part of the reason.[6] The English term "supplements" hardly captures the feel of the vibrant clutter of pastel and glittered goodies that are tucked as neatly as possible under the cover of the *imōto* magazines.[7] Typically between seven to ten items adorned in manga characters, ranging from stationery, stickers, and posters to pens, self-assembly cardboard boxes, and even cell phone straps are included in the cellophane supplements packet. Supplements are provided by the publishers packaged in a clear plastic bag and are inserted into the front cover of the manga by store owners who also bind the magazine with twine to prohibit stealing the goodies inside. Figure 3.2 flaunts the supplements that will be available in the next month's issue of *Nakayoshi* (*Nakayoshi* 2002b).

While supplements have an illustrious and competitive history, their function has remained the same: to encourage each child to buy her own copy of the manga magazine. When I asked manga artist Miyazaki Yuri about her first experiences with manga in grade school she explained, "My first was the one I am writing in now. . . . My friend bought it and got great supplements, which I wanted as well. So I bought it. I read some manga, but really I liked the supplements." Yamaguchi Akira, one of the more cut-to-the-chase, businesslike editors I interviewed, laid it out simply: "Supplements are included to deter people from passing the magazines around; this way you want your own. You buy your own magazine because you want the supplements." As Miyazaki and Yamaguchi attest, the supplements encourage children to buy the magazines, from among a plethora of choices, and the hope is that from there they will become interested in manga, leading to further purchases throughout their lives.

The paradox in this discussion is that supplements are no longer a substantial part of boys' manga for this same age group, despite greater sales and competition among publishing houses. Perhaps it is in part the sense of community fabricated through *shōjo manga* magazines that encourages girls to share magazines, necessitating the inclusion of supplements to instigate individual purchases. Likewise, supplements are frequently found in special issues of fashion magazines for girls and women, to encourage the reader to buy a copy and to reward loyal readers. But what is different about *shōjo manga* supplements is the sheer volume (multiple items every month in the case of the youngest magazines) and the creation of a link between manga and girls' consumer culture.

This highlights the secondary function of supplements: in the case of these youngest manga magazines, they are all linked to manga, covered in illustrations of characters from manga currently running in the magazine. While Miyazaki just liked the cute and cool supplements her friend had, editors use them to fuel interest in their popular manga. As one young editor explained it, "The supplements are really to make a manga more popular. Of course, we would like to sell more magazines, but the purpose really is to make a manga title more popular and desirable so that its books will sell.

Figure 3.2. June 2002 *furoku* announcement (partial), *Nakayoshi*, May 2002, 16. (Courtesy of Kodansha)

This is also the purpose of anime and character goods—selling manga. This is where we make money." Thus, the supplements increase manga's popularity, and they are desirable because of the manga's popularity.

Attracting new readers to their magazine and thus their manga lineup is the name of the game for *imōto* magazines, and between them the competition is fierce. Great supplements are one way that magazines from different publishing houses compete with each other for the attentions of these new readers. As the tagline in *Nakayoshi*'s advertisement for the next month's supplements proclaims (figure 3.2), "*Kawaisa Number One!! Chō tsukaeru dai 9 furoku*" (Number one in cuteness!! Big 9 super usable supplements) (Nakayoshi 2002b). During my fieldwork, the dynamics of supplements in the world of *shōjo manga* magazines was in flux. The industry-wide rules governing them, established in the early postwar years, held that they must be constructed of paper, must fit within the cover of the magazine (however awkwardly), must be visible (even if just a corner) from outside the plastic bag that holds them, and, finally, must be the same size as the magazine. Thus, stationery, paper dolls, self-assembly paper boxes, stickers, and the like, have long made up most of the supplements in manga magazines.

However, in 2001 the main publishing houses passed new regulations enabling an expansion in the materials that could be used to create supplements. Starting with the January 2002 issues, supplements included plastic character figurines, pens, mobile phone straps, mirrors, plastic cosmetic cases, and bags of all sorts, alongside the more traditional stationery and stickers. As it was explained to me, the publishing houses decided that plastic, metal, and other materials should be allowed for use in supplements in order to reinvigorate the industry, driven by the fact that girls' attentions are increasingly divided by new media and technology and that plastic items can be made so cheaply in China today. By stepping up the range of supplements, publishers hope to be able to better compete for young girls' loyalties in today's plastic-saturated kids' consumer market. Particularly in the first year, there was a *furoku sensō* (supplement war) as magazines filled their supplement sets with every imaginable thing in an effort to outdo each other and sell more magazines. And their sales did, indeed, pick up.

Girls' consumer culture is fraught with little items adorned in cute characters, epitomized by Hello Kitty. And in the manga world, supplements represent the link between manga as popular culture and manga as consumer goods. Ōtsuka Eiji argues that the *shōjo manga* supplement system blossomed in the late 1970s alongside the creation of Hello Kitty and her friends, feeding the development of Japanese consumer culture with young women consumers at the helm (Ōtsuka 1991a, passim). Still today, not only are the manga and manga magazines themselves for sale, but in an effort to entice more readers they provide more tangible plastic consumables in the form of supplements. Girls from this young age are becoming consumers both through purchasing the magazines and later manga books, and through the desire for character goods, even if, and precisely because, they are identical to those their friends have. Here girls' consumer desires are extended beyond the pages of manga into the realm of character goods. The consumer potential of manga encapsulated in the supplements is really just the first rung on the ladder to full consumer participation encouraged by *shōjo manga* magazines, mail order goods, and survey prizes to further girls' induction into contemporary consumer culture.

### Mail Order Goods

Mail order goods in *shōjo manga* magazines require a little more active participation on the part of girls, providing another link between these magazines and consumer culture more generally. *Zenin* means "everyone," and *zenin* service is an opportunity for readers of *shōjo manga* magazines to order special character goods through the mail. Unlike supplements, the mail order service is a mainstay of mainstream *shōjo manga* magazines and is found in all genres and levels of magazines. Its offerings are usually character goods available only through mail order for a limited time and thus provide another way readers can acquire desirable goods related to their favorite manga. The sense of immediacy and expiration encourages both readership and consumption.

Displayed prominently on glossy foldout pages in the front of the magazines alongside the ads for next month's supplements, mail order goods occupy a place of honor in *shōjo manga* magazines. The manga-related watches seen in figure 3.3 were available through *Ciao* mail order goods in the summer of 2002 (*Ciao* 2002b). As can be seen, this service provides nicer, more durable character goods than supplement offerings, although they are not quite free. As Takigawa pointed out, "The mail order goods are like freebies on top of the supplements, but are things that can't fit into the magazine, like bags. Readers can write in to get these items and only pay postage." While not all magazines offer mail order goods every month, typically between three to five items are offered at a time, and sometimes they are offered for several months running. During peak times, when magazine sales spike—Golden Week (May), summer vacation (August), and New Year's (January)—a wider selection of special mail order goods is offered.

In order to obtain mail order goods, the readers must send a special form found at the back of the magazine to the publishing house. Because the readers of these youth magazines are generally in grade school, great care is taken in the instructions. The process is greatly simplified and explained by a manga-like character. On the left-hand side of each page there is an

Figure 3.3. *Zenin service* goods page, *Ciao*, July 2002, 8. (Courtesy of Shogakukan)

application form that the reader must cut out and mail in to request the mail order goods. Along with this form the reader is required to send in stamps for the return postage of these items. Typically, mail order goods "cost" only around four hundred yen, but on special occasions certain items may require up to eight hundred yen in stamps or even a postal money order.[8] Because there are an unlimited number of mail order goods, orders are placed according to the number of applications received. On average for the *imōto* magazines, between eighty thousand and one hundred thousand girls send in for the mail order goods each month, according to several of the editors I spoke with.

Essentially, the mail order goods service provides the same motivation to readers as supplements—it promotes manga and requires that you buy a copy of the magazine. The application form *must* be cut out of the magazine—copies are not accepted—and thus girls who want the character goods have to buy their own copies of the magazine. In some cases mail order goods are extended over several months, requiring the purchase of two or more magazines in a row in order to obtain the desired goods. Mail order goods function like supplements to encourage new readers to enter the manga system. But it takes the reader a step further along the consumer continuum because the goods require some extra money, roughly the same amount that the magazine itself costs. As several editors pointed out, they are reliant on their readers to be able to use their allowance for the magazine and/or mail order goods, and that keeps the prices relatively fixed and low. Furthermore, mail order goods discourage girls from simply disposing of the magazine when they are finished, which has influenced girls' reading culture by making it less transient than that of boys' manga. Thus, mail order goods further the consumer potential of *shōjo manga* magazines introduced by supplements, encouraging girls to participate actively in both the magazine offerings and consumer realm.

### Ankēto Kenshō (Survey Prizes)

The final link between *shōjo manga* magazines and consumer culture more generally can be found in the survey prize offering. Literally "prizes," *kenshō* are a limited selection of goods that readers can "win" by filling out a survey (*ankēto*). Like mail order goods, survey prizes are not just available in the *imōto* magazines, but are a mainstay of the mainstream *shōjo manga* magazines. Survey prizes provide girls with another method of obtaining goods ornamented with their favorite manga characters; this time the currency of exchange is not money, but readers' opinions, or "what girls like."

The survey prize pages take up the first few pages of every *shōjo manga* magazine, right alongside the supplements and mail order goods pages. The goods offered as survey prizes vary from month to month and from magazine to magazine, and are age appropriate. For example, in May 2002 *Nakayoshi* offered a range of cute and stylish purses and bags perfect for going out on a warm spring afternoon, shown in figure 3.4 (Nakayoshi 2002a). As seen in this example, survey prizes are not always linked to manga. As often as not, they are simply consumer goods that the editors feel girls will like—they're fashionable, cute, and cool. Survey prizes can be as simple as stickers, pencil cases, or temporary tattoos and as elaborate as keyboards, Game Boys, and CD players. Typically there are anywhere from ten to thirty goods, ranging in value, offered to the three hundred to five hundred readers whose surveys are lucky enough to be chosen.

To be eligible to win a survey prize, readers answer the questions provided in the application page near the end of the magazine on a postcard, indicate their top three choices of prizes, and return it to the publishing

Figure 3.4. Survey *kenshō* page, *Nakayoshi*, May 2002, 17. (Courtesy of Kodansha)

house by the deadline (usually the day the next month's magazine comes out). The readers' comments solicited through the survey prize system are the primary way editors find out what readers think of the manga sampled in their magazine. The survey questions vary, with questions about current manga, most typically "From the list below, please choose and rank your top three favorite manga from this issue of [magazine name]"; similar questions about the non-manga matter found in the magazines; questions about the content and quality of a new serial manga showcased that month; questions about the readers' history with the magazine, such as "How long have you been reading it?" and "Why did you make your first purchase?" and questions about lifestyle, computer usage, hobbies, and the like.

Many of the editors I spoke with indicated that *shōjo manga* get many more surveys returned than any other genre of manga, and within that the *imōto* magazines win hands down. The *imōto* magazines receive several thousand (3,000 to 7,000) in an average month while the older magazines receive only several hundred postcards a month. When I asked editors how many postcards they receive each month, the inevitable answer was "Well, basically it depends on what prizes were offered that month." Hence, there is a direct link between popular prizes and the comments received.

Readers' opinions are used to determine what kinds of topics readers will be interested in, the direction that their tastes and trends are leaning, and simply what manga they like and why. Examples of this interplay between readers' comments and manga narratives were plentiful in my discussions with editors and artists. The most common changes were in character prominence and romance; often a side character becomes a main heartthrob or sidekick due to readers' response, and likewise characters and plotlines can be demoted or dropped altogether if unpopular. Since manga magazines are used to see what manga will sell, readers' opinions are used to determine what manga to make into books, anime, character goods—the more lucrative side of the business. Thus, survey prize submissions are a main tool for determining what manga will sell in the long run and what direction the manga and magazine overall should take.

Like supplements and mail order goods, survey prizes serve to link the readers of *shōjo manga* magazines to the wider consumer world. Through the survey prize system, a select number of lucky readers can win desirable consumer goods in exchange for their opinions about manga and manga magazines, and their hobbies, interests, consumer habits, and lives more generally. As noted above, the more popular the prizes, the more feedback the editors receive about their magazines and the manga therein. In this way, the process of creating popular manga involves the readers as consumers not only through their purchasing of manga magazines, and subsequently manga books themselves, but also through their desire for other *shōjo* consumer goods.

Displayed prominently on glossy foldout pages in the magazines' frontispiece, supplements, mail order goods, and survey prizes are pages where girls begin to participate in the creation of manga by giving their opinions and collecting character goods, along with reading the manga. These goods and services encourage readers to buy the magazines while also promoting the manga within, along with their cute characters. In their role as the gateway, *imōto shōjo manga* magazines in particular interpellate young readers as consumers of manga and so much more. Althusser uses the term "interpellate" to explain the way that ideology "hails" us as individuals into specific social categories (or subjects); in this case, beyond *shōjo manga* readers, girls become consumers (Althusser 1971, 170–177).

As Nakagawa explained, the editors try to create a "fun experience" through the magazine itself. "This is what we keep in mind for [our magazine], and it also helps keep sales even—we are not reliant on one or two popular titles," he added pragmatically. This "fun experience" amplifies the active nature of reading, eliciting reader participation through reading manga, as well as providing ample ways to obtain related character and lifestyle goods. The participatory experience of *shōjo manga* magazines fashioned by the editorial teams fosters a community of readers who share similar experiences, thus intertwining readership and consumption for manga and beyond. The concurrence of pragmatic business decisions, the creation of rewards for buying one's own copy of the magazine or sending in comments, and an overall focus on creating a space for readers to participate are all ways in which the editors of *shōjo manga* magazines foster a community for readers as a consumer base, one that will continue to purchase manga magazines, books, and goods from the publishing house throughout their lives. As I will elucidate in the following sections, the community ties do not stop here, but rather, readers' pages and the Manga School fabricate a *shōjo manga* magazine community through the construction of a conversation between readers and between readers and artists.

## NINGEN KANKEI: HUMAN RELATIONS AND READER COMMUNITY IN SHŌJO MANGA MAGAZINES

Gracefully poised and stylish as ever, manga artist and octogenarian Ueda Toshiko sipped tea in the middle of a long table in the café at the Yayoi

Bijutsukan (Yayoi Art Museum) near Tokyo University. About twenty of us (scholars, colleagues, schoolmates, and fans) gathered for tea and conversation with the renowned artist in conjunction with the exhibit Postwar *Shōjo Manga* History—The Debut of the *Otenba* (Tomboy) (Nakamura and Horie 2001). For an attentive audience, Ueda *sensei* answered questions and mused about her childhood in occupied Manchuria, as well as her career as a manga artist. "Really," she reflected, "I see my life and my career as concerned with the study of people, of humanity, through stories and characters, to help make the lives of the readers brighter" (Ueda 2001).

This notion of humanity, or human relations (*ningen kankei*), came up time and again when people I met tried to define *shōjo manga,* whether prompted or not. In such conversations boys' manga were described as filled with stories about heroes (winning and defeating the odds) and friendship, while girls' manga emphasized human relations, emotions, and love. These seemingly universal gender categories—action for boys and emotion for girls—still dominate the mainstream manga industry, even as crossover titles are increasingly visible. As discussed in chapter 2, in the history of manga the focus on *ningen kankei* in *shōjo manga* was codified in the late 1960s through the early 1970s. As women artists became more and more prevalent in the realm of manga for girls, one of the main innovations was a focus on interiority. Rather than the more action/dialogue-based plot construction of the boys' manga, these new female artists began to experiment with how to express emotion, inner thoughts and feelings, memories, and musings—the stuff of human relations. In these stories intimacy is produced as a gendered category, and young women artists are valued precisely because they are intimate with readers.

Augmenting the *ningen kankei* content of the genre, *shōjo manga* magazines actively focus on interpersonal relations through the participatory pages within the magazines. This can be seen in readers' responses to manga—survey postcards, fan letters, and illustrations—and reflected back in the readers' pages. Through a dialogic process editors create a space where readers can participate (*sanka shite kure*) in the realm of manga. First, they solicit readers' comments and combine them with the outpouring of fan mail. Then editors selectively publish a collection of fan comments and illustrations, along with artist's comments and thoughts. Thus, these pages serve as a bulletin board where readers can learn about each other and about their favorite manga, see their own ideas and images in print, and even ensure that their favorite artist received their comments.

When I asked editors and artists how they "hear the voices of their readers," the reply was fairly standardized: (1) from the survey prize submissions; (2) fan mail; and (3) field trips and meet-the-artist events, in that order. The information gathered from the survey is, for the most part, confined to a ranking of titles and brief comments. However, several magazines have expanded from the traditional postcard format to listing a range of questions on a magazine page and asking the readers to send in answers on their own paper, allowing for room for more questions and lengthier answers. Furthermore, in recent years manga publishers have expanded their content onto the Internet, soliciting readers' feedback via their Web pages.

But the surveys are not the only way that editors (and artists) hear from readers. Fan mail makes up another form of communication, however transient. Beyond the surveys, readers who are particularly smitten with a manga title will often simply write the artist a letter, in care of the publishing house. Received via mail, fax, and e-mail, such fan letters are a daily occurrence for popular manga artists. While the information provided on the prize surveys is primarily used to rank popular manga and help gauge what readers like or dislike about the magazine as a whole, fan mail is largely addressed to the artists themselves and is concerned explicitly with manga stories. Not surprisingly, this kind of communication is significantly more common in the youngest magazines, where readers tend to be, and are encouraged to be, more involved.

Sitting in the publishing office carrels amidst the din of the office at night (when it is most lively), young artist Miura Junko and her editor Saejima let me join in on a typical meeting. "These are the letters from just the past few weeks," Saejima said as she divided up a five-inch stack of postcards and letters and handed them to Miura *sensei* and me. Pink prevailed in the stack of letters and postcards I perused. They were filled with personal information, compliments about her manga, questions for Miura *sensei,* and illustrations of Miura's characters. "These are on the stationery which was a supplement last month," Saejima said as she pointed to several letters on pastel paper adorned with Miura's characters, "and these ones here came with chocolate or cookies. We automatically throw out any food that comes." She continued, "We check all the letters which are addressed to the artists for *abunai* [dangerous] content and then show them to the artist."

Most of the letters were from grade school girls saying they liked a particular story or character and encouraging Miura *sensei* to *ganbatte* (keep working hard). "They often tell me about their everyday lives, which is a good gauge of what life is like for them, since I am a little older," Miura claimed. She said that she skims through most of the letters, as we were doing that evening, but doesn't have time to read them thoroughly or respond. While the job of the editor is ultimately pragmatic, to sell more magazines and make popular manga to sell as books and the like, for the artists readers' comments can hold a slightly different meaning. The artists are able to not only gauge how much and why readers like their stories and artwork, but can also determine what other topics readers are interested in. While fan mail is not systematically solicited with prize offerings, it is encouraged through numerous postings of the publisher's address, fax number, and e-mail address, accompanied by comments such as, "Tell us what you think."

The final way that editors learn what readers like is through fieldtrips and events. Several times a year, usually during spring break and summer vacation, the mainstream publishing houses invite a group of one hundred or so readers to tour the manga division. Similarly, once a year many schools throughout the country take fieldtrips to Tokyo. On these school trips the children visit a variety of companies, and one of the choices is a publishing house, wherein they visit the manga division. In these structured events the children learn about how manga are made, and the editors are able to ask more questions about what the kids are interested in. As one editor put it, "We ask readers' opinions any time we get a chance, since they are the backbone of manga." Clearly, the "any time" suggested here is actually relegated to a few structured avenues; however, these special events do allow readers some space to participate in the construction of manga magazines, and indirectly in the creation of manga.

Pragmatically speaking, editors are reliant on readers' opinions and readers' interests at some level. After all, if no one bought the magazines or the manga, there would be no manga industry. The survey prize system, along with the readers' pages, solicits girls' opinions on what manga are interesting, what themes are appealing, and what their lives are like. This notion of trend spotting was a topic of grave concern to many of the editors with whom I spoke. Veteran editors Minami Yoshio and Okamoto Hajime argued, "One of the most important tasks of manga magazine editors is to stay a half-step ahead of readers. A whole step ahead is too much, readership drops off, but if you aren't a little ahead they get bored. You constantly have to guess what a half-step ahead is. It is really a hard business." Similarly, Saejima explained her technique for assessing what will be popular as survey prize goods: "I sometimes spend my free time at Kittyland in Harajuku, where I can watch the kids in the store and see what is coming next. Today's grade-schoolers are really growing up quickly; they love makeup even though they are in grade school. I didn't know it until I went looking; I never would have thought of it, but it is everywhere. Now we can offer makeup accessories on our survey prize pages and they are really excited!" As these accounts suggest, editors use a combination of methods to deduce what their readers will like in order to sell more manga.

Yet the making of manga magazines is typically driven by the *giri giri* (last minute) pace of monthly deadlines, and the groundwork for any magazine begins about six months in advance. Saejima's discussion of the selection of supplements is particularly telling. "Right now it is only June, but we are already planning the supplements for November's issue with winter and Christmas themes. Gradually you begin to not know what actual season it is; you are planning so much in advance. It is always *saki ni saki ni* [next, next]. So we have to think, what would be good this year, and then we talk to Sanrio or other manufacturers to see what we should do. What is coming, what is coming?" Saejima's seasonal confusion attests to the fact that supplements at least require more planning than the typical fare of manga magazines. Furthermore, the critical feature of supplements is that they are tied to manga characters or stories. Thus, the editors have to have a sense what manga will be popular, or at least ensure that it is still running in their magazine, in six months. Thus, because of the prevalence of character goods in girls' culture more generally, they are creating interests a half-step ahead. This notion of trend spotting is a concept I will discuss at the end of this chapter.

In discussions about the ways that readers participate in the *shōjo manga* magazines, the readers' pages were one of the main components mentioned. The collecting of readers' opinions in and of itself is a basic marketing research technique, and readers' pages are a part of *shōjo manga* magazines for all ages, although the youngest magazines make the most of them both in terms of space and enthusiasm.[9] The editors select a range of fan letters, illustrations, and readers comments and display them in the magazine itself. Clearly exciting for the selected young illustrators, these pages do more than flatter a smattering of readers and offer proof that the artists receive their mail. The layout and design of the readers' pages mimic a conversation between readers, between readers and artists, and even between readers and the editorial division of the publishing house. This participatory event serves to foster a sense of community, and one that is very productive for the *shōjo manga* industry.

Figures 3.5 and 3.6 from *Hana to yume,* October 2001, exemplify some of the readers' pages found in the main magazines during my fieldwork. The theme of the readers' pages in this example is *Hanamushi* (Flower bugs), to go along with flowers in the title of the magazine. Each magazine has a theme for their readers' page—for example, circus (*Ribon*), radio show (*Ciao*), and paradise (*Nakayoshi*). Within the rubric of these pages there is a mixture of free submissions and requested entries; a fusion of readers' com-

Figure 3.5. Hanamushi, *Hana to yume*, October 2001, 451. (Courtesy of Hakusensha)

ments, artist info, and editorial advice; and a combination of items related to manga and some simply related to girls' everyday lives.

Most magazines have a drawing corner devoted to displaying illustrations of current manga characters sent in by readers, as can be seen in the *kakihōdai* (all you can draw) section in figure 3.5. Several magazines ask

Figure 3.6. Hanamushi, *Hana to yume,* October 2001, 452. (Courtesy of Hakusensha)

their readers to send in illustrations with a theme for a special corner each month. Selected drawings are displayed in a later magazine, and sometimes they are eligible for prizes. Similarly, the "Free Talk" section, where some of the funny stories from everyday life that readers send in are printed, is common fare in the readers' pages. Such an example can be seen in figure 3.6: "Kyoto, Tomaru: I decided to confess my feelings to K-kun who I really like. I was too shy to tell him directly so I left a note in his desk. But the next day K-kun was absent. Moreover, we had to rearrange our seats. The desk with my note to K-kun now belongs to R, who is notorious for being quiet. Now he keeps making eye contact with me. I'm too scared to ask him!!" (*Hana to yume* 2001b). Likewise, many of the readers' pages include snippets or short interviews with an artist or two. In the case of *Hana to yume*, at the bottom of a two-page spread each artist is asked to provide a little blurb on a predefined topic. In figure 3.6 the topic was "What do you do to watch your health?" The sixteen artists in this particular magazine all wrote something like, "I watch variety shows (they are funny). Does that count?" "Recently I have been challenging myself to eat a variety of raw veggies. An odd battle with lettuce (but I am feeling better)," and "I do lots of things that I know are bad, but I can't quit. I am an unhealthy type" (*Hana to yume* 2001b). Lastly, each readers' page section has a small corner where readers are invited to make suggestions for enhancing the pages themselves.

Finally, on a structural level there is another interactive component to the readers' pages in *shōjo manga* magazines. These pages are utilized to train new editors about the voices, interests, and concerns of *shōjo manga* readers. Saeki described the importance of the readers' page in an editor's career: "This page is where we let the newest editor (*shinnyūsha*) work so that they can come to understand our readers. This is the page closest to our readers and we want them to quickly understand the readers, so this is what the newest editor does. They read the postcards and fan mail to know what the readers are thinking, what they like to wear, what they want to be. We raise (*sodateru*) the new editor this way." Several other editors voiced similar strategies for "raising" young editors (*kōhai o sodateru*), those in their first few years, through reading lots of manga, as well as through the construction of the readers' page. This training method doesn't require much knowledge of *shōjo manga* magazines but familiarizes the editor with the magazine and its readers. Several indicated that this is especially true for young male editors who did not grow up reading *shōjo manga* and must gain a sense of both the genre and its readers.

By including the readers' pages as a fundamental section of the manga magazine, editors construct a site for reader participation. These pages mimic a conversation as the editors, and presumably the artists, respond to readers' ideas, comments, and creative endeavors by organizing them and displaying them for others to read. But these pages are not written in the tone of your average adult male editor.[10] Quite the contrary, the text that surrounds the readers' entries are written in the tone and voice of an average reader. The cute characters that inhabit each readers' page frequently comment on the readers' funny stories or illustrations using a style of speech reserved for close friends. For example, "*Ciao* Paradise" uses a short comic strip to provide readers with details about how to send things in to the readers' page. Cute characters provide guidelines for submissions. "Lime: If you don't write your name and address we can't print your postcard. Peach: Color is cool but bad! Black shows up the best! *Gomu* (Gum eraser): And write clearly so it is easy to understand. Mosaic: Send away" (*Ciao* 2002a, 469). While this interchange is clearly conversational, it is punctuated with numerous exclamation marks, stars, and hearts and uses ending particles that elicit an informal and even childlike tone. The conversational language of the readers' page structures a feeling of community between the readers as they "talk" to each other, the characters in the pages, artists, and editors through this magazine section.

It is here that *shōjo manga* magazines bear the most resemblance to other teen magazines in Japan and elsewhere. Sarah Frederick's analysis of the role of readers' pages in women's magazines in the prewar period discusses them as sites of participation and community ( 2006, 98–101). The *shōjo manga* magazines of today grew directly out of the early prewar magazines for women and children, and the mediation of these features remains. But relation to readers is not solely the purview of Japanese women's media. Dawn Currie sums up this tendency of girls' magazines in general nicely: "From their inception, magazines for girls adopted this personal form of address, integrating their textual messages into the intimacy of readers' lives" (1999, 41). This is true for *shōjo manga* magazines as the personal and girlish form of address reaches beyond manga stories and into girls' lives. In essence, the readers' page is an extension of the human relations encountered and cultivated in the manga themselves, as readers' questions and comments about a particular manga are placed side by side with issues from their own lives. In these pages artists, editors, and readers are in dialogue, however tenuous, relating to each other through and about manga. Not only can readers get advice on problems at home and school, as well as the ubiquitous boy trouble, but they can also let their own preferences and interests be known to the artists and editors, as they can hear from other girls their own age who enjoy the magazine and its manga. In part because the content of *shōjo manga* typically concerns human relations, and because the focus today tends to be on everyday life in Japan, the lines between characters, readers, artists, and even editors are blurred in such conversations. The community created in the readers' pages is imagined in Anderson's sense because the participants will not meet face to face, and in fact many participants (as readers and fans) will never be directly represented in the pages of the magazine; it is also fabricated consciously by the way that editors craft readers' pages from a range of reader feedback shaped by notions of "what girls like" that are at once descriptive and prescriptive.

The *ningen kankei* articulated in *shōjo manga* stories is extended into girls' everyday lives through the creation of a sense of community within the pages of *shōjo manga* magazines. This can be seen in part through the questions about girls' likes and lifestyles in surveys, in the availability of non-character goods as both mail order goods and survey prizes, and finally in the space provided in the readers' pages for girls to write in about their own crushes, problems, and life issues. Thus, the readers' pages are girls' manga culture writ large in that they mimic the communal ways that girls read and consume manga and character goods. As we will see in the next section, this integration is taken a step further in the Manga School, wherein a handful of readers have the opportunity to become manga artists.

## LIVING THE DREAM: THE *SHŌJO MANGA* SCHOOL

In recent years much of the scholarship on manga in the West has focused on the untapped energy and creativity found in the amateur manga and fan subculture within the *dōjinshi* comic markets in Japan (Kinsella 1998, 2000; Thorn 2004; Orbaugh 2003b). When I began to formulate my research on the *shōjo manga* industry, armed with experiences at and articles about *dōjinshi* markets as well as tales of superstar artists like CLAMP, I assumed that publishers scouted the chaotic halls of these comic markets for new raw talent. As I quickly found out, this could not be further from the truth. The majority of the editors with whom I spoke were at pains to distance themselves from the likes of *dōjinshi*. With caveats for success stories like CLAMP, most editors explained that they did not go to comic markets or even pay attention to *dōjinshi;* quite the contrary, they find all their artists from the midst of their readers.[11]

Today, the most fundamental step on the road to becoming a manga artist is the Manga School, where readers can send in their manuscripts for the chance to get an editor and debut.[12] Each magazine includes a Manga School submission page that provides instructions on how to submit a manuscript to the Manga School. These pages also outline the various prizes that, at the time of my research, ranged from 300,000 to 500,000 yen ($3,000 to $5,000) and the chance to debut; to the Honorable Mention, Effort, and One More Breath prizes, which included smaller monetary prizes and a description of the artist's work and score displayed in the Manga School pages; to the A, B, and C Course prizes, which display the winner's name and marks for what needs to be improved. From the Effort prize on up, the budding young artist will be assigned an editor who will consult on her work and prepare her for the possibility of debuting. The cultivation of artists from readers is another link to the earlier prewar women's magazines, where serialized novels and short stories were solicited from readers in exchange for money and a chance to be published (Frederick 2006, 119–120). But the postwar manga industry has taken this strategy to new heights, establishing it as the main route to a life as a manga artist, especially in the *shōjo manga* division. Today, more than the small monetary prize that accompanies winning, getting assigned a magazine editor is the real reward, for it provides a connection at the publishing house, something absolutely necessary for manga artist success.

Depending on the magazine, there can be anywhere from thirty to seven hundred Manga School submissions for editors to sort through. Each manuscript is ranked along the following categories: overall sense, story, character development, character drawings, frames, and strength of drawing style. The number of points scored determines prize levels, and thus the highest prizes are not awarded every month. Figure 3.7 samples the Manga School pages from the April 2002 issue of *Ribon*. In this case the highest prize was the Honorable Mention, and twenty-five-year-old Kobayashi Yoshimi (pen name) received the prize money and contact with an editor at *Ribon,* and a Debut Study fee of ten thousand yen each month for six months to encourage her to keep working. In these four pages, thirteen submissions are described and critiqued, with the top prizes getting the most coverage. The artist's pen name, prefecture, and age are given alongside an image from the manuscript and the score (*Ribon* 2002b, 473–476). Of course, the number of submissions analyzed in each issue of the magazine depends on the number of top prizes awarded, but typically between ten and twenty are showcased.

Winning a Manga School contest does not ensure that an artist will be able to debut in a *shōjo manga* magazine. In fact, only about five to ten

Figure 3.7. *Ribon* Manga School 2002, *Ribon*, April 2002, 473. (Courtesy of Shueisha)

artists debut in each magazine each year. For an artist to finally debut, she must win the *Shinjin Shō* (Newcomer Prize) held by each publishing house only a few times a year. These contests are not limited to *shōjo manga* and include all genres of manga. Anyone can submit a manuscript to the *Shinjin Manga Shō,* including those who have won a Manga School contest and are working with an editor. Editors help these young artists craft a manga that can win the *Shinjin Shō* so that they can debut as a manga artist. Like the Manga School, the top few works submitted to the *Shinjin Shō* are discussed and critiqued in each of the main magazines and lucky winners even receive manga artist feedback on their work.[13]

While it may seem logical that the older magazines would cultivate artists most strongly, it is, in fact, the reverse. The *imōto* magazines promote the Manga School most vehemently and consistently. Many of the older magazines hold contests every other month or even three times a year, but for *Ribon, Nakayoshi, Ciao,* and *Hana to yume,* the Manga School is a mainstay of the magazine environment offered every month. Indeed, many older *shōjo manga* magazines populate their pages with artists who are already popular in the younger magazines. In this way artists, like readers, can "grow up" and move up the magazine ladder within a given publishing house. For example, Yazawa Ai was a wildly popular artist in *Ribon* in the 1990s, and in 2000 she began her current hit, *Nana,* for *Ribon's* older-sister magazine *Cookie,* which caters to older teens and college students. Thus, just as the magazine system relies heavily on the *imōto* magazines to lure and create new readers who will move up the magazine ladder as they get older, artists are likewise groomed primarily from the earliest fan base and climb up the rungs of magazines as they mature.

What is important about the Manga School system is precisely the focus on learning the ropes of manga creation through the magazine. Rather than searching for artists at art schools or the amateur markets, as one might imagine, artists are raised from readers. As Udagawa Toshiya, a middle-aged editor, explained, "Like all publishing houses, we rely on the schooling method to find artists. Thus, all the magazines, boys and girls, young and old, pull their artists from their readers. That artists and readers are the same is crucial." Again we see a focus on the salience of readers, at least in the rhetoric employed by editors in our discussions. But here there is a concrete example of the importance of readers for these magazines, for from their midst almost all new artists emerge. Takigawa was clear on this point as well, saying, "We rely on its readers, and actively help them become manga artists."

The Manga School rears artists in several ways. Not only is it readers themselves who submit manuscripts, but the Manga School pages in each issue serve as a course for how to draw manga. Udagawa explained this most clearly: "The reason this contest is called a 'school' is that the top percentage are given feedback on their stories." The top manuscripts are not only written up in the magazine Manga School section, but budding young artists can receive comments from an editor directly and begin working towards a debut. And all submitters have the option of receiving written feedback on their manuscripts if they so desire. Furthermore, whether their own manuscripts are critiqued there or not, readers can get a sense of how to draw a strong and interesting manga through the comments and tips found in the Manga School pages. Several of the editors I spoke with used the term *sodateru* (to raise or bring up) again to discuss this Manga School system. It raises or rears artists from a young age, as witnessed by the overwhelming popularity of the Manga School in the youngest magazines. It is through the *imōto* magazines that the bulk of manga artists are cultivated. And these young artists are quite literally taught how to create manga through the magazine competitions.

But there is yet another level to this schooling system. It is not simply that manga readers become manga artists, but that the system is strongly wedded to the magazines and even more to the publishing houses themselves. As Hayasaka Yūsuke explained, "So through these ten or so pages [Manga School pages] in each magazine readers or potential artists can find out what this magazine likes and how to draw manga. They are shaped by the magazine, and yet the magazine watches for new creative (not just rule-following) artists. It is the play between these that creates the new talent. Regrettably, it is becoming stricter as it grows; it was freer when it started. Now artists really are created from the magazine so you tend to get more and more of the same." Thus, potential artists learn what kinds of styles and themes a particular magazine prefers as they learn to draw and write manga. Accordingly, the magazines themselves have some bearing on the manga produced. Granted, an aspiring artist may submit to several magazines and most likely chooses those she likes best, but the fact remains that the magazines raise manga artists. I asked Komatsu Tetsuo if a young artist needed to read a particular magazine in order to debut there. He replied, "We get all of our authors from the school now, and there is some sense of raising authors, but more for the publishing house overall than just a magazine. But for example, the magazine *Cookie* is only two years old, and we say that soon a breed of *Cookie* artists will have been raised." As Komatsu suggests, beyond raising manga artists for one magazine, although each magazine may have its own flair, this system creates artists for the publishing house more generally. For artists do not work as freelancers contracting out to the highest bidder. Rather, each publishing house has its own system, and artists work directly for a specific publishing house in the mainstream industry.

Throughout my interviews, it was clear that almost all artists are now reared through this Manga School system. Minami, another seasoned editor, admitted that this system has changed the industry. "In the old days, the *shōjo manga* golden years, it was famous artists who were household names, who kept the magazines selling and popular. It used to be 8/2 [80 percent known authors and 20 percent new ones], then it went to 4/6, and now it is completely reversed, 2/8. Now new authors make up a high percentage and authors don't stick around for as long. The potential of artists is key and that is somewhat lost with this new system; they don't have the same chance to fully develop." This sense that *shōjo manga* lost momentum after the end of the golden years was prevalent in many of my interviews, especially with older editors, but what is important here is the role of new artists. That the bulk of the magazines consist of newer artists rather than seasoned big names changes the shape or atmosphere of the magazines and manga industry as a whole. Miyazaki Yuri confirmed this sense of turnover when we spoke.

> **Miyazaki:** I am planning on stopping [being a manga artist] when I turn twenty-six.
> **Jennifer:** Why do you want to stop?
> **Miyazaki:** That is just what I always thought. I don't know what I will do next, maybe be a housewife, but I won't do this forever.

The twenty-year-old artist was never any clearer on why she would stop being an artist, but she was very clear that this was not forever, much to the dismay of her editor, since Miyazaki was quickly becoming a top artist. In part, rapid turnover could be said to breed more creativity or a fresh face to manga, but artistic control increases as artists gain more experience, and the comparative dearth of older artists lacks a level of maturity, a point I will discuss at length in chapter 4.

As I have outlined through this discussion of the Manga School system, there was a sense among those with whom I spoke that from the very first experience with a manga magazine budding artists are being reared from among the pool of readers. The Manga School is the final level of production educating young artists step by step in the ways to create an *omoshiroi* (interesting, funny) manga that will sell to their friends and younger sisters. Thus, not only is community between readers and artists fostered through the readers' pages, but through the very fact that artists are raised from readers. Each reader has the opportunity to learn how to become a manga artist through participating in the manga magazines and beyond. The intimacy created between readers and artists is not simply of fan and artist, but each reader could herself become an artist, and, in fact, the artists are themselves a part of the community of readers. Here, community is fabricated through participation and the cultivation of readers not just as consumers, but as potential artists.

## Community Fabrications

In the process of creating manga magazines, editors tack back and forth between various domains: the business end of selling manga, the creative end of working with and even cultivating artists, and the marketing end of understanding and instigating readers' interests. The bottom line of the manga industry is selling manga. Manga magazines at their most basic showcase manga in the hopes of leading to further purchases and a semblance of publisher loyalty. Each of the aspects discussed in this chapter help to further this goal. The inclusion of supplements and mail order goods requires girls to buy their own copy of the magazine rather than share with friends. These features, along with the survey prizes, fan the flames of interest in a particular manga through the creation and distribution of character goods, be they paper, plastic, or even electronic. As novice editor Kodama Kaori bluntly put it, "The purpose is selling manga. That is where we make our money." This profitability is the most basic function of manga production and the goal of magazine production.

However, through the business of making and marketing manga there is an interesting interplay between readers and the magazines themselves. The participatory aspects of manga magazines encourage the reader to do much more than simply buy and read manga. The glittery supplements, glossy mail order and survey goods pages, conversational readers' pages, and lessons of the Manga School have become a sort of contact zone between the various parties involved in the *shōjo manga* magazine culture. Here readers can acquire character goods, read each other's thoughts and ideas, learn about their favorite artists, and learn how to become artists. Nevertheless, this space within *shōjo manga* magazines is consciously constructed by editors. Readers are encouraged to participate (*sanka shite kure*) within the pages of the magazine in a variety of ways and in so doing are, at least in part, raised (*sodateru*) as readers, consumers, and artists. Yet this notion of encouraging readers to participate in the manga magazines speaks to what Henry Jenkins has called "affective economies." Jenkins argues that in affective economies media marketing has begun to focus on the emotional attachments consumers make that shape purchasing decisions (2006, 60–61). Long before the new media Jenkins is concerned with came along, the editors of *shōjo manga* crafted various ways to engage their readers emotionally with the manga, character goods, and magazines. In the interplay between creating a space for readers to participate in the magazine and raising readers, consumers, and artists, a sense of community is fabricated. This fabrication in *shōjo manga* magazines ultimately serves the publishing houses' bottom line, and the idea of such a sense of community is integral to the way that *shōjo manga* is understood. At some level, *shōjo manga* magazines have evolved beyond their economic initiative to create a locality where human relations, business matters, dreams, and talent collide.

# CHAPTER FOUR

# Affective Labor

Gender, Generation, and Consumption in the
Production of *Shōjo Manga*

Manga grew up alongside the first generation of postwar children.
The fledgling industry struggled for its footing in the early years,
providing much needed entertainment for the children of the fifties
and early sixties. As those children grew older, they continued to
be enamored with manga, and the genre expanded into teen and
then adult titles. From among this first generation of postwar
children came the great manga artists of the late sixties and
seventies, stars like Fujiko F. Fujio, Ikeda Riyoko, Ishinomori
Shōtarō, Takemiya Keiko, and the like. For a time manga was
considered at best pulp fiction and at worst a danger to young
children, but by the eighties, manga was embraced as national
culture.
—Compiled from numerous interviews and conversations

This standard account of the postwar history of manga, culled from countless interviews and conversations, tells the story of the rebirth of an industry
and the generation of children who were inspired by it and, in fact, made
it what it is today.[1] While clearly a view through the rose-colored tint of
hindsight, this account nonetheless leads us to think about the relationship
between the readers and the creators of manga. The tenet that manga, the
mass medium, grew up along with the first postwar generation of children
presumes that these youngsters exerted dual influence on the genre, both
as readers and as artists. And as we saw in the previous chapter, today
almost all artists are cultivated from the ranks of readers, further solidi-
fying this relationship. This formulation caught my attention when I first
began research on manga because it insinuates a more dynamic relationship
between production and consumption than typically has been addressed in
research on popular culture.

In the history of *shōjo manga* this tale of readers growing up with manga,
becoming manga artists, and reinvigorating the industry is also a story
about gender. Tezuka Osamu, Chiba Tetsuya, Ishinomori Shōtarō, and the

like, were the forefathers of *shōjo manga*. However, by the early 1970s most of the artists writing for *shōjo manga* were women. Since then, within the industry, classic gender relations have played out through the predominance of older male editors and young women artists. In the logic of the industry, the production of manga requires someone who understands what young female readers will buy, and this role has been filled by young women artists who rise up primarily out of the ranks of readers, whereas their *sarariiman* editors provide a level of objectivity and business prowess to the endeavor. However, young women editors, many of whom bring with them the investment of personal experience with *shōjo manga,* are examples of the ways that the distinct roles of reader and editor sometimes converge. This is affective labor in that the manga stories themselves manipulate affect, and yet the labor itself is affective for the artist and some editors, particularly young women. Thus, in this chapter, it is through the gendered and generational dynamics of production that I examine the broader relationship between production and consumption in the *shōjo manga* industry today.

## Inside the *Shōjo Manga* Industry

This chapter is framed around questions of structure and agency in the *shōjo manga* world. Setting the stage for a discussion of how individual editors and artists negotiate human relations to produce *shōjo manga,* I begin by outlining the structure of the manga divisions where I conducted my interviews. This opening discussion situates individual editors and artists firmly within the corporate structure in which they work.

Media and publishing jobs have long been competitive in Japan, and most publishers hire only one cohort a year. The publishing houses where I conducted my research are among the top publishers and as such attract recruits from Japan's leading universities.[2] These days even the biggest publishers hire only between eight and twenty-five employees a year, of which one to five are assigned to the manga division.[3] Accordingly, there is a competitive application process including an exam and multiple interviews to enlist new employees. Recruits are able to specify the division where they would like to work, but ultimately the decision as to what their job will be is up to the company. An applicant may very well apply to work on an economic magazine and end up editing manga, or vice versa.

In addition, once hired it is typical to move around in-house throughout your career. Sharon Kinsella explains that at Kodansha there were a few editors who are selected to work in one division for their entire careers in order to become management in that division, but the bulk of the editors are moved around significantly (Kinsella 2000, 167–168). This system clearly varies from publishing house to publishing house, as I met several high-level managers at other publishers who had moved around extensively. According to those I spoke with, at least three internal transfers in the first ten years was standard. Depending on how long they had worked at a given publisher, most of the editors I interviewed had held positions at one other manga magazine, if not more, and many had spent some time in another division. For example, one veteran editor began his career as a *shōjo manga* editor, where he worked on three different magazines over the course of fifteen years; then he was moved to an entirely different realm, an adult men's magazine, where he worked for seven years. Finally, he was moved back to the *shōjo manga* division, where he has remained. Another young woman editor expressed relief when she was moved to the *shōjo manga* division, a subject closer to her own heart than the men's news magazine where she had started her career. The structures of work life in the publishing industry outlined here are part and parcel of company life in postwar Japan. This is, after all, big business.

Each of the publishers covered in this study has a manga division, which is divided up into at least two separate sections—a *shōjo manga* division and *shōnen manga* division (see appendix B).[4] Next, the *shōjo* and *shōnen* divisions are each segmented into several sections corresponding to target age. For example, at Shueisha's *shōjo manga* division, the Dai 1 Henshūbu (Division 1) is made up of the younger magazines *Ribon, Margaret,* and *Cookie* while the various ladies' manga are in the Dai 2 Henshūbu (Division 2). The two divisions are then segmented by magazine, categorized by intended readership (primarily age, then theme). Each manga magazine division is headed by a *henshūchō* (editor-in-chief), frequently has a *fuku-henshūchō* (vice editor-in-chief), and employs from three to fifteen *henshūsha* (editors). These rank-and-file *henshūsha* are in charge of working directly with *mangaka* (artists)—and each manages between ten and twenty artists.[5]

Like most large-scale corporations, when a new recruit enters a publishing house in a full-time capacity, he/she does so on one of two career tracks: *sōgōshoku* (integrated/managerial track) and *ippanshoku* (clerical track).[6] Established in response to the Equal Employment Opportunity Law of 1986, this two-track system enables firms to treat women equally in terms of recruitment, hiring, job placement, and promotion while it also ensures a gendered division of labor—men are almost always on the integrated track and women are usually on the clerical track (Brinton 1993; Kawashima

1995, 271–293; Ōmori 1993, 79–102). The integrated or managerial track requires a commitment to overtime whenever necessary and possible geographic transfer, but also includes the ability to move into managerial positions. In contrast, the clerical track does not require as much overtime commitment or geographic transfer, but neither does it allow for vertical movement within the company, and it virtually assumes a woman will quit working when she marries or has a child. Encouraging women to quit after marriage or childbirth leaves them no opportunity to move up the ladder because they are not on the managerial track. Almost all of the women editors I spoke to were on the clerical track.

At the bottom of the publishing house hierarchy resides a host of consulting and other part-time staff who take care of the nitty-gritty magazine details. The various staff positions are composed primarily of designers, other contract workers, and part-time employees easily hired and fired as the whims of the economy deign. Following wider labor trends in part-time hiring, in the *shōjo manga* divisions in which I interviewed, these employees were almost exclusively female and hired on a short-term contract basis, despite working forty or more hours a week.[7]

Finally, artists are the capstone of *shōjo manga* production, and yet they are tangential to the publishing house corporate structure. Artists, even the most famous, are hired on a contract basis. Due to the competitive nature of the manga publishing industry, contracts frequently include exclusivity clauses stipulating that the artist will work only for that publishing house while the contract is in effect.[8] Artists also must agree to share ownership of their characters and stories with the publishing house, since the resale of manga titles as books and the proliferation of character goods, anime, and video games bring in substantial income for the industry and artists alike. Their position outside the publishing houses is literally played out in the geography of the industry. Artists work at home, venturing to the publishing house only for meetings with editors to hammer out story lines and draft details, and even this is frequently done by fax or phone.

In terms of compensation, artists are paid by the page depending on seniority/popularity (typically ranging from eight thousand to ten thousand yen for a new artist at the time of my research). Thus, an artist just starting out and publishing a short manga every few months cannot make enough to live on, but once her manga are recompiled into a book, her income increases substantially. In addition, artists get more money for other requested illustrations, like cuts (character pictures for character goods distributed with magazines) and the cover of the next month's magazine. As an artist increases in popularity, her work increases in profitability and distribution, and money inflow increases for both the publishing house and the artist. Still, research at the site of manga production highlights how artists are at once critical to the creation of manga and yet are mediated by editors focusing on magazine production and book sales.

This detailed outline of the structural organization and hierarchical underpinnings of the manga industry underscores the fact that the making of manga is at its base a corporate enterprise. But it is also one composed of individuals who interact to create manga. The negotiations between individuals across corporate structures in the process of creating *shōjo manga* are the focus of the remainder of this chapter.

## *Ningen Kankei* (Human Relations): Negotiations between Editors and Artists

*Ningen kankei* infuses *shōjo manga* magazines through both the content of manga stories and the fabrication of a community within the magazine pages, as discussed in the previous two chapters. But *ningen kankei* is also integral to the production of *shōjo manga* through editor and artist relations—relations that are structured by both gender and generation.

The specter of editor and artist relations haunts the manga industry. Tales of cruel editors circulate throughout the manga world and occasionally beyond. In my own interviews with both editors and artists this topic was clearly a source of tension. Yet everyone admitted that this relationship is at once the crux and the crucible of manga production. Even though editors work primarily behind the scenes and are rarely in the limelight in the way that popular artists are, their managing role is notorious. Tales of heavy-handed editors sequestering artists in tiny apartments for days on end in order to meet a deadline, chastising the artistic skills of veteran artists, and generally dominating their creative counterparts abound. *Ningen kankei* is always at some level about negotiating complicated power relations, and in this section I examine the human relations through which *shōjo manga* is created.

The job of a *henshūsha* (editor) can be misleading to a Western audience, as it indicates a stronger managerial position than the term "editor" connotes. As one veteran editor explained it, "Unlike our Western counterparts, Japanese editors do not simply proofread texts, but coordinate putting things together, actually working with the artists to make the stories and then the magazine. The editors who work on a given magazine have a great deal of influence over its style and content." Of course, the extent of collaboration depends on the artist and the editor, but most accounts held with this general description.

Returning briefly to the corporate social order, editors-in-chief (*henshū-chō*), and even the vice editors-in-chief (*fuku-henshūchō*), typically do not work with artists, but instead manage the division, overseeing all aspects of the magazine production. Takigawa Masahiro explained the hierarchy. "The *henshūchō* is actually the one who takes responsibility for everything, so he has ultimate control. He has say in many decisions along the way; editors run everything by him on a weekly basis. There are times when he overrides a decision, but if you have a good *henshūchō* who trusts his editors, as in my case, that is not necessary. The *henshūchō* has final say on the magazine and takes responsibility for the numbers." As Takigawa elucidated, editors meet on a weekly basis to make decisions about the upcoming issue and submit progress reports to that end. It is in these editorial meetings that the making of manga magazines and manga itself is micromanaged, and as pointed out above, the editor-in-chief sets the tone for these meetings and the magazine.[9]

It is the rank-and-file editors who work directly with artists to create manga. While it varies from magazine to magazine, each editor is in charge of around twenty artists. These include a mix of veteran artists who know the ropes and publish serial titles on a regular basis, artists who have debuted and are early in their publishing careers, and *shinjin* (newcomers) who have won a Manga School contest but have yet to debut. Different levels of artists receive/require different levels of time on the part of an editor. Young artists who have not yet debuted tend to send in a manuscript every month or two, while artists who are writing serials correspond with their editor on a weekly, if not daily, basis, depending on how close to the deadline it is.[10]

The main job of an editor is working with artists to create interesting manga—manga that will sell. At every stage of the process editors weigh in on the content, tenor, and artistic quality of the manga story. In the original planning of a story, the editor's role may range from simply approving an artist's *puroto* (prototype), helping the artist flesh out the story, or telling the artist that their draft isn't interesting, to suggesting a story line to the artist. Similarly, after the artist has sketched the *nēmu* (rough draft of an episode, in pencil), editors have a great deal of input as to whether or not the story, characters, and pacing work. In the meetings at which I was present, the editor's copy of the *nēmu* was covered in red pencil marks and the editor walked the artist through necessary changes, many of which involved rearranging and resizing frames to better direct the flow and punch of the story. A *nēmu* may go through only one edit before moving on to the *genkō* (final draft of manuscript), or it may go through several. Finally, the editor proofs the *genkō* and, when he or she is satisfied, passes it up to the *henshūchō* for final approval. In each of these stages the editor and artist meet to solidify the creation of manga;[11] this is how manga is made.

Because manga editors play such a strong role in the creative process, editors discuss the making of manga as a negotiation between artists and editors. Several editors likened their jobs to that of a sport coach or movie director—that is, someone who works behind the scenes yet is a part of the creative process. Takigawa again provides insight into this process. "So much of the job has to do with human relations: understanding readers, working with other editors, interacting with artists and designers; you are the intermediary. All artists work slightly differently, their communication styles, work pace, and needs are different and you have to change and adapt to each, in a way. So listening, adapting, and communication are crucial to the job of editors—*ningen kankei*." In interview after interview publishing personnel explained that the main theme that characterizes editor and artist relations is human relations. Whether this process goes smoothly or not, or is fraught with tension, depends on a variety of factors, including the temperaments of those involved. Miyashita Kenji outlined this process. "The process of making *shōjo manga* is relative. Basically, it's cooperation between editor and artist. But every decision in this process is made by both together. Generally, the more famous the artist is, the stronger [the] role she has. On the contrary, the newer the creator is, the weaker her role is. It is always difficult for me to make decisions with artists because the relation between editor and creator is unsettled. There is no one method, but what is important is *ningen kankei*—'communication with human-beings.'" Similarly, as Sōda Naoko, in her second year as an editor, explained,

> Relationships between editors and artists really vary a lot. I feel like I learn from rather than am in charge of more veteran artists. But at the same time in such situations I am closer to the reader's age than the artist, and read a lot [of *shōjo manga*] as a young girl, so my personal input, between the readers and artists, is useful. With new artists, they are even closer to readers than I am but don't know the publishing world, so I am better able to help them out, make it smoother for them. It just depends on the situation.

Miura Junko, a young artist, also commented, "I had heard so many horror stories about editors that I actually breathed a sigh of relief when I met [my editor] and found her to be young, kind, and cheerful." Thus, at the heart of the matter, lie *ningen kankei* as editors and artists work together to create manga, balancing creativity, what readers want, and profit margins.

Here we get a glimpse of the power relations involved in these relationships. The editor and artist play different roles, depending on who has the most experience. But this notion of negotiation and *ningen kankei* that many of my interviewees expressed is undoubtedly biased, particularly in light of the fact that today new artists make up about 80 percent of those published in the average *shōjo manga* magazine, while only 20 percent are veteran artists. What Takigawa and others were finessing with sociological terms like *ningen kankei* was the inherent power relations in the editor and artist relationship. Artists in positions of power over their editors are few and far between; the fact remains that editors, at all levels, have ultimate say in what the end-product manga looks like, subject to the editor-in-chief. The power dynamics are clear in most cases—the economic viability of the magazine and the editor's perspective get priority in the end over and above artistic integrity and enthusiasm.

Yet there is another factor that complicates the *ningen kankei* of editor and artist relations in the creation of *shōjo manga* in particular: gender. Not only is *shōjo manga* a fundamentally gendered genre, but the manga industry itself is organized by gender. The segmentation of manga for boys and for girls is palpable upon entering the manga division, as the girls' manga areas shimmer with pastel while the boys' areas are boldly primary. But beyond the gendering of the target audience, in the case of *shōjo manga* in particular there is a gendered division of labor: 75 percent of *shōjo manga* editors are men, while 99 percent of the artists are women (mostly in their teens to late twenties).

For the most part, this division of labor is all about the business practices of the *sarariiman* managerial system. The postwar miracle was predicated on the tripartite social system of work, home, and school. The *sarariiman* system provided a living wage and pension as part of the social contract that advocates that women (as wives and mothers) take care of the household and children. The publishing industry is part and parcel of this system. Editors are traditionally *sarariiman*, full-time employees on the managerial track, and thus tend to be men. However, this gender divide speaks more broadly of gendered relations of production. As Saeki Yoshimi, an editor in his late thirties, suggested, "Male editors can be more objective in their impressions. They can focus on details like the overall selling points of the characters, their charm or market potential, and the progression of the story—this is slow for example, or are the characters okay, what is the overall drama progression. . . . For men there is some natural distance that helps more than an a priori relationship to the *shōjo* magazines." The young female editor Kodama made a similar point. "When I first started working here I was really surprised how many men edited *shōjo manga*. But men add a new perspective because they have no preconceptions (*sen'nyūkan ga nai*) [of *shōjo manga*]." In this line of thinking, young women make good artists because they are closer to the readers, but women editors are naturally too close to the genre. Likewise, male editors add a new perspective while keeping the overall business goals in perspective.

Thus, the presumption of a gendered division of labor, where the distance required for business decisions falls on the shoulders of male editors (typically older) and the creativity involved in drawing manga falls to the female artists (typically young), dominates the production of *shōjo manga*. The answer seems to be as simple and as serious as gender ideology. In this configuration, young women artists are valued for their affinity with readers, while their older male editors evaluate a wide range of factors, always watching the bottom line. The gendered bifurcation of perspective has been fundamental to the production of *shōjo manga* for most of the postwar era.

Creating manga is the point where editorial business know-how and artistic creativity meet, and *ningen kankei* are paramount. While accounts of good and bad editors do hinge on personality and managing style at some level, the power relations inherent in this relationship dictate the tenor of negotiations. As outlined here, the relationship between editors and artists relies on communication skills structured by gender relations and sharpened by the whims of economics.

## Dream Job or Daily Grind: Working Life in the *Shōjo Manga* Industry

This chapter is shaped around the corporate structure of *shōjo manga* production and the personal narratives of those who create it. Thus far I have outlined the structural parameters of how *shōjo manga* is made using the voices of the creators—editors and artists. I turn now to focus on the experiences of editors in order to examine the meanings they make of their role in *shōjo manga* production, elucidating the way that younger manga industry personnel often blurred the boundaries of producers and consumers in the ways that they talked about their jobs, the readers of their magazines, and the genre of *shōjo manga* more generally. Part of my original interest in the *shōjo manga* industry lay in the relationship between editors, artists, and readers. As such, I focused part of each interview on the editors' or artists' own personal histories with manga, and how they came to produce it. It is to these personal accounts of why editors sought a career in publishing and what role manga played in their lives that I will now turn, in order to think about the role of consumption in the realm of production.

As mentioned above, jobs in the large manga publishing houses are highly competitive and coveted. According to Kinsella most of the editors in the men's division at Kodansha were attracted to publishing because it provided all the perks of big business in Japan.

> Despite changes to the rigid structure of the professional labour market during the 1980s, and the increased popularity of working for small flexible companies, employment in a large publisher, such as Kodansha or Shogakukan, is still regarded, by university graduates, as highly desirable. These are large, well-established companies which provide a range of welfare programmes and perks for employees, as well as the security of life-time employment, accompanied by wage rises guaranteed with ability, if not seniority (*nenkō seido*). Employees also enjoy the high social status, personal confidence and power bestowed on them by becoming an employee of a prestigious and all but indestructible company. (2000, 166–167)

This notion of big company life held true for many of the editors that I worked with as well.[12] Like Kinsella, the editors I conducted my research among were white-collar workers straight from Japan's top universities applying almost exclusively to big companies in their job searches.

However, when I asked each editor why he/she looked for a job at a publishing house, their answers added a perspective not captured by Kinsella's primarily class-based analysis. Most discussed a desire to work in mass media more generally, along with a search for a less rigid work environment. Many applied not only to several publishers, but also to big companies in the fields of radio, television, newspapers, and advertising. Veteran editor Minami Yoshio, in his late fifties, waxed nostalgic, explaining this interest in terms of Japanese culture and postwar history. "My generation was the first postwar baby boom and we grew up immersed in the mass media—radio, television, movies, and *kashihon manga*—as it was rapidly developing in Japan. We soaked it in and went on to be the first media-savvy generation to work in the entertainment industry and infuse it with our multimedia childhood experiences." Similarly, Odagawa Toshiya argued that in postwar Japan the entertainment industry has been vital. "At college I studied to be a journalist. But in Japan, entertainment is more interesting than journalism; it has more influence on society so I looked for work at a publishing company [entertainment genre]." As both of these editors attest, working in mass media has been an attractive pursuit throughout the postwar because of its prevalence and stature. For many of the editors I spoke with, working in a publishing house was appealing because it was a main form of mass media as well as a stable *sarariiman* job.

Additionally, several editors indicated that working at a publishing house provided a more creative job experience than the typical *sarariiman* fare. Almost half of the editors I interviewed majored in Japanese literature in college and cited their love of reading as their inspiration in seeking a job in publishing. As Hayasaka Yūsuke, an editor in his late thirties, explained, "I went to Tōdai (Tokyo University, the premier university in Japan) and majored in literature because I have loved fiction ever since I was a child. When I graduated there were two kinds of jobs that I was interested in, both of which involved creating fiction: manga editing or working in the TV drama industry." A few editors expressed early interest in being fiction writers, and one even published a few manga before entering the editing business.

But while many wanted to be involved in the creation of fiction, as Hayasaka suggests, most did not indicate that they wanted to be writers. Young editor Suda Junichirō epitomizes this view. "I really wanted to work closely with authors, although not only manga, but books, short stories, or manga. I wanted to work with people who write *monogatari* [stories]. I have always been interested in stories like that. I tried to write a little as a kid, but from about middle school I knew I wouldn't be a writer and from then on wanted to be some kind of *monogatari* editor, to work with creative authors/artists." Suda's admission paralleled the reasoning given by several of the younger editors I spoke with. They may not have felt they could be writers themselves, but still wanted to be a part of the creative process. For many, manga editing was not their only goal, but the creation of fiction, of which manga is one viable genre, was a big draw. Furthermore, when I asked editors whether the actual job of editing manga differed from their expectations, many of the younger ones expressed surprise that making manga actually involved the production of magazines rather than working on manga stories. These editors envisioned spending their time creatively working with artists; the power of creation was what was appealing to this group. This desire to do creative work has implications for the production of manga, amplifying the editor's role in shaping manga stories themselves.

Overall workplace environment was the final motivation editors gave for pursuing a career in publishing. In the words of Miyashita Kenji, a relative newcomer to the editing business, "I really wanted something creative and free, exemplified by not having to wear a suit or keep business hours. Even though editors are really busy it is a freer career." Kodama Kaori, another young editor, agreed. "The great part about being an editor is that you can come to work whenever you want, although you have to get your work done. There is practically no one around until almost noon. And most people stay until 7 or 8 p.m., depending on how close it is to monthly deadlines. It is big company life without big company life." I experienced this more informal working life throughout my fieldwork, as I witnessed the difference in office atmosphere between the quiet of early afternoon, when it is still sluggish, and late evening, when everything is abuzz with activity.

Similarly, dress code, or a lack thereof, was another factor mentioned as a part of the casual atmosphere many editors were looking for in a career. While the older editors who worked as division heads tended to wear suits, the average editor was casually dressed, with jeans and T-shirts or button-downs being the most common attire—certainly not what one imagines *kaisha* life to be like. This desire for a mixture of job security and flexibility is not surprising, given social concerns about youth and work that emerged in the 1990s, highlighting a new employee's hesitancy to simply embrace the big *kaisha* life that dominated much of the postwar era. Thus, for young people looking for steady and reliable middle-class employment, but without the strict schedule and business dress code of most companies, working in a publishing house is a perfect match.

## MANGA HISTORIES: *SHŌJO MANGA* EDITORS AS MANGA CONSUMERS

While almost all of the editors and artists I spoke with read some manga when they were growing up, many of them admitted that they had no intention of editing manga when they began their publishing careers. As mentioned previously, new employees do not get to choose where in the publishing house they will end up working, and most move around significantly in the first ten years. Many of the editors I interviewed envisioned themselves editing literature, dictionaries, biographies, nonfiction, and the like and were nonchalant about manga itself, but about a quarter of them had manga editing in their sights when they set out job hunting. For this set of editors, producing manga was a specific way of being involved in the creation of fiction in a more relaxed work environment. Harada Tomohiro was one such editor.

> Throughout my life I read a lot of manga and watched a lot of movies. I have really liked manga from long ago. Manga is different overseas where it isn't so common, but here manga is such a main genre. I loved manga as a kid and a teen; novels just seemed too hard and didn't seem to catch me in the same way, and that is still true. Of course, I still read all the literature biggies and many are great, but for me, I guess the age has changed and manga is the main form of expression. Manga is accepted and really makes you think; it feels close. I continued to read manga all the way through my twenties; that's all I did in college [*laughs*]. So I thought it would be great to be a part of that, be a part of making fiction.

For Harada and several others I spoke with, their own experiences growing up with manga were a part of their career decisions. Being part of the creation of manga, which had enhanced their own lives, was an important aspect of the way they talked about their jobs. Editors who tended towards this perspective were notably excited about their work—the fun of working with artists to help create manga and doing something they liked—even if it is really hard work at times. These avid manga editors eagerly discussed what manga they read apart from work, something that I did not encounter in all my interviews.

Returning to the history of manga, which opened this chapter, the story holds that manga grew up alongside the first postwar generation of children. If that is the case, then what of the generation that grew up with manga already firmly established? It is this generational difference that can be seen clearly among the editors in this study. All of the those who indicated a strong link to manga were in their early twenties to early thirties. This is not to indicate that all younger editors loved manga or that no older ones did, but the lifelong engagement with manga tended to differ between editorial generations. The older generation of editors, whether they expressed indifference or pride in relation to manga today, cited less of a relationship to it from their childhood. Yamaguchi, in his fifties, provides a telling example.

> **Yamaguchi:** I didn't read a lot of manga growing up and I wanted to work publishing literature when I started here. . . . Back then, when we started here, not many people really wanted to work in manga. Now it has changed and many of our applicants want to be manga editors.
>
> **Jennifer:** What changed?
>
> **Yamaguchi:** When I was little manga was considered frivolous—people only read it on vacation or if they were home sick as a present, but you never took manga to school. But today, it is different; those who grew up reading manga are adults and they have a different consciousness about manga.

An editor in his mid-thirties, Ishihara Katsunobu, highlighted this change through a more contemporary example. "Many of our applicants the last few years credited their interest in a career here with their love of Yazawa Ai's *Tenshi nanka jya nai* [I am no angel], which ran in the early 1990s." Editors young and old touched upon this new trend wherein many new recruits to the publishing industry apply because of their interest in manga specifically, and a title from that publishing house in particular. While many of these publishing initiates will not end up working with manga for their whole careers, if at all, the interest is telling. This point is remarkable because it was cited as a relatively new phenomenon despite the fact that manga sales in general reached their peak in the 1990s and the golden years are considered to have been in the 1970s. This kind of anecdotal evidence was commonly cited in my interviews and in discussions to portray changes in the relationship that younger generations have to manga, highlighting that the manga generation has entered the job market as well as the artist pool.

Finally, I want to return for a moment to issues of gender. Whether they were avid manga fans or mostly read manga for work, most of the male editors distanced themselves from the genre of *shōjo manga*. The words of Maruyama Akira about his days editing *shōjo manga* are emblematic. "I read manga as a kid, but not *shōjo*. I had older sisters so I was not unfamiliar with the genre, but I didn't really read it. . . . Ishinomori [Shōtarō] also had no idea about young girls, so we fumbled along together to learn what the readers liked, and I guess we did okay [*laughs*]." Many of the male editors I interviewed admitted to reading manga as children, but qualified it with "but not *shōjo*." Several explained that for male editors the first few months on the job are spent primarily reading *shōjo manga* to get a sense of what exactly it is, as though it were an entirely new world. There are a few exceptions; I did have a few younger male editors admit, sheepishly, that they read their sister's *shōjo manga* and were familiar with it when they began their careers. The majority, however, did not admit to sharing such an affinity.

In contrast, many of the female editors cited their youthful experiences with *shōjo manga* as important to them, and to their current jobs. Sōda clarified her overall perspective as we concluded our interview. "Again, more than any other work, for me working as an editor is from [my] experience of being a girl reading manga." Saejima expressed a similar relationship to her love of manga, any manga, and her work as an editor.

> In college I was in the Japanese literature division and I knew I wanted to work writing *monogatari* and *shōjo manga* in particular. Even now I still like people and I think that is true for most girls. I remember greatly the feeling of reading a manga and thinking of the main heartthrob, "He is so cool" and wanting to be closer to my friends, things like that. That kind of content is still a big part [of *shōjo manga*]; that is what is so great about manga—no matter how it changes, peoples' true feelings don't change and that is reflected.

For these editors the line between their jobs and one of their favorite pastimes is blurred. In the course of our conversations, several of the young women editors excitedly discussed their favorite manga titles past and present with me. Upon learning that we both enjoyed Yazawa Ai's *Nana*, Ōsaki Midori proceeded to discuss the latest *tankōbon* (book), which had been released the night before. I hadn't seen the issue yet, to which Ōsaki exclaimed, "That is a great part of working here, we [publishing houses] send each other copies of everything hot off the press so I get to read all the newest manga for free at work, after hours, of course." For these young women, and a few of the men, *shōjo manga* was both a main form of entertainment and a job. The unique perspective of women editors provides a view of the *shōjo manga* industry between that of producers and consumers, a point I posit in the final section of this chapter.

## Between Production and Consumption

In the narrative history of manga that begins this chapter, the postwar generation of children grew up reading manga and in turn helped the industry grow through their purchasing power, through demand for more mature titles as they grew, and as emergent manga artists themselves. On the flip side, the industry expanded as this generation grew, branching into teen and then adult manga, harnessing the enthusiasm of this first postwar generation into stories and yen. In the case of *shōjo manga,* from the early 1970s on young female artists have been critical to the industry because of their potential affinity to young girls. Through the Manga School contest readers are raised to be artists, learning the technical ropes from current artists and editors and trying their hand at writing manga. Thus, young artists are taught the parameters and styles of the *shōjo manga* form through reading the magazines and submitting their own manga for critique and, hopefully, the opportunity to debut. In these instances it is easy to see how, in the creative role of artists, the identities of producer and consumer are blurred, a factor that is fundamental to the creation of *shōjo manga* today.

Artists have always lived a somewhat otherly existence in the realm of mass-media analysis, often escaping the label of "producer," with its insinuations of corporate culture, and the manga industry is no exception. Indeed, as discussed above, artists are both central to the creation of manga and yet collaborators in the production process itself. But this chapter focuses primarily on the mass-media producers of manga, the editors who create *shōjo manga* magazines and work with artists to create manga. Editors have traditionally been *sarariiman* managing the creativity of artists and harnessing them into the structured mass-media industry, thus shaping the genre of manga. That these editors are *sarariiman* first and manga producers second is clear. Their job is to manage the creation of manga in manga magazines, always with a watchful eye on the bottom line. However, the process of determining what will sell demands a delicate balance between reformulating the tried and true (or the homogeneity and predictability that Horkheimer and Adorno decried) and gauging what readers will like and, thus, will continue to pay for (Horkheimer and Adorno, 1972). Traditionally, these two angles were covered by the use of older male editors—company men—and young women artists who were viewed as closer in both age and sentiment to the readers. However, in the example of the younger generation of editors and particularly the young women, these roles sometimes collide.

While the young women editors I interviewed are unequivocally company employees first and foremost, many of them expressed a certain stake in the production of *shōjo manga.* Typically this was because of their own personal histories with manga and often *shōjo manga* in particular. These editors who view themselves as consumers of manga as well as editors who get to work at creating manga are at once producers and consumers. They are in a unique position to concretely think about "what readers will like," albeit often based on personal preferences and experiences, while evaluating the business end of making manga, meeting deadlines, and shaping the stories and characters to fit the tried and true aspects of the genre. If what is at stake in discussions of production and consumption is the question of where meaning is made—as ideology spoon-fed to the masses or in the process of consumption—these editors are in a position to think about both—not in the simple guise of gender essentialism, but because they feel connected to both the readers and the texts in a different way than older male editors or scholars have assumed.

Furthermore, these young women editors, like artists, are betwixt and between the realms of manga production through their liminal employment status. The *ippanshoku* track, discussed at the beginning of this chapter, encourages women to work until marriage or childbirth, ensuring that moving up the corporate ladder is not their main objective. While the women editors I spoke with were clearly serious about their jobs, they were not planning to work there forever. Similarly, manga artists do not often remain in the business for their whole lives. As mentioned in chapter 3, the Manga School system shifted the publishing dynamic, leading to fewer veteran artists. Miyazaki Yuri's declaration that she wouldn't create manga forever, even though she didn't know what she would do next, puts the female editors and artists in a similar relationship. Between the connection with and desire to create manga and the structural liminality of both female manga artists and editors, the lines between producers and consumers are blurred.

Manga editors utilize contests and prizes to solicit readers' feedback, even in cases where this is solely to determine which manga are the most popular and thus will sell more books, anime, video games, and the like. What the readers are interested in is a part of the making of manga. This is true in most culture industries today; millions of dollars, yen, and euro exchange hands daily in the name of market research and focus groups. Yet how exactly do the business end of making manga and readers' opinions merge? In my conversations editors gave examples of characters that were marginal and became central because of readers' love of them. Saejima provided a particular example while flipping through a manga book. "In this one we wanted a serious drama, different from the previous title we created, but the readers kept wanting more of this guy [*points to character*]. He is just funny, for comic relief, but readers wanted that style, so we made it funny." Here we see a point where readers' feedback is directly articulated into the making of manga so that the title will remain popular, perhaps at the expense of artistic integrity.

The editors I interviewed discussed the tension between keeping readers and attaining new readers in the face of economic hard times and steep competition in a variety of ways. Minami bluntly outlined the tension. "They [manga] are, after all, ultimately mass media. To be really successful as an editor, magazine, or manga division, you have to be able to cater to readers specifically, while also trying to reach more and more people. This is the real trick. Today, with all the competition it is harder than it used to be." For some of the editors, readers held even greater significance than simply purchasing power would suggest. Takigawa and Shimizu both held particularly strong editorial philosophies.

> **Takigawa:** The good and bad thing about working as a manga editor is that there is insecurity involved; there is no real way to feel like you have "know how" because the terrain is always changing. The readers change and that changes everything. Everything in this business depends on the readers and it is hard to chart what they will do. Also, so much of the job has to do with human relations, understanding readers, interacting with artists, other editors, and designers; you are the intermediary.

> **Shimizu:** The important thing for editors is to have the confidence to really listen to the readers and try and understand them, and to create an environment that is easy for artists to write in. The editor needs to be strong, but not overpowering, to provide the space to write and to manage between the readers and artists, helping the transmission and nothing more. Editors should not dictate or raise artists. The readers raise the artists. Japanese readers are really sharp; if you really pay attention to what they want, you will produce great stuff. Not a simple sense of what will be popular, but a deeper level of listening. Today's editors have lost that. Japanese people read manga from a young age and really learn what to appreciate. I am not talking about what you might call fans, but the average Japanese reader.

These editors felt that listening to readers can be more than a matter of simple market research collected in surveys, but something that editors actually rely on. The philosophical attitudes expressed in these quotes were not expressed by all whom I interviewed but were attributed to "good editors," those who aren't too heavy-handed and are successful intermediaries between readers, artists, and the bottom line.

As Maruyama Akira summed up the process, "At its best, making manga is not a one-way but a two-way conversation among editors, with artists, and between artists/editors/readers." If we take Maruyama's claim at face value and agree that the making of manga is, at its best, a two-way street, the lines of communication are certainly mediated. Henry Jenkins aptly identifies this phenomena when discussing the changes in new media models, writing, "Rather than talking about media producers and consumers as occupying separate roles, we might now see them as participants who interact with each other according to a new set of rules that none of us fully understands" (2006, 3). However, what Jenkins is identifying in new media we see in the *shōjo manga* industry, which is traditional media, rooted in the postwar corporate culture.

While the editors for whom interactions with artists and readers was paramount stood out among my interviews, for the small number of mostly female editors who were positioned as producers and consumers, this philosophy was inherent in their approach to their jobs. Ōsaki Midori summed up *shōjo manga* as follows: "They are for the readers; I am an editor here, but a reader for others, so editors are frequently in both positions at once." Also, remember Sōda Naoko, who, as quoted in the epigraph that opened this book, wanted to provide a fun and carefree life like she enjoyed in high school for the readers of her magazine. For editors like these, understanding what readers want and enhancing their lives is a part of what will sell manga. In these editors we can see the way in which the roles of producer and consumer can be slippery. These editors are still *sararii*-men and women attuned to what will sell, and that is their job, but some are also deeply invested in the genre of manga, which they grew up with and loved, making them both consumers themselves and more easily identified with the consumers of their products.

*Shōjo manga* production, in this instance, is affective labor. Returning to Hardt and Negri's definition, affective labor produces both material and immaterial goods, but most importantly it produces and manipulates affect and constructs relationships (2000, 293; 2004, 147). The creation of *shōjo manga* is affective labor on two fronts. It produces affect through stories about human relations, intimacy, and interiority, and these stories are both material (books, magazines, character goods, etc.) and immaterial (stories that are rearticulated in other forms of popular culture). But the production of *shōjo manga* is also affective labor because for the young editors discussed at the end of this chapter (as well as artists), the creation of manga is something they are personally invested in; they feel close to readers and close to the texts that they produce, as do artists. The affect comes in precisely where production and consumption meet for these young editors.

This is not to suggest that *shōjo manga* production is the only place where this confluence of production and consumption happens; in fact, video-game, music, television, and movie production necessitate people invested in the medium working as creators. However, the fact that it is a part of the way the history of manga is told makes it an apt case study through which to theorize the affective labor involved in media production. Since the 1980s there has been a spate of scholarly research, across disciplines, that theorizes the various ways that meaning is made at the site of consumption, as a more nuanced corrective to the class- and production-based assumptions of the Frankfort school. Discussing the ways that consumers (mis)use commodities and media texts is an important turn in thinking about the ways we engage with mass media. Beginning with the assumption that consumers read and understand media texts in a variety of ways, I have tried to take this theorization back into the realm of production. The young (women) editors of *shōjo manga* are an especially apt example of the use of consumption models in the production of media texts.

By taking an ethnographic look at the people who inhabit this industry, the men and women behind the scenes, we see that while the processes and institutionalization involved in the production of manga are structural and bureaucratic at best, there are individual people with their own histories, relations, hopes, and dreams behind the culture industry machine. All of these factors—bureaucracy and creativity, gender and generation—affect the creation of manga, both in terms of process and content. Undeniably, the basis of any industry is profit, and the manga industry is no exception. In this chapter I have taken the dominance and cultural productivity of the industry as a starting point, but then turned to examine the social dynamics that are negotiated in the process of publishing manga. At some level producers of manga must be attuned to what their readers want in order to gauge what will sell, but beyond this superficial bottom line many of the younger editors and artists I spoke with perceived themselves as having been variously shaped by this very medium when they were growing up. Thus, through the affective labor of young editors we see a betwixt-and-between space within the process of production that relies on reader interests—that is, consumption—in multiple ways.

A view of production, attendant to the jobs, understandings, and personal experiences of editors and artists of *shōjo manga,* leads us to question the dichotomy between production and consumption as they have been theorized. Not only does this research flesh out what happens in the process of production, the way that the needs of readers, artists, and editors are managed, but it also illuminates the way that today many producers in the culture industries are also consumers. Like scholars, producers are often attentive to the meanings and uses consumers make of their texts/products, particularly in the culture industry. And for the group of young editors, readers of manga themselves past and present, the dual role of producer and consumer is natural and is in part why they chose to work in the industry. While we cannot simply ignore the power relations inherent in the culture industry, understanding the process through which these texts are created provides a more complete understanding of production and consumption in the contemporary moment.

CHAPTER FIVE

# *Material Gals*

Girls' Sexuality, Girls' Culture, and *Shōjo Manga*

In the towns, something began to happen in this period, in the late 1980s and early 1990s. From that time things like *kogyaru* began to emerge. Whatever town you were in, whatever young girls you looked at had become catalysts. Namely, the making of trends, the ability or talent to make trends increasingly came from young girls. In other words, young girls out and about were not just consumers. This time it was opposite. They had become the catalysts of consumer society.
—Interview with Yonezawa Yoshihiro, 2002

"Gals!"—Kotobuki Ran is the world's most invincible *kogyaru*. Even today, she's a daredevil, rampaging through Shibuya. But now that she has discovered her classmates' *enjo kōsai* activities . . . ? Raging hot-blooded, pure-hearted streets!!
—Fujii Mihona, "Gals!" 1999

The *kogyaru* as heroine of Shibuya, depicted in the promotional tagline for "Gals!" above, is telling of the relationship between *shōjo manga* and the discourses about girls that surfaced in the 1990s. "Gals!" by Fujii Mihona, is a typical millennial *shōjo manga* that ran in Shueisha's *Ribon* magazine from late 1999 through 2003. The antics of the gals (*gyaru*) Kotobuki Ran and her schoolmates, Miyu and Aya, policing the streets of Shibuya vigilante style, dressed in *kogyaru*-chic, captured the hearts of young girls throughout Japan. The combination of materialism, sexuality, and cute in this story of the life of teens in Tokyo is exemplary of the discussion of schoolgirls that imbued the 1990s, when sexy-cute girls seemed to dominate the streets and, as manga scholar and cultural critic Yonezawa Yoshihiro suggests, even drove consumer society. In this chapter, I examine the way this national gaze into the life and times of schoolgirls was incorporated into and amplified through one realm of the girls' culture industry by unraveling the complex negotiations between the *shōjo manga* industry, discourses about girls' sexuality, and youth culture itself at the turn of the century.

Taking up where the history of *shōjo manga* left off (in chapter 2), this chapter examines representations of girls' sexuality in contemporary *shōjo manga*. In the 1990s, as the nation seemed nearly consumed with discussions of schoolgirl sexuality, the representation of sex in *shōjo manga* increased. Throughout this chapter I ask how this national preoccupation with schoolgirls as trendsetters and consummate consumers is reflected and refracted in the pages of *shōjo manga*. Through textual analysis of "Gals!" along with ethnographic examples I analyze how editors and artists manage the boundaries between "what girls want"—the audience they serve and must satisfy—and wider social and political concerns about girls' sexuality in the 1990s. Ultimately, I argue that *shōjo manga*, which is for and about girls, is both contingent on and contributes to wider social concerns about girls.

## Representations of Sex in *Shōjo Manga*

The leading *shōjo manga* magazines for readers from grade school through high school have always been mainstream and thus tamer than some of the other manga magazines available. In the world of *shōjo manga*, depictions of sex are a relatively recent phenomenon, and one that proliferated in the 1990s. *Shōjo manga* scholar Fujimoto Yukari outlined this metamorphosis for me.[1] Before the 1970s there was no sex at all in *shōjo manga*. In the 1970s bed scenes[2] were banned, but from then on they gradually began to appear. The innovations of the *24 nengumi* intensified the drama of love stories in *shōjo manga* and bed scenes began to appear in the mainstream magazines, although they were still rare and iconic more than graphic. According to Fujimoto, by the mid-1990s the levels of sexual activity in *shōjo manga* had greatly increased, as discussed in chapter 2 (Fujimoto 2002).

But even in the twenty-first century, when mass media boundaries are increasingly porous, age segmentation is still an important part of *shōjo manga*, and sexually explicit content, like other adult themes, progresses as you move up the magazine system.[3] In the *imōto* (little sister) magazines (*Ribon, Nakayoshi, Ciao,* and *Hana to yume*) aimed at the youngest readers, around fifth year in grade school, there is no nudity or scenes depicting compromising positions. Here, romance stories, which can continue for years, still may culminate in a kiss. Magazines for the next generation (*Margaret, Shōjo friend, Shōjo comics,* and *Lala*), aimed at junior high girls, include a little more content dealing with sexuality, and while bed scenes are more prevalent, explicit sex scenes are relatively rare. Finally, magazines such as *Cookie* (Shueisha), *Dessert* (Kodansha), *Bessatsu shōjo comic* (Shogakukan), and *Shōjo comic cheese!* (Shogakukan), which are aimed at high school or college girls, sometimes include more explicit references to and depictions of sexuality.

In particular, several magazines for high school girls emerged in the 1990s to target the "new" teen trend of sexual proclivity—for example, *Cheese!* (1996, Shogakukan) and *Dessert* (1997, Kodansha).[4] Both of these magazines were started when the recession had already begun to affect the publishing houses, and the trend was to cut back rather than add to the existing repertoire. But these two magazines were aimed at enticing (and keeping) readers in their teens who were interested in contemporary issues, namely sex. The taglines for these magazines speak volumes about their content and aim: *Cheese!*—"*Ren'ai mōdo ON! magazine*" (Love mode ON! magazine), and *Dessert*—"*Omoshirokute H, soshite kandō!*" *Rabu sutori comikkushi* (Interesting H, so moving! Love story comic magazine). Both magazines are focused on love stories, and *Dessert* has slang for sex, "H," in its tagline.[5] Similarly, "H" appeared in many of the story titles for both *Cheese!* and *Dessert* during my research. There was even a special issue of *Cheese!* in December 2001 with the theme "*Lolita: Kiken sugiru jun'ai*" (Lolita: Too dangerous true love). Similarly, in June 2002 *Dessert* devoted an entire issue to "*Minna no H: Uwaki!? Wakare!? Koi to H no kiki kara dasshustu suru hōhō*" (Everyone's H: An affair!? Breaking up!? Methods for escaping the crisis of love and sex). The buzz phrases are all there to catch the eye and reel in the imagination. Clearly, these new magazines meld the traditional focus on love stories found in *shōjo manga* with racier content.

However, even the more overt magazines are not graphically explicit compared to the dripping photos found in many *seinen* (young men's) and adult manga. The sex scenes are still infrequent, typically two to six per magazine. As the image from "Watashi no meganekun" (My boy in glasses) by Sumoto Amu in figure 5.1 exemplifies, the scenes tend towards lots of cuts and close-ups eliciting the frantic feeling of the action rather than full-on sex scenes (although the latter are not unheard of). The content may be racier and have sex at the fore, but the stories themselves still explore the ins and outs of love and friendship, issues that girls are facing in the real world.

## From *Shōjo* to *Gyaru*: "Gals!" as *Shōjo Manga*

This chapter focuses on a case study of "Gals!" as one example of the ways that wider preoccupations about girls and sexuality were articulated in *shōjo manga* magazines. More serial than narrative, "Gals!" follows the antics and adventures of Kotobuki Ran and her friends Miyu and Aya as they hang out in Shibuya. Ran is from a police family and, although she vows never to be a cop, she and her friends monitor the streets of their favorite hangout vigilantly, chasing off bad guys and girls alike. I chose to focus this textual analysis on "Gals!" precisely because it was a wildly popular manga aimed at grade-school girls during much of the heated discussion about schoolgirls and sexuality. Looking at the ways that this discourse about high-school girls' materialism and sexuality frames the plotline of this *shōjo manga* for younger girls enables us to examine how social issues are absorbed and amplified in *shōjo manga* more broadly.

"Gals!" is a typical *shōjo manga* in several ways: content, cuteness, cohort, and combat. First of all, the bulk of the narrative is about high-school girls' everyday life: school, hanging out with friends after school, shopping, and discussing important issues such as whether or not to dye one's hair, what color cell phone is best, or who is the cutest guy from the

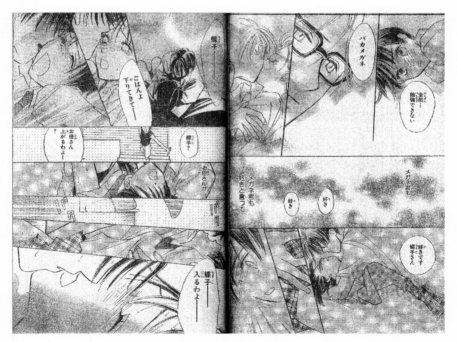

Figure 5.1. Cuts and angles capture the heat of the scene in "Watashi no Megane-kun" by Sumoto Amu, in *Cheese!* July 2002, 368–369. (Courtesy of Shogakukan)

premier Tokyo high school, along with the weightier issues of *ningen kankei* (human relations) discussed throughout this book. As I argued in chapter 2, beginning in the 1980s everyday life in Japan became the most prominent trope of *shōjo manga,* and the trivia and details in "Gals!" are no exception.

Similarly, while Ran and her friends (and rivals) are all explicitly *kogyaru,* they are also typically *shōjo manga* cute. Their clothes, conversation, and context may scream *kogyaru,* but their doe eyes and demeanor evoke the saccharine cuteness found in *shōjo manga.* Particularly because "Gals!" ran in *Ribon* and thus targeted grade-school readers, cuteness was critical to its success. As the image in figure 5.2 attests, Ran is a cute young schoolgirl. Her cheerful vitality is depicted in her stance and expression, and her eyes reveal her innocence and heartfelt exuberance.

Furthermore, the girl gang portrayed in "Gals!" is consistent with another trend in *shōjo manga,* the cohort. Because friendship and relationships are central to the genre, *shōjo manga* has long focused its stories on the protagonist and her group of friends, rather than solely on one lead character. Ran, Miyu, and Aya patrolling the streets of Tokyo and hanging out with their male friends and love interests, is, again, the standard fare of *shōjo manga* and girls' culture more generally.

The text accompanying figure 5.2 elicits another characteristic of contemporary *shōjo manga*—the *otenba* character. It reads,

> **Kotobuki Ran, Early summer in my second year of middle school**
> *I bleached my hair and added a red streak to get ready for summer,*
> *    but my teacher yelled at me as expected.*
> *The adults around me keep telling me to be serious, but I'm like,*
> *    "Whatever."*
> *I hate studying; I hate making an effort; It's super fun hanging out*
> *    in Shibuya!*
> *To be honest, there is nothing I am afraid of these days.*

*Otenba* is actually an older word meaning "tomboy" and was used to characterize the vivacious and strong-willed girls who frequently enlivened the stories of *shōjo manga* in the 1950s and 1960s. Ran and her friends are contemporary colleagues of the likes of Sapphire (*Ribon no kishi,* Tezuka Osamu), Fuichin (*Fuichin,* Ueda Toshiko), and the like (Tezuka 1953, Ueda 1957–1963).[6] Yet while the *otenba* of the past were frequently precocious, mischievous, or even pranksters, in the 1990s these feisty young girl protagonists took on a new characteristic—a mixture of sexy and cute.

Figure 5.2. Cute and carefree 1990s *otenba*, Ran Kotobuki. Fujii Mihona's "Gals!" 1999, 1:149. (GALS!© by Mihona Fujii/ Shueisha Inc.)

Because "Sailor Moon" by Takeuchi Naoko was one of the first *shōjo manga* titles to capitalize on this trend, it exemplifies the turn. Tsukino Usagi is a crybaby, a poor student, klutzy, and loves to eat. And yet when called she morphs into a super-heroine, Sailor Moon. Adding to her girly cachet, it is a piece of jewelry, a brooch, that spurs Usagi's transformation into Sailor Moon, and her weapons include her boomerang tiara and a moon prism wand. Most strikingly, while Usagi is all girl, Sailor Moon is decidedly a woman. The magical makeover that turns Usagi into a superhero includes longer legs, a shorter skirt, and cleavage (Allison 2000, 134–138; Grigsby 1999, 191–192). Here we see the merging of the cute of *shōjo manga* with the sexy of *roricon* (Lolita complex) culture.[7]

Created a decade later, Ran shares several key features that characterize the new *shōjo manga* heroines of the 1990s: she is cute and sexy, girl and hero. While Sailor Moon was a volatile and vivacious heroine, she was all female; Ran, on the other hand, is frequently described as "a hot-blooded person (*nekketsu*) prone to getting all worked up."[8] In contemporary *otenba* flair, Ran is always ready and willing to pick a fight in order to help people she cares about, but unlike Sailor Moon, she lives firmly within the reality of everyday Japan and embodies sexy-cute without requiring a transformation. As the slogan "Raging hot-blooded, pure-hearted streets," quoted at the beginning of this chapter, exclaims, in "Gals!" the innocent cuteness of *shōjo manga* is wedded to issues of girls' sexuality at the turn of the twenty-first century. But the question remains: why did sexual content increase in *shōjo manga* in the 1990s? In order to answer, I turn to an account of the wider social preoccupation with girls' sexuality that broiled in the 1990s.

### *Kogyaru* and the *Enjo Kōsai* Phenomenon

The recession, which began in the 1990s, begat hardships that rocked not only the core of the financial powerhouses, but also the postwar social management system, with its ostensibly seamless infrastructure of workplace, home, and school acclaimed as the very impetus for the Japanese miracle. As the bubble burst and the economic miracle began to deflate, it seemed as if the social fabric of Japan was collapsing as well. Throughout the 1990s and into this new century there has been widespread anxiety about the effects that the economic miracle and its social system (especially through their downfall) have wrought on Japanese society.[9] This apprehension about social collapse was primarily channeled into angst about youth. In general, from the nineties on there has been a pervasive feeling that youth today have no sense of values or purpose, a sentiment voiced ad nauseam in the media, among academics, and even within the halls of the Diet. The moral panic that emerged in the 1990s coalesced around the issues of violence and sexuality among teens, falling along gendered lines.[10] Violence was the source of concern for boys, as news stories of young boys who "snapped" (*kireru*) and committed acts of violence—frequently against classmates—abounded.[11] Sexuality was the dominant fear for girls, evinced by the *enjo kōsai* (assisted dating) phenomenon. As early as 1993, news stories about promiscuity among junior high and high school girls began to saturate the media. Such reports were written in a tone of disbelief at the new trends, all involving issues of sexuality and consumption, that seemed to have taken schoolgirls by storm.

    *Kogyaru* is typically written in katakana (the syllabary for foreign words, and emphasis), and so its etymology is debated. The term originates from either "small gal" or "high school gal," but either way it refers to a fashion trend that hit the streets of Tokyo in the late 1980s and early 1990.

*Kogyaru* blends the notion of *kawaii* (cute) that has dominated *shōjo* culture throughout the postwar with a carefree, sexy attitude, adding an urban flair. The scene of schoolgirls crouched in corners or at the end of train cars after school, chatting loudly while rolling up their school uniform sleeves and skirts, gluing baggy, loose socks (*rūsu sokusu*) in place, and applying extra makeup stowed in their designer bags is the everyday stuff of *kogyaru*. As Kinsella aptly points out, ultimately *kogyaru* fashion transformed the schoolgirl uniform into an almost "prostitute-chic" look (Kinsella 2002, 230). Sexy and cute had merged in the fashion of the schoolgirl.

*Kogyaru* style is not limited to tailoring school uniforms. Similarly combining a sexy-chic with cuteness, *kogyaru* can be seen in non-uniform short skirts, fur-lined jackets, mini-Ts adorned with cute characters, and clunky sock-boots. Whether in uniform or not, *kogyaru* typically accessorize with a mixture of sexy and cute, combining Hello Kitty and other such character goods with elaborately decorated nails and temporary tattoos, and mobile phones, likewise adorned, are the number-one accessory. Finally, *kogyaru*'s hair is also styled. Dying one's hair blond, known as *kinpatsu*, as well as *meshu* (streaking one's hair), was popular in *kogyaru* circles and beyond through the 1990s and into the new millennium.[12]

Yet Yonezawa's mention of the materialization of *kogyaru* as the turning point for girls' role in 1990s society, cited at the beginning of this chapter, is telling, for discussions of the escapades and experiences of *kogyaru* seemed to grip Japan at the turn of the century. Young girls out and about in Shibuya held considerable sway over the media and marketers in Japan at the start of the new millennium. Kinsella argues that, in fact, schoolgirls had themselves become a "brand" as the image of sexy schoolgirl (forever in uniform) not only proliferated through media reports about their lifestyles, but also in the advertising realm (Kinsella 2002, 229). Schoolgirls could be found adorning ads for products now associated with them, like mobile phones, designer goods, and snack foods, as well as a range of random products such as cameras, computers, and the like. This sense, that it is girls who set the trends and drive consumer society in contemporary Japan, is something I encountered time and again on the fringes of my research. This was perhaps epitomized by the pervasive images, in the media and on the streets, of young girls with thumbs flying as they deftly text messaged each other on their mobile phones. Such phones, adorned with flashy frills and cute accessories, are the secret weapon of this new consumer vanguard. Schoolgirls had become the wave of the future, the trendsetters for Japan in the new high-tech Internet age.

The identification of woman as consummate consumer is not new; she has always been at once fashionable and threatening in her changing behaviors (De Grazia and Furlough 1996). In fact, the 1980s was simultaneously dubbed the women's age (*jōsei jidai*) and heralded the coming of age for Japanese consumer society (*shōhi shakai*) (Skov and Moeran 1995, 1–74). Furthermore, visible consumption by women and girls has frequently elicited a flurry of media attention, positive and negative, descriptive and productive. Laura Miller aptly links the visibility of *kogyaru* and fears about consumption and sexuality to the discussions of *moga* (modern girl) almost a century earlier (2004, 226).[13] Indeed, the *kogyaru* as consumer vanguard was soon quickly linked to a moral decline not just because of her sexy attire, but also because of her association with the phenomenon of *enjo kōsai* that dominated discussions of schoolgirls throughout much of the 1990s.

*Enjo kōsai*, translated as "assisted dating," refers to the practice of schoolgirls giving their time and, sometimes, sexual favors to older men in exchange for money to buy designer goods. Typically, the phenomenon consisted of high school, and occasionally junior high, girls meeting men via *terekura* (telephone clubs) or *dēto kurabu* (date clubs) in order to set up a "date" for a prearranged sum of money. Advertised ubiquitously on free advertisement tissues handed out in front of train stations and posted all over phone booths, *terekura* were locations where men could pay for a private room to await a call from a young girl to set up a date. The clubs had networks of girls they could call to connect with the eagerly awaiting client. Mobile phone Internet and e-mail networks made such transactions all the easier; a man could simply post a proposal—"20,000 yen for dinner" or "40,000 yen for dinner and sex"—at a specific bulletin board or newsgroup and wait for a girl to respond, or vice versa.[14] The dates could consist of anything from dinner, to a walk in a park, to kissing, to sex.

The term *enjo kōsai* was coined by the media in countless articles, books, and television news documentaries about the wayward girls that populated Japanese schools at the end of the twentieth century and into the twenty-first century. Immediately, a wave of concern about the welfare and mindset of high school girls swept the nation. Scattered across the major newspapers by August 1994, one could hardly miss panicked headlines such as "27% of middle and high school girls phone *terekura* and 2 shots (phone dating service)" (*Nikkei shinbun*), "Today's junior high girls . . . one out of four say 'I have experience' with *terekura*" (*Yomiuri shinbun*), "Even junior high girls have experience with *terekura*. Is it really bigger than we thought?" (*Asahi shinbun*) (Miyadai 1994, 1). Mountains of articles, news stories, and

PTA and government reports, as well as books, both academic and popular, accumulated quickly, all of them trying to figure out what was happening and how many girls were involved (Kinsella 2002, 228). A background scene from Kirino Natsuo's best-selling thriller *Out* epitomizes the ubiquity of the schoolgirl watch of the 1990s. Kuniko is watching TV.

> A special feature on high school girls came on, and Kuniko found herself setting aside her chopsticks and focusing on the program. A girl with long, straight, dyed-brown hair was talking. Her face had been disguised with digital blurring and her voice was distorted, but Kuniko could tell the she was pretty and stylish.
>
> "Men are wallets, just wallets," she was saying. "Me? What did I get out of them? A suit, a ¥450,000 suit." (2005, 18)

One could hardly turn on the TV in the mid-1990s without witnessing such a scene, and these deviant schoolgirls cropped up in the pages of *shōjo manga* as well.

The *enjo kōsai* phenomenon, and the widespread response to it, was not simply about promiscuity among youth in general, as was the case with the "friends with benefits" phenomenon in the United States (Denizet-Lewis 2004), but rather about girls *selling* their intimates and intimacy to businessmen, typically in their thirties to fifties. The endless loop of schoolgirls who appeared on the news, with faces pixilated and voices disguised, and in print media of all sorts, all voiced the same response to questions about why they would do such a thing: "For money to buy myself things." Louis Vuitton, Prada, Gucci, not to mention karaoke and mobile phone bills—these seemed to be a girl's best friend in Japan at the turn of the century. And they all came with big price tags. The media discourses about *enjo kōsai* bemoaned the level to which these youth had become so shallow, seemingly surviving only for brand-name goods and to hang out with friends, at any cost.

What is most poignant about the discussions of and interviews with girls engaged in *enjo kōsai* is how inextricably linked the trend was to the recession in Japan. Both girls in interviews and the media attributed these behaviors to the increasing difficulties in keeping up the lifestyle of the 1980s in the face of hard times, as the following exchange from a magazine article reveals:

> T: If my parents would give me money I would uphold the ordinance.[15] We say we want money, but how much do you get each month?

R:  10,000 ($100)

T:  Me too.

K&M:  It depends.

R:  But 10,000 yen is way too little, I do karaoke and go out to eat
    . . . but of course I spend most of it on clothes. I also want brand
    goods. Right now I want a Prada wallet! . . . So I get money from
    ojisan. Returning to a poor life would be hard now, I don't want
    to, I won't. (Shūkan Josei 1997, 214–215)

As this girls' roundtable discussion from a mainstream girls' magazine suggests, rather than peasant parents selling their daughters into prostitution in order to help feed the family, this form of amateur prostitution was driven by girls who felt they didn't get enough pocket money. Living as a teen in Tokyo is expensive, especially if you try to participate in the glamorized life depicted in magazines, manga, and novels, or on TV. Perhaps this was simply a case of teen desire gone awry in the age of globalization, but what is clear is that in the national perception it was a signifier of the collapse of the postwar miracle economy and the social and cultural structures that underpinned it.

We cannot discuss the issue of girls "for sale" without addressing who is buying them—the role of the *oyaji* (old man) or *ojisan* (uncle) himself.[16] Significantly, it was always *sarariiman* who were presumed to be the clients in *enjo kōsai* transactions, with all that that image entails—absentee husbands and fathers returned home late at night from a hard day's work and required play.[17] For the most part, the focus of discussions of *enjo kōsai* revolved around the girls themselves, while the problems inherent in the practice of buying girls' companionship or bodies was only indirectly touched upon. This is not to suggest that the *oyaji* or *ojisan* were portrayed in a positive light; in fact, when they were depicted they seemed primarily hapless, sad, and occasionally perverse. However, the moral panic that surrounded the issue of *enjo kōsai* did not explicitly concern the loss of morals on the part of the nation's businessmen, husbands, and fathers.

Sociologist and leading social critic Miyadai Shinji champions the misunderstood youth who have been all but blamed for the collapse of Japan—socially and morally, if not economically.[18] Relying in part on interviews and discussions with a range of girls throughout the 1990s, Miyadai argues that *enjo kōsai* and other forms of after-school sex work are examples of girls' desire for and creation of a sense of sexual self-determination. In his two books on contemporary girls, Miyadai outlines his theory that the events, practices, and behaviors of schoolgirls within this milieu can be understood as an assertion of the right to make choices about their bodies and sexualities in the face of the monolithic and highly structured/structuring system of school standards (1994, 1998). In a similar turn, both Kinsella and Miller argue respectively that *kogyaru* sexuality is a form of subcultural resistance on the part of girls. Miller argues that through *kogyaru* fashion, which is misunderstood by wider society, girls are crafting new forms of femininity in search of an identity different from the good wife/wise mother, *kyoiku mama*, or even saccharine cute of the 1980s (2004, 231; 2006). Kinsella, on the other hand, focuses on the evolution of the schoolgirl uniform and discourses about schoolgirls in media throughout twentieth-century Japan, arguing that the *kogyaru* phenomenon is a rebellion against the media anxiety about girls' sexuality (2002). Each of these scholars persuasively argues that *kogyaru* and *kireru* boys are the excess that spill out of the constraints of the school system in late capitalist Japan; they are the sign of rupture and movement to a new era rather than the cause of collapse.

Thus, schoolgirls themselves were the consumers and the consumed, trapped in a loop of selling themselves (their personal items, personas, and bodies) in order to buy designer goods and fashionable lifestyles. At the same time, they had become both the producers and the produced, as they found their own means for attaining the things they wanted in the face of difficult economic times (by hawking their wares—whether image, clothing, or flesh) and through their role as a "brand." All of this played into national fears about the shallowness of a rampant consumer society (linked to women as the ultimate consumers) and girls' sexuality, which is always of interest to the nation in its potential. In the 1990s schoolgirls became at once the sign of collapsing social systems—family, work, and school—and yet the hope for future generations as trendsetters. Despite the fact that the *enjo kōsai* fears completely subsided by the turn of the twenty-first century, the discussions of girls, sexuality, and materialism have remained a part of discourses about girls. *Shōjo manga* traffics in images of girls as entertainment for girls, and the preoccupation with schoolgirl sexuality discussed here certainly affected such images and the way those images were perceived.

## *Etchi, Keitai,* and Shopping: The *Shōjo Manga* Connection

As the epigraph from "Gals!" that opened this chapter highlights, this national view of the schoolgirl as sexually and materially deviant mingled with the sassy but sensitive girls that populated *shōjo manga* in the 1990s. I turn now to an analysis of how these issues of girls' sexuality and consumption, which surfaced in the 1990s, percolated into *shōjo manga*. As a main form of girls' entertainment, *shōjo manga* is always in dialogue with wider trends in girls' culture (what girls like), as well as with social concerns about what is appropriate for girls. By looking at one concrete example of a *shōjo manga* title that dealt directly with the schoolgirl panic—"Gals!"—I examine the way that editors and artists engage with trends in girls' culture and discourses about girls more generally, arguing that such responses are at once descriptive and proscriptive.

Returning to the epigraph that opened this chapter, "Gals!" features a group of *kogyaru* policing the streets of Shibuya. Even the title elicits the *kogyaru* atmosphere of the 1990s. During my fieldwork, the manga was one of *Ribon*'s best sellers, and the anime based on "Gals!"—entitled *Chō gyarusu!* (Super gals!)—was one of the top girls' anime.[19] That *kogyaru* fashion and *enjo kōsai* situations had trickled down to become trendy topics suitable for grade-school girls' entertainment, reaching even the youngest girls, signals the way that schoolgirl issues and images had become omnipresent by the late 1990s.

*Kogyaru* style and lifestyle are central to "Gals!" The fashion trend is captured through the panache of Ran and her cohort, as well as through their constant quest for money for fun and designer goods. Figures 5.3 and 5.4 exemplify the look of the characters throughout the series. Ran and her friends are 100 percent *kogyaru* in both their school uniform style (figure 5.3)—baggy socks, short skirts, and oversized sweaters—and in their street fashion (figure 5.4)—the flamboyant flair of fur-lined collars and mini-Ts, miniskirts, and platform shoes. Both looks are accompanied by a plethora of rings, bracelets, hair accessories, and the ever-present *keitai* (cell phone) (figure 5.3). As I argued in chapter 3, *shōjo manga* magazines are one way that young girls are initiated into girls' culture, learning about fashion and the latest trends, and "Gals!" with its incredibly popular portrayal of *kogyaru* fun is no exception.

Yet while Ran is emphatically *kogyaru*, she does not participate in *enjo kōsai*; in fact, she fights against those who take advantage of girls in Shibuya. As the warning in the left-hand margin of figure 5.5 indicates, the message of "Gals!" is that *enjo kōsai* may be a reality of contemporary high school life, but it is not sanctioned. Found in the artist's notes in the margin of the first book, the warning is written like a police safety notice and reads, "*Enjo kōsai* '0'—City Declaration, Tokyo."[20] Importantly, in the scene that

*(Left)*
Figure 5.3. The *kogyaru* in schoolgirl attire. "Gals!" Fujii Mihona, 1999, 1:118.
(GALS!© by Mihona Fujii/Shueisha Inc.)

*(Right)*
Figure 5.4. The *kogyaru* all decked out. "Gals!" Fujii Mihona, 1999, 1:4–5.
(GALS!© by Mihona Fujii/Shueisha Inc.)

accompanies this warning, Ran discovers that a fellow classmate, Hoshino
Aya, is participating in *enjo kōsai*. The following encounter ensues.

> Ran finds Hoshino on the street in Shibuya and asks, "Are you waiting
> for an *oyaji*? Stop doing *enjo kōsai*. It's not worth it."
> Hoshino yells, "Leave me alone. It's my choice so no one can
> complain."
> ". . . Why do you want money," Ran replies.
> Hoshino, looking sad and embarrassed, explains, "My parents are
> really strict, my curfew is six and I am not allowed to have an after

school job. Plus my grades have to be the top or else they get really mad. I just want to hang out like everyone else, and go shopping too!"

We see a close-up of Ran's face with a sparkle of sympathy in her eyes, ". . . sold your body already?"

Hoshino, also in close-up, replies, " . . . not yet, until now I have only gone on dates. But maybe today . . . I think I will have to. . . ."

"It's fun being a *kogyaru* even if you don't have money," Ran pleads. "Don't you have any pride?"

"I really don't care anymore," Hoshino resignedly explains. "I felt so guilty at first, but now I don't feel anything. Anyway, it's fine as long as I don't sell my heart."

[*Begin Figure 5.6*] ". . . So, except for your heart, you are nothing less than a thing?" Ran queries.

"Exactly, is that so wrong?" Hoshino answers.

Figure 5.5. No *enjo kōsai* is the message in "Gals!" Fujii Mihona, 1999, 1:42–43. (The scene is continued in figure 5.6.) (GALS!© by Mihona Fujii/Shueisha Inc.)

Exasperated, Ran slaps Hoshino. In the next frame she exclaims, "Don't be so childish! Things don't feel any pain!! Aren't you alive!? If you're hit you feel pain, if you're cut you will bleed, right?! If you don't feel pain, it's as if your heart is dead as well. Go try to cut apart your own body and sell it, if you can't do that, you shouldn't talk so big!!"

The scene ends with Ran's friend Miyu telling Hoshino, "Having fun with me and my friends will be much better than hanging out with some *oyaji*. We will listen to your troubles too, you know." Hoshino, now called by her first name, Aya, becomes one of Ran's *kogyaru* sidekicks. (Fujii 1999, 42–46)

In this interchange all the components of the *enjo kōsai* phenomenon are at play. Hoshino argues that it is her choice and hers alone;[21] furthermore,

Figure 5.6. (Continued from figure 5.5.) Ran sets Aya straight in "Gals!" Fujii Mihona, 1999, 1:44–45. (GALS!© by Mihona Fujii/Shueisha Inc.)

her parents are strict and she just needs some fun away from all the pressure, which is why she engages in *enjo kōsai*. However, she doesn't think it is fun. Hoshino describes herself as "no longer feeling guilty but not feeling anything." Here we get an account of the general malaise towards the rigors of everyday life in postwar Japan that characterized much of the discourse around Heisei youth. However, it is not this disaffection, but rather Ran's heartfelt speech about humanity and self-liberation, that sets up the plot that drives the series, girls policing the streets of Shibuya. It turns the standard discourse of worrying that all *kogyaru* are doing *enjo kōsai* (and demoralizing the nation) on its head, making anti-*enjo kōsai kogyaru* the champions. The message of "Gals!" to its young readers is clear—*enjo kōsai* is not worth it. However, this anti-*enjo kōsai* attitude does not translate to a critique of the materialism that suffused discourses about *kogyaru* and *enjo kōsai*. While discussions of *enjo kōsai* directly linked rampant materialism with a collapsing social fabric, "Gals!" uncouples them. In "Gals!" the practice of *enjo kōsai* itself is condemned, but the materialism that underlies it is exalted. In fact, the message of materialism in "Gals!" goes further than a mere reflection of the latest fashions seen on the streets of Shibuya; the tension and quest that drives the plot of "Gals!" is not one of heroic altruism, but heroic materialism. While Ran criticizes Hoshino for participating in *enjo kōsai* in order to get money for fun, she is constantly in search of money herself to buy designer goods. In fact, Ran's father, a policeman, keeps track of how many "good deeds" she does in Shibuya, and for every ten he gives her the paltry sum of five hundred yen (five dollars at the time). Thus, she makes her money for brand-name goods fighting *enjo kōsai* and other bad elements, although the payoff is not nearly as good. Hence in "Gals!" the *kogyaru* style and materialism is preserved—even paraded—but the *enjo kōsai* image is purged.

Furthermore, like the wider social discourse, the image of *kogyaru* throughout "Gals!" is mixed. On the one hand, the heroines are all *kogyaru* and discussions of *kogyaru* lifestyle, amusements, and fashions make up a significant portion of the content and appeal of this manga. Ran and her friends spend all their time hanging out in Shibuya, shopping and doing karaoke, while modeling the fashions that epitomize this subculture. On the other hand, many characters throughout the story line assume the worst about *kogyaru*. Beginning with the main heartthrob, Otohata Rei, who declares time and again, "I don't like *kogyaru*" and "I hate *kogyaru* style," various people assume that Ran and her friends are participating in *enjo kōsai* or are just otherwise unruly and unsightly. Indeed, neither Ran nor her

friends are typical good girls: Ran is a hothead, always fighting with someone, Miyu used to be a gang leader who engaged in knife fights and other
unsavory behavior, and, as we have seen, Aya participated in *enjo kōsai* for
a time. Complex main characters of this sort are typical of manga, but this
case also brings up the question of what representation of *kogyaru* "Gals!"
is putting forward. While general society, in reality and within the pages of
"Gals!", is wary of *kogyaru,* Ran and her friends, like their real counterparts, appropriate the identity as a way to empower themselves, as Miyadai
argues of the real *kogyaru.* "Gals!" takes this notion of self-empowerment
a step further by having Ran, Miyu, and Aya police Shibuya to make it a
better place for having fun. In true *shōjo manga* fashion, the "Gals!" gang
embodies both the "girls just wanna have fun" attitude of *kogyaru* and the
grander purpose of trying to help people in trouble, even if their help is ultimately given in exchange for money to buy designer goods.

"Gals!" provides insight into some of the ways in which the *enjo kōsai*
and *kogyaru* phenomena have been (re)articulated in *shōjo manga.* At the
turn of the century *kogyaru* was becoming a standard part of the image of
schoolgirls even in the sweet love comedies typical of *Ribon's shōjo manga.*
Here, *kogyaru,* with her fusing of cute and sexy, is embraced as a part of
girls' culture in the 1990s. At the same time, they draw the line at *enjo kōsai*
practices for the benefit of the young readers of *Ribon* and "Gals!" through
Ran, Miyu, and Aya's vigilantism and their message, "It's fun being a *kogyaru* even without money. . . . Having fun with me and my friends is much
better than an *oyaji*" (Fujii 1999, 46). The demonizing of *enjo kōsai* and
glorifying of *kogyaru* is exemplary of the ways that editors and artists tack
back and forth between notions of what girls want, what will sell, and what
they should want.

## "What Girls Want": Producing *Shōjo Manga*

"What is *shōjo manga?*" was the question with which I concluded all of
my interviews with editors, artists, and scholars of manga. A seemingly
naive question, one perhaps only a foreigner would ask, the inquiry always
proved to be the hardest for my respondents to answer. After a chuckle and
a pause for reflection, everyone responded by explaining, "*Shōjo manga* is
what girls want." Definitions of "what girls want" varied from person to
person and have varied over time, but the overall perception was that girls
themselves shape what makes up *shōjo manga.* In the rest of this chapter I
explicate the way that editors of *shōjo manga* navigate the tension between

"what girls want," "what girls should want," and "what will sell," all of which are as productive as they are descriptive.

Before turning to the voices of editors, I want to return to the discussion of this phrase "what girls want" from chapter 1. From a business perspective, editors used "what girls want" to discuss what will sell, a notion that was always at the fore in discussions with editors. However, "what girls want" was also the reason given for the preference for young female artists close to the readers' own ages—they are better able to decipher what girls want. And finally, "what girls want" is productive of what girls will want. The prominence of *shōjo manga* in girls' popular culture in Japan ensures that popular titles influence other media, fashion trends, and the like. Through the media-mix system wherein popular manga titles are also promoted through primetime anime and video games, all of which bring with them a mountain of character goods, manga character style comes to infuse girls' culture. Foucault's notion of the power of discourse is clearly at play here (1980). In this usage, discourse is a system of representations that in the guise of describing a subject actually define it; rather than merely listing the characteristics of a subject, discourse creates the very thing it is trying to describe. Just as editors feel beholden to follow the taxonomy of trends that girls themselves are setting (especially as they are understood as the movers and shakers of late capitalism in Japan), the stories and images they create actually fuel girls' culture as well as discussions of girls in the 1990s. As we have seen with the example of "Gals!", social issues were amplified through the story line, reemerging in recognizable form and yet tailored to the *shōjo manga* format. At the same time, the valorizing of *kogyaru* materialism as self-expression joins the conversation about girls as producers and consumers of contemporary Japan, this time in the guise of a story by, about, and for girls.[22] These are the complicated levels of ideology at work in the stories editors tell themselves about themselves, and it is these levels that I will unpack here through the example of the increase of sexual content in *shōjo manga* in the 1990s. I begin with editors' points of view.

The idea that *shōjo manga* reiterates girls' culture because it is created to be "what girls want," which was promoted by many of the editors I spoke with, is suggestive of the way in which *enjo kōsai* and *kogyaru* entered the world of *shōjo manga*. The mechanism through which these issues entered the *shōjo manga* realm was highlighted to me in an interview with two top manga executives. Sitting in a third-floor conference room, veteran editors Okamoto Hajime and Minami Yoshio mused about the history of manga at their publishing house and the state of manga today. Minami remarked,

"Returning to *shōjo manga*, popular themes are always changing. For example, a while ago it was volleyball and we made manga focused on volleyball, and then it was tennis; playing on tennis teams was what girls wanted to do, and we made manga about that. But today, you know what the number one *shōjo manga* theme is? H [slang for sex]." With a tone at once bemused and resigned, Minami was informing me of the shifting trends of what girls are interested in—it used to be volleyball, now it is sex. Spoken during one of my earliest interviews, this statement and the *shikata ga nai* (it can't be helped) tone with which it was delivered struck me. This tone, which I encountered on other occasions, washes the editor's hands of responsibility for the increase in sexually explicit manga for girls, insinuating that such a turn is just a part of the changing times in contemporary Japan. Whether it is good or bad, editors are at the whim of the market, Minami implied.

*Shōjo manga* editors and artists have long had to contend with how to deal with issues of sexuality—whether to represent them, and if so, how—as can be seen in the changing trends outlined at the beginning of this chapter. Udagawa Toshiya, a young executive editor, explained, "*Shōjo manga* has always had a focus on the complicated relations involved in being adolescent. So we deal with problems, issues, and tastes of those in their difficult adolescent years. This is somewhat different for boys and girls: girls' manga deals with deep friendships and human relations, although now boys' magazines are doing this more as well." Certainly, one of the key issues that arises in adolescence is sexuality.

During the golden years, in the late 1960s and early 1970s, *shōjo manga* was fanciful and set in exotic locales such as Europe, and the stories developed the dreamy and effervescent quality for which *shōjo manga* came to be known. However, in the 1980s *shōjo manga* returned to representations of everyday life in Japan; while still fanciful and whimsical, the settings, contexts, and backgrounds were set in the reality of girls' everyday lives. Thus, in the 1970s the first explorations of sexuality in *shōjo manga* were between two beautiful boys set in exotic locales, distanced on two fronts; today, *shōjo manga* explores sexuality among "real" girls in Japan. Okamoto and Minami touched on this issue in the context of changes they have seen in the manga world and the world at large. Okamoto ruminated,

[For girls today] if you look at the real world, what makes their hearts race (*doki doki suru*) is no longer in the world of manga, but their own world. The real world makes them *doki doki suru* now. So now manga also touches on this world. Really, that is what we try to create [in *shōjo manga*], "*doki doki suru,*" but today that is H. The *doki doki suru* part still remains, it is not gone, but [it] has changed. This is not just in the manga world. Sex is not new; there has always been interest in it, but with cell phones used for dating, things have changed. So we [as editors] have to wonder if we should take from this reality or not. Certainly, it depends on the date; some may have sex on dates or not, but manga, too, is affected. *Shōjo manga,* too, changes with the times out of necessity, but that can be hard for us old editors.

*Doki doki suru* is one of the quintessential characteristics of *shōjo manga*—with romantic undertones, it means to make one's heart flutter or race. *Doki doki* romance stories always have the question of sex lingering in the wings. But according to Okamoto, *shōjo manga* now has competition from the real world to make the hearts of high school girls flutter, and that real world includes sex. When I asked Iijima Akiko about the love story focus of the magazine she edits, she replied, "Some say that compared to regular *shōjo manga* there is more H in [our magazine], but it is not our intention to sell more sex. The main characters in our manga are in high school, and according to high school kids today, there can be no love without sex. If we are going to have a real love story expressing love feelings, then there will be representations of nature and sex. Therefore, these are love-story comics, through and through." Thus, according to these editors, sex is a part of regular everyday life for girls today; girls have changed and *shōjo manga* has changed along with them.

I want to push the simplistic argument that these editors put forward claiming that *shōjo manga* merely reflects "what girls want." What is most telling about the confessions of these editors is that they start with the assumptions implicit in the wider discourse about schoolgirls in the 1990s discussed above. The pervasive anxiety over *enjo kōsai* and the conflation of schoolgirls and sexuality that resulted fostered the idea that girls today are more interested in sex than their earlier counterparts. The supposition that sex has become a part of everyday life for girls, and so, too, it becomes a part of *shōjo manga*, ignores the role that manga plays in wider discourses and girls' culture more generally.

This *shikata ga nai* attitude about the new "H" trend was reiterated by many I talked to when this issue came up. Yet there is an ambiguous relationship between these editors' discourses about sex and their readers inherent in such comments. While on the one hand their ultimate goal is to sell magazines, and thus provide readers with moving stories that will keep them reading, they also showed signs of disapproval towards the state of events in 1990s' Japan. Many of these editors are older men and acted paternalistically both towards their artists and their readers. Thus, we see a resigned and even moralistic attitude on the part of many editors towards the increase in sexual themes in *shōjo manga,* while the very representations of schoolgirl sexuality in these stories fosters the trend it follows.

One example of editors grappling with the juxtaposition between the descriptive and productive sides of "what girls want" can be seen in the 2002 release of a book entitled *10000 nin ni kiita onna-no-ko no H* (The questionnaire to 10,000 girls about their H experiences) (Dessert Editorial Division 2001).[23] This book was compiled by the editors of *Dessert* (Kodansha) from surveys about girls' sexual experiences and opinions distributed in the magazine during 2000 and 2001.[24] Framed as a conversation between two characters, a princess and a maid, the book uses graphs, text, quotes, and manga images to report the results of surveys collected by the *Dessert* editorial staff.

The questions range from collecting basic information (age, year in school or employment, general sexual experience) to short-answer questions specifically aimed at those who are still virgins, such as "What worries you the most about having sex?" "Do you have any questions about sex you can't ask anyone else?" and "When you dream about your first time what is the situation?" to questions for non-virgins such as, "How old were you when you first had sex?" "Have you ever been to a love hotel?" "Did your relationship with the boy change after you had sex?" and "Do you have any advice for the virgins out there?" (Dessert Editorial Division 2001). The layout of the book, with its manga character framing, and the candor of the quoted girls' answers is reminiscent of the readers' pages of *shōjo manga* magazines that are put together by the editors as a community space so girls can interact with each other through the magazine (see chapter 3). There is even a section called "Isha no heya" (Doctor's room) where the princess asks for information about birth control, pregnancy, and STDs, interspersed with survey data (Dessert Editorial Division 2001, 91–106).[25] In this way the book serves as an information guide for girls about general issues of teen sexuality. The book ends with the following dialogue between the princess, the maid, a butler, and a doctor.

> **Maid:** Princess. Now do you understand the situation of sex among young girls?

Princess: Yes. I understand really well now. "H" varies from person to person.

Doctor: So, you should not feel rushed.

Princess: I know.

Butler: The most important thing is that you have sex with someone you really like.

Princess: Right. That is what the girls themselves said.

Princess: I, too, will keep trying. (Dessert Editorial Division 2001)

The editors close the book with a positive message, not of abstinence but of caution couched as the summary of the collected survey data. The editorial board is thus able to collect data on the sexual experiences of their readers in the wake of the *enjo kōsai* phenomenon and put forth an educational text to help girls navigate this tricky terrain.

Yet while the content of the book is explicitly for girls and utilizes their voices through quotes from the surveys collected, the book cover speaks to an entirely different audience. The cover features a picture of the princess and maid characters, yet unlike their demure counterparts inside, they are gun-toting, loose socks, and miniskirt-wearing coquettes (figure 5.7). Rather than the typical *shōjo manga* fare, *kogyaru* or not, this image plays into a different realm of imagining girls, that typical of *roricon* (Lolita complex) found in young men's manga, anime, and video games. *Roricon* is a genre that developed in the amateur manga world, bringing the innocent cuteness of *shōjo manga* characters into sexually explicit young men's manga (Shigematsu 1999, 129–132). The cover indicates that the editors of *Dessert* are advertising their book to an audience beyond the readers of their magazine and *shōjo manga* in general. Furthermore, the information band that surrounds the cover displays the following text in schoolgirl handwriting, replete with hearts and emoticons: "Wow!!! I am a virgin but (I am so embarrassed) I want to get suggestions from various people (Okayama Rei 16 years old)." Below this, in bold print, it reads, "A record of the H experiences of 10,000 girls in their teens." And the spine reads, "Full of honest H stories and information" (Dessert Editorial Division 2001). The enticing language here reads much less like an informational book for girls and more like scintillating reading for those interested in schoolgirls' sex lives. Here the editors are contributing directly to the discourses about how sexually active girls are "in their own words" prevalent in the *enjo kōsai* phenomenon. Although *enjo kōsai* activities are not touched on in this volume at all—it is all presumably sex among peers—it still explicitly plays into the voyeuristic propensity for discussions of schoolgirls and sex. In a sense this follows the duplicity in discourses about *kogyaru;* anxiety about girls' sexuality reproduces them as quintessential sexual producers.

This discussion has brought us full circle to the issue of wider apprehension and assumptions about girls and sexuality from the 1990s on, as it has percolated through *shōjo manga.* As the examples in this section attest, *shōjo manga* as a genre and those who create it find themselves betwixt and between. On the one hand, as publishers whose job it is to sell, manga editors feel compelled to create texts that will maximize their profit margins, and in doing so they have to pay attention to "what girls want," in their words. In this case, the answer was sex. That teens in contemporary Japan would not be satisfied with saccharine romances that end in a kiss is not surprising, and certainly *kogyaru* fashion and sexual content are a part of girls' culture in the new millennium. On the other hand, as adults in the era of recession, some editors also expressed concern over these changing mores of kids today, resignedly discussing this turn to sexuality in *shōjo manga.*

Figure 5.7. Cover of *10000 nin ni kiita onna-no-ko no etchi,* Kodansha 2002. (Courtesy of Kodansha)

Their influence, along with the history of the genre, leads to a somewhat more cautious approach to sex than is seen through much of the manga genre. As we saw in "Gals!" the context, fashion, and content is *kogyaru,* but the sexual conduct itself is missing. Likewise, sex scenes in magazines for high school girls have increased and run the gamut from more suggestive to quite explicit, but the magazines still cater to an emotional tone that helps girls navigate the rocky terrain of adolescence.

However, by highlighting *shōjo manga* as "what girls want" these editors are minimizing their role in furthering discourses about girls and sexuality. Manga is a main medium of popular culture in postwar Japan and has become the background, if not the foundation, for much of the mass media in Japan. As such, the manga industry participates in the construction of youth culture and beyond by its very ubiquity. The stories of everyday life, love, and friendship within the pages of *shōjo manga* are at once in dialogue with girls' culture and productive of it. Thus, *shōjo manga* does not simply reflect the desires of girls; it mediates them. *Shōjo manga* producers (artists and editors) garner ideas and assumptions from girls' culture and wider discourses, amplifying them into fantasies for and about girls. In their pivotal role within this nexus, artists and editors are at once capitalizing on a trend and, yet, through their very stature, are creating "what girls want." *Shōjo manga,* through its creators, is one point where wider discourses that link schoolgirls to sex in the 1990s are put into dialogue with girls' culture, resulting in both a perpetuation of such discourses (girls are interested in sex) and a route for self-conscious interaction with such discourses.

In this chapter I have examined the way that wider social issues of gender and sexuality in Heisei Japan were reflected and refracted in the pages of *shōjo manga* through the case study of "Gals!" Wider societal preoccupation about schoolgirl sexuality, emanating from the *enjo kōsai* and *kogyaru* phenomena, set the stage for changes in the content of *shōjo manga.* Yet the mainstream manga industry is part and parcel of the commodification of youth culture. Thus, social trends such as *kogyaru* are incorporated into and amplified through the pages of *shōjo manga.* Tacking between notions of "what girls want" and what is appropriate for its readers, the *shōjo manga* industry navigates tricky terrain, ultimately participating in the construction of girls' culture and discourses surrounding girls' sexuality in millennial Japan.

# Shōjo Manga *at Large*

**Japanese Schoolgirl Watch—"What a Girl Wants"**
In Tokyo, teen trends come and go faster than bullet trains.
As soon as Sanrio's My Melody cell phone straps were all the
rage, it-girls in Shibuya wouldn't be caught dead with them.
For companies that cater to these *kogals*, spotting the next fad
is like throwing udon against the folding screen to see what
sticks. Luckily, the cool-hunters at GirlsLab (www.girlslab.
com) discovered a way to divine what's cute and hip. The
research firm teamed up with *Nicola* to put questionnaires on
the glossy bubble gum mag's pages and phone-friendly Web
site. Lured by the chance to win prizes like pink iPod minis and
Samourai perfume, girls answer dozens of queries, like "What
brands of clothing go well together?" and "Explain how you
have successfully asked for gifts." Videogame company Namco,
confectioner Lotte, and underwear maker Wacoal have signed
on to find out what makes the teens tick.
        —Brian Ashcraft, "Japanese Schoolgirl Watch," 2005 [1]

Beginning in 2002 *Wired* magazine added a column called "Japanese
Schoolgirl Watch" to their "Play: Culture. Gear. Obsessions." section, an
odd move for a technology guru magazine. The short blurbs in the "Japanese Schoolgirl Watch" detail the latest trends among Japanese schoolgirls,
ranging from emoticons for mobile phones, to black spray paint to cover
up bleached hair at school, to the "cool-hunters at GirlsLab" cited above.[2]
That is to say, some are related to technology and some are not. Granted,
*Wired* has always included information on the subcultures that surround
new technology, but the question remains, What does that have to do with
Japanese schoolgirls? Following the surging popularity of Japanese popular culture, *Wired* has tapped into the almost obsessive preoccupation with
schoolgirls that gripped Japan itself throughout the 1990s. One can hardly
escape her ubiquitous image—the schoolgirl clad in sailor-style school uniform and knee-high socks smiles at us coyly from billboards and television ads from the pages of manga and magazines—Japan's new mascot. As
the "Japanese Schoolgirl Watch" in *Wired* evinces, these schoolgirls are not

only a national brand, but, on the coattails of Japanese popular culture, also have become an international label.

Each chapter in this study has examined a point where the realms of production and consumption are intertwined, from the history of manga wherein a generation of children grew up with manga and as adults forged the industry, to the use of readers' pages and the Manga School to raise readers and rear artists in the industry, to discussions of "what girls want." The relationships among editors, artists, and readers—producers and consumers—are intimate. I have argued throughout that the production of *shōjo manga* is a form of affective labor, as editors and artists who are invested in the genre and feel an affinity with readers create affect through their texts, through the sense of community and sites for participation in the magazine, and in their own conception of their jobs. Yet this affective labor at once creates relationships and community while reifying the salience of gender and the role of women as the consummate consumers.

But this intimacy is a national one: in my interviews editors and artists were clear that the audience they write for is Japanese. Foreign fans were seen as intriguing, but not a factor in the creation of manga. When I was conducting my research (2000–2002) this global market was just beginning to get some attention within the manga industry. While anime has a history of coming and going in the American market, manga has been much harder to import, and mostly for technical reasons: anime requires mostly subtitles or voiceovers, while manga has to be translated and the pages and frames flipped. [3] It wasn't until anime had gained an established market and Japanese character goods started to infuse the American market that manga was substantially imported to the United States. Thus, opposite its emergence in Japan, on the global scene manga follows anime, and manga has become big in the English-speaking world in the past decade.

The ways that consumption is entailed in the production of manga is enhanced in the U.S. market. In fact, the U.S. market for manga has been driven almost exclusively by fan interest with the help of emerging information technology. This system sits somewhere in between a production-based economic model and a consumption-based one. On the one hand, it was the demand for more manga and anime by the fans of anime, communing at conventions and then on the Internet, that U.S. publishers began tapping into, indicating a more flexible consumer-based model. And yet, fitting with a Fordist model of production, Japanese publishers have a vast store of manga already made for a national audience, and with the help of distributors like Tokyopop, VIZ, and Del Rey, who straddle the two nations, they find markets for and translate manga. But, at least thus far, these new consumers have not reached back to the realm of the producers; that is, while publishers are intrigued by foreign markets and are happy to make money there, there is no explicit consideration of them in the production process. This happens at the realm of distribution and is very low risk for the Japanese publishing houses.

Since I left the field in the summer of 2002, Japanese popular culture had come to infuse the global scene. One of the biggest changes that has occurred in the interim is that *shōjo manga* has gone global. In this epilogue, I draw attention to the changes wrought on the *shōjo manga gyōkai* (business world) in recent years, most notably in relation to new media and the new markets. In keeping with the questions examined throughout the preceding chapters, I ask, How might faraway markets affect the blurring of production and consumption seen in the industry itself, as well as notions of "what girls want," discussed throughout this book? Thus, this final chapter zooms out from an ethnographic analysis of the production of *shōjo manga* to the context of this moment wherein Japanese popular culture is a hot commodity, inquiring how issues of gender and intimacy, production and consumption in late capitalist Japan translate to the global milieu.

## Shōjo Manga and New Media

The Internet is one site where Japanese popular culture is circulated, and it is still one of the easiest ways to obtain J-pop (Japanese popular culture) from overseas. However, before I turn to discuss manga on the global scene, I examine the ways that the manga industry in Japan has begun to make more use of emerging media forms. The manga industry has long had ties to anime studios, toy manufacturers, and video-game producers through the contracting of copyrights and stories for cross-marketing purposes.[4] It is this conservative pattern of selling the rights to titles and characters, with ultimate editorial and artistic control remaining in-house, that has characterized the publishing industry's relation to both new technology and foreign markets.

During my fieldwork, each of the main publishers in this study was beginning to explore the full capabilities of the Web. Beginning in the late 1990s publishers began using the Internet to display the contents of upcoming magazine issues and advertise newly released books, as well as sell books. In 2000 the publishing houses still primarily used their Web sites for advertising purposes, advising interested readers of new releases and displaying the table of contents for the newest magazines. Due to infrequent use of credit cards and mistrust of security features, Web commerce was comparatively slow to take off in Japan. Thus, while each publisher had an online bookstore in 2000, they accounted for only about 4 to 5 percent of total sales. However, during my fieldwork, www.amazon.co.jp, as well as a local online store called Book One (www.bk1.co.jp), devised other payment methods, such as paying at a bank or convenience store or delivery to a local bookstore, which greatly boosted online sales.

From 2001 through 2002, each of the main publishers started to promote their wares on the Web more actively, and manga was a big part of this trial. On manga Web pages, Flash and other programming tools were used to promote popular titles by providing interactive videos and other activities. Likewise, artist commentary and interviews as well as reader feedback formats were beginning to be included on magazine Web pages. Yet the seeming lack of interest in the Internet and new media more generally surprised me as I was conducting my earliest interviews. Because so many manga are made into anime and video games, all of which seem linked to new media, I assumed the manga industry was as well, and today it certainly is.[5] But what became clear in my interviews was that many of the editors I spoke to viewed new media as a threat to manga's existence. They are, after all, print publishers.[6] In conversations about the decline in manga sales and readership, new media—video games for boys and mobile phones for girls—came up time and again. Rather than viewing the Internet explosion that was happening at the turn of the millennium as a new frontier that could in fact keep manga alive, there was a palpable nervousness about it. But that has changed today—the mainstream *shōjo manga* Web pages today practically jump out of the screen, filled with flashing, scrolling, and twinkling images, splattered with pastels.

Not surprisingly, the manga magazines aimed at older readers make more use of their Web pages than those aimed at the youngest ones, due to reader access and interest. Similarly, boys' manga utilized this medium before girls' manga did, although girls' manga integrated mobile-phone versions earlier than their male counterparts. Beginning in April 2002 the national education system began to teach all grade-school students about Web use, making editors at even the youngest magazines begin to take the resource more seriously.

The Internet is heralded as the conveyer of new models of communication, and the interactive sections of manga magazines are translated easily into cyberspace. Today, manga readers can log on to their favorite magazine

Web page and find sample manga to read, extra information about manga, interviews with artists, bulletin boards for discussing the latest installment of a favorite manga, and details about upcoming events, magazine issues, manga books, and character goods.[7] The Web pages typically have a survey with prizes one can win and information about becoming a manga artist. Most of the interactive aspects of magazines discussed in chapter 3 are now supplemented and available on any computer or mobile phone (through special mobile-phone-friendly sites as well). As I argued in chapter 3, these participatory components of *shōjo manga* magazines provide a space for readers, artists, and editors to interact in the creation of manga, but they also shape readers as consumers and potential artists. Because of the seamless integration of community and commerce enabled by the Web, the online extensions of these magazine features further suture the commercialization and community of *shōjo manga*.

Manga publishers continue to play with the potentialities of the Web, trying online manga samples and even a cell-phone-sized version for commuters. While the bulk of their content still revolves around selling the print editions, the biggest new trend in 2006, especially among the mainstream publishers discussed in this manuscript, was to release popular titles in a variety of formats—online, mobile phone, and the like (Shuppan Nenpō 2007, 35). Similarly, the final change in publishing-house Web pages since my time in Japan is that each one has a more extensive English site, and these promote manga exclusively. In fact, Shueisha announced in the fall of 2009 its plans to begin selling mobile-phone versions of its most popular manga in twenty-eight countries (ICV2 2009). Thus, engaging with new media both provides manga publishing houses with the means to compete with other forms of popular culture in Japan and links them to audiences outside of Japan.

## Manga as Cultural Ambassador

In recent years international venues have been embracing manga and anime at the level of pop culture and high culture, commercial goods, and art. As I was conducting my fieldwork in Japan, manga seemed to have infiltrated the art scene, as the critically acclaimed art exhibits of Nara Yoshitomo and Murakami Takeshi claimed roots in both traditional Japanese arts and manga. Both artists received national fanfare for their exhibits in Japan in 2001, *after* having stirred up the international art worlds. Importantly, Nara and Murakami met with acclaim in the West precisely for the way their art played with a mixture of traditional art forms and techniques as well as popular culture styles. These globetrotting artists have themselves crossed back and forth between the art world and that of commercial culture, as their artwork and characters can be found adorning T-shirts, novel covers, and a variety of goods in recent years.[8]

The Nara exhibit I Don't Mind, if You Forget Me featured paintings, three-dimensional installations, sketches, and an assortment of character goods on display at the Yokohama Museum of Art from August 11 to October 14, 2001 (Nara 2001). For Nara it was his first solo exhibition in his home country after showing in Europe and the United States. Nara is known for dualistic paintings and sculptures that focus on one character animal or child that seems at once cute and sinister, gentle and cruel. The oversized heads and large eyes of many of his pieces draw from the stylings of shōjo manga and yet have their own distinct feel. The curator of the exhibit, Amano Taro, likens Nara's work to woodblock prints, shōjo manga, and other contemporary artists who play between popular and applied arts (Matsui 2001).

Like Nara, Murakami has also won international critical acclaim for his work that is explicitly anime and manga influenced. As the exhibition guide to the 2001 exhibit Summon Monsters? Open the Door? Heal? Or Die? (Shōkan suru ka doa wo akeru ka kaimono suru ka kaifuku suru ka zenmetsu suru ka) explains, "Beginning around 1993, he [Murakami] began making paintings and sculptures featuring his original cartoon character, Mr. DOB, straightforwardly incorporating the subcultural genres of manga and anime (cartoons and animated films) and the otaku (nerd) culture of Japanese youth which supports them. This work eventually earned high praise at home and abroad as a form of pop art reflecting the current state of Japanese culture (Murakami 2001)." His characters, Mr. DOB and Miss Ko[2], play with the lines between low and high art, signaling Murakami's engagement with popular culture, especially manga and anime. Murakami consciously created a new artistic style he calls "super flat" in reference to the two dimensionality of manga and anime, which mimics contemporary urban life, according to Murakami (Murakami 2000). The continued global popularity of both Murakami and Nara is an example of the way that manga has become part of the backdrop to contemporary popular culture, Japanese culture, and, increasingly, even global culture.

From 1999 to 2002 the Japan Foundation sponsored an exhibition that traveled throughout Europe entitled Manga: Short Comics from Modern Japan. As a part of the Japan Foundation's collection of touring exhibits designed to "present Japanese art and culture to the outside world," this exhibit was in high demand in the early twenty-first century (Natsume and Hosogaya 2001, 4). Manga was clearly being showcased as a unique Japanese art form, a part of modern Japanese culture, to be showcased to the world.

Similarly, in 2005 an art exhibit entitled *Shōjo Manga! Girl Power! Girls' Comics from Japan* made the circuit around art schools in the United States. According to Masami Toku, the curator of this exhibit, there were two main goals for the project. "One is to examine the world-wide phenomenon of Japanese comics (*manga*) not only in Japan but in other countries, including the United States. The second purpose is to enlighten audiences—teachers, students, and community—and develop their media and visual literacy" (Toku 2005, 4). Paired with lectures and symposia, *Shōjo Manga! Girl Power!* provided viewers with a concise overview of the history of *shōjo manga* with original prints from prominent *shōjo manga* artists. In this event, too, we see the promotion of manga as an art form but also as a cultural product to provide audiences with visual literacy in today's image-saturated world.

All of these exhibits, which brought manga into the global art scene in different ways, signal a new role for manga in Japanese culture, this time as cultural ambassador.[9] As Susan Napier discusses, while Japan was renowned for woodblock prints and attention to design at the turn of the twentieth century, at the turn of this millennium manga and anime are taking up the mantle (Napier 2007). In the past few years the Japanese government has begun to capitalize on the global popularity of Japanese popular culture by holding forums with scholars from all over the world to discuss the creative potential for marketing Japan via its creative content. This new way of promoting Japan is evident in the pamphlet "Creative Japan," produced and distributed by the Ministry of Foreign Affairs.[10] Written as an introduction to contemporary Japan, the brochure claims, "It is impossible to fully convey here the magic of contemporary Japanese culture, which draws on a creative tradition with unbroken links to the past. However, we offer this brochure in the hope that it will enable people from other parts of the world to gain a greater understanding and appreciation of Japanese contemporary culture"(Ministry of Foreign Affairs 2007). With short introductions to manga, anime, games, art, fashion, food, literature, architecture, design, and technology the brochure promotes international relations and an understanding of contemporary Japanese culture. Taking this notion of cultural ambassadors a step further, in 2009 three young women were appointed "cute ambassadors" and charged by the foreign ministry with promoting Japanese popular culture throughout the world (Kaminishikawara 2009). In these examples we see a direct instance of manga and anime as cultural ambassadors to the world. The question remains, How is the manga industry in Japan responding to this success, driven at least in part by global desires?

## *Shōjo Manga* in Global Proportions

By the end of my field research, Japanese popular culture, including manga, had become a global force to be reckoned with.[11] During the 1990s manga emerged from the nooks and crannies of obscure fan culture to line the shelves at Barnes & Nobles, Border's Books, Virgin Megastores, and the like, throughout the United States and Europe. Nevertheless, as of the turn of the century, within the manga industry the national market was by far the largest segment; in fact, despite the sizable increase in exported manga beginning in the late 1990s, exports are still a minor portion of the industry totals. Furthermore, in spite of the countless books and articles that have appeared in Japan recounting and theorizing the rise of Japanese popular culture's recent global popularity (Amano and Sumiyama 2002, Hosogaya 2002, Iwabuchi 2001, Kyotani 1998, Natsume 2001, Ōtsuka 1998), the major publishing houses and animation companies still consider foreign markets an afterthought.[12] And in the hierarchy of markets, Asia is second to Japan, followed by Europe and Australia, and then the United States. To qualify this point, the largest publishing houses have quite established markets throughout Asia, and with the increasing popularity of anime and manga, the markets in Europe and the United States are growing. However, this has just recently become a major undertaking for these publishing houses. Most exports have been and are still initiated by outside interest rather than internal motivation; consequently, these publishing houses primarily work through local publishers rather than distributing and translating themselves.

In interviews with artists and editors I found a level of curiosity about foreign markets, but overall disinterest. Time and again I was told that it is great to have foreign readers, a nice perk, but ultimately the audience they are writing for is that which is closest to their hearts—Japanese girls. The publishing industry has yet to embrace these new markets in the way that the toy companies have in the past decade, flooding international markets with Pokémon, Yu-gi-oh, and Beyblade goods to the delight of children all over the world. In fact, many of my interviews ended with a discussion of the potential for a *shōjo manga* market in the United States. Many of my interviewees were interested in whether I thought it would sell given the lack of a strong girls' comic tradition as well as the paucity of children's magazines in the United States (something that publishers of manga here have also had to contend with).

In the intervening years since my fieldwork, this attitude towards foreign markets has begun to change. Companies that translate and market Japanese manga have increased in the United States in the past decade. Accordingly, bookstores in North America and Europe have sections dedicated specifically to Japanese manga. In the past few years each of the major publishing houses covered in this study has made significant structural inroads into the American market. Tokyopop, located in Los Angeles, started primarily in manga publishing in 1996. Unlike the other major manga publishers in the United States, Tokyopop doesn't have an exclusive relationship with any one publishing house in Japan. This both provides them with the freedom to select the titles they want to translate and market more freely, and burdens them with the necessity of negotiating rights on a case-by-case basis. VIZ LLC, located in San Francisco, has been one of the main translators and publishers of manga in English in the United States since 1987, and was a subsidiary of Shogakukan. In 2005 VIZ merged with ShoPro to become VIZ Media, a joint venture owned by Shogakukan (40 percent), Shueisha (40 percent), and Shogakukan Productions (20 percent) (VIZ Media 2005). Thus, VIZ publishes manga from the Shogakukan family (Shogakukan, Shueisha, and Hakusensha). Similarly, in 2005 Kodansha began a joint venture with Random House, starting the Del Rey manga line, which publishes Kodansha's most popular titles (Del Rey Manga). Both of these new mergers represent a foothold in the U.S. market, a change from simply fielding requests for the right to translate titles.

Finally, not only have publishers taken a bigger interest in selling manga books overseas, but in the past few years they have begun to try their hand at selling manga magazines. Shueisha and Kodansha in particular have been selling Chinese versions of their most popular magazines in Taiwan since the late 1990s and have since embarked on the Western markets. In 2002 the first English-language issue of *Shonen jump* was released by VIZ Media, and in 2005 the first issue of *Shojo beat,* a girls' manga magazine, premiered. Similarly, in 2003 Hakusensha started a *shōjo manga* magazine in German called *Daisuki* (I really like you). Thus, despite the reticence towards a Western manga market that I encountered in my fieldwork, in the intervening years the publishing industry has begun to test this market, in some significant ways.

## Producing Japan/Consuming Japan

Finally, I want to think about the ways in which the mainstream manga publishing houses' recent interest in new media and international markets might affect the issues of gender and intimacy, production and consumption that drive this study. Thus, I return to the particulars of *shōjo manga*. In several of my discussions with editors and scholars about the potential for a U.S. *shōjo manga* market, the lack of comics for girls was the first point raised. I was asked why girls in the United States didn't like comics, for which I had no real answer. Of course, there are girls/women who read comics in the United States, and there are some comics that explicitly cater to them, but for the most part there is no solid tradition of a girls'/women's comic genre. More than that, American comics generally are deemed boys' toys. Thus, it was only on the tail of the growing popularity of *shōnen anime, shōnen manga,* and *shōjo anime* that *shōjo manga* was formally introduced.

VIZ's first attempt at defining *shōjo manga* for its American audience appeared on the back cover of books as follows: "shō•jo (sho'jo) *n.* 1. *Manga* appealing to both female and male readers. 2. Exciting stories with true-to-life characters and the thrill of exotic locales. 3. Connecting the heart and mind through real human relationships" (inside cover, VIZ *Shōjo Manga series,* 2003). Here we see the quintessential focus on *ningen kankei* and intimacy for girls, discussed throughout this book, but less strictly gendered. In fact, this definition markets *shōjo manga* as for both boys and girls. While the American manga market was originally primarily a men's market, this is starting to change, as the increase in *shōjo manga* and anime titles available in English attests. When talking to American anime and manga fans about why they like Japanese popular culture, one reason that always comes up is the complexity of plot, characters, and character relations.[13] *Shōjo manga* takes human relations to another level, and as the VIZ description highlights, this is its big selling point for men and women internationally.

However, *shōjo manga* has another main selling point: it is from Japan. Unlike earlier anime imports, manga today plays up its Japanese roots. When you open a cover of a manga in English, the first thing you will see, more often than not, is a warning that you are reading the last page. Japanese books are read right to left, and most manga in English follow suit. Because manga in the United States has been fan driven, issues of authenticity have been played out through arguments about whether to subtitle anime or use dub-over voices, and whether to flip the manga or not. To date, for the most part the Japanese style is winning out in the manga world.[14] Even *Shonen jump* and *Shojo beat*, both of which are trying to reach out to new audiences, play up their Japanese origin rather than hide it. For example, the August volume of *Shojo beat* carried the following article.

> **Traditional Japanese Foods for All Occasions**—Whether part of a sacred tea ceremony or simply a snack on the go, food plays a huge role in Japanese culture. Here we introduce traditional Japanese foods and beverages, some of which you will encounter as you read this month's *manga* stories, and show you how to make them. Just pick a mood, then pick a menu! (Vardigan 2006)

Featuring such summer delights as cold soba, barley tea, and shaved ice, *Shojo beat* is selling Japan as much as manga, even if it is an idealized or even romanticized version. In fact, *Shojo beat* markets Japan, and especially Japanese popular culture, between the manga serials. This brings us full circle to the editors and artists who create *shōjo manga*. This manga for Japanese girls, which at once relies on and reifies notions of "what girls like," as I have argued here, becomes the mediator of Japanese culture in this global context. Manga has become more than an international commercial product; it is also an emissary of Japan.

Within the context of the global success of Japanese popular culture, this study returns to the roots through an ethnographic examination of the *shōjo manga* industry. A formative legacy of postwar Japanese success, manga have become the main story weavers for contemporary Japan, supplying fantasy and fiction for television, films, books, video games, and more. Within this, *shōjo manga* is a subgenre, but one that has been seminal both to manga itself and to girls' culture throughout the postwar era. Thus, through an examination of *shōjo manga* we get a sense of the stories that Japan tells itself about itself in the global capital world of the late twentieth century. Several editors I spoke to described their magazines as places for girls to come and interact (*sanka shite kure*), and I have written this study, too, as a place to interact with *shōjo manga*, engaging all the while with issues of gender, production, consumption, intimacy, and community—the issues of our times.

# APPENDIX A. Magazine List

This is a list of the *shōjo manga* magazines covered in this volume; it is by no means a comprehensive list and does not include the special editions *(zōkan)* associated with these main magazines *(honshi)*.

| English Translation | Japanese Title | | Est. dates | Publisher |
|---|---|---|---|---|
| • *Best friends* | なかよし | *Nakayoshi* | 1954 | Kodansha |
| • *Girls' friend* | 少女フレンド | *Shōjo friend* | 1962 | Kodansha |
| • *Special volume friend* | 別冊フレンド | *Bessatsu friend* | 1965 | Kodansha |
| • *Juliet* | ジュリエット | | 1984 | Kodansha |
| • *BE LOVE* | | | 1980 | Kodansha |
| • *Kiss* | | | 1992 | Kodansha |
| • *Dessert* | デザート | | 1997 | Kodansha |
| • *Ciao* | ちゃお | | 1977 | Shogakukan |
| • *Girls' comic* | 少女コミック | *Shōjo comic* | 1968 | Shogakukan |
| • *Girls' comic cheese!* | 少女コミック チーズ！ | *Shōjo comic Cheese!* | 1996 | Shogakukan |
| • *Special volume girls' comic* | 別冊少女 コミック | *Bessatsu shōjo comic* | 1970 | Shogakukan |
| • *Petit flower* | プチフラワーズ | | 1980–2002 | Shogakukan |
| • *Flowers* | フラワーズ | | 2002 | Shogakukan |
| • *Petit comics* | プチコミック | | 1997 | Shogakukan |
| • *Kiss Kiss* | ちゅちゅ | *Chu chu* | 2005 | Shogakukan |
| • *Ribbon* | りぼん | *Ribon* | 1955 | Shueisha |
| • *Margaret* | マーガレット | | 1963 | Shueisha |
| • *Cookie* | コッキー | | 2000 | Shueisha |
| • *Chorus* | コラス | | 1994 | Shueisha |
| • *Flowers and dreams* | 花とゆめ | *Hana to yume* | 1974 | Hakusensha |
| • *Lala* | ララ | | 1976 | Hakusensha |
| • *Melody* | メロディ | | 1996 | Hakusensha |

# APPENDIX B. Manga Division Organizational Chart

This chart outlines the general organization of the publishing house manga divisions. The chart is truncated due to space constraints—for example, Editing Divisions 1 and 2 each have typically three to five magazines, and each magazine has five to fifteen editors. Finally, each editor is in charge of ten to twenty artists.

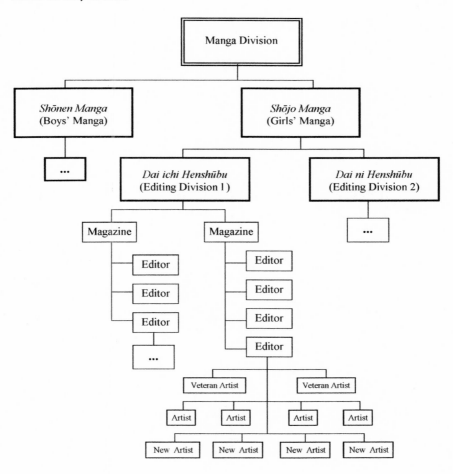

# NOTES

## Chapter 1. The Heart of the Matter

1. Due to the competitive nature of the publishing industry and the generosity of those who spoke with me at length about *shōjo manga* and their own careers, I have used pseudonyms and other discretions throughout this manuscript to ensure anonymity. Discussions with manga scholars whose works are published are exceptions to this rule.

2. Much of the affective labor performed in today's economy is considered women's work, sometimes referred to as "care work." Following Hochschild's groundbreaking work on emotional labor (1983), feminist scholars have theorized the dual social and material implications of women's unpaid reproductive work within the home and traced the roots of reproductive labor into the labor market. Care capital articulates the not-just-material work involved in caregiving, acknowledging that today such work is increasingly done outside of the home and even across global borders, within both the formal and informal economy (Aguilar and Lacsamana 2004, Ehrenreich and Hochschild 2002, Hochschild 2000). In the context of Japan, Miriam Silverberg's analysis of the café girl in early twentieth-century Japan characterizes her work and the moral anxiety that surrounded it as a kind of affective labor, one that flirts with prostitution (2006, 92).

3. Fan fiction is that written by fans about the characters they love—e.g., Star Trek, anime, etc. Cosplay is the practice of dressing up as a favorite character. For insightful analyses of these phenomena, see, respectively, Jenkins 1992 and Napier 2005.

4. The term *gyaru* is clearly from the English word "gal." Because *kogyaru* is typically written in katakana, there is debate about whether the *ko* stands for "small" or comes from the *kō* (high) from *kōkō* (high school) (Kinsella 2002, 230; Miller 2004, 228). Chapter 5 examines the relationship between *shōjo manga* and *kogyaru* directly.

5. *Enjo kōsai,* translated as "assisted dating," refers to the practice of schoolgirls giving their time and, sometimes, sexual favors to older men in exchange for money. *Enjo kōsai* emerged as a social concern in the early 1990s, receiving much attention from the media, the government, scholars, and parents alike. Likewise, during the late 1990s and early twenty-first century, fears about the

plummeting birthrate were manifest in a flurry of discussions about "parasite singles." This less than flattering nomenclature refers to young women who postpone marriage and child rearing or who opt out altogether, characterizing them as lazy girls living with their parents rent free, spending all their money in the city with friends (Yamada 1999).

6. To complicate matters further, manga are also referred to as *komikkusu* (comics) in Japan. While *komikkusu* clearly retains some of its Western origins, the terms are used interchangeably both by the publishing industry and in common parlance. For the sake of consistency and clarity, I have chosen to use the word "manga" to refer to Japanese comics and "comics" to refer to U.S. comics.

7. Throughout this book I have altered the standard style for citing books and magazines slightly in order to clarify when I am talking about a manga magazine title and when a manga series. Thus, even though most manga become books and their titles should be italicized, I will keep them in parentheses to distinguish them from manga magazine titles for readers unfamiliar with the vagaries of the manga world.

8. Even within these main publishers there are a few other, hard to categorize *shōjo manga* magazines. *Petit Flower*, now *Flowers* (Shogakukan), *Chorus* (Shueisha), *BE LOVE*, and *Kiss* (Kodansha) are all marketed as *shōjo manga* rather than ladies' comics but target readers in their early twenties and older.

9. Sarah Frederick's and Barbara Sato's respective work on women's magazines in the early twentieth century provide salient historical precedents for the discussion of *shōjo manga* throughout this book (Frederick 2006, Sato 2003). In particular, Frederick theorizes the relationship between readers and editors in women's magazines in the 1920s, and my research serves as an in situ account of quite similar dynamics within the pages of *shōjo manga* magazines and within the walls of the *shōjo manga* publishing industry today (Frederick 2006).

10. Outside of the big mainstream publishing houses there are many that specialize primarily in manga. Hakusensha, one of the publishing houses this book focuses on, is one such exception. However, the bulk of the genre is produced within the mainstream publishing industry.

11. I have chosen not to use the macrons in the names of Kodansha, Shueisha, and Shogakukan in keeping with the way that each of these publishers romanizes its own name on English publications and Web pages.

12. By focusing on the top four *shōjo manga* publishing houses I cast my net wide in order to capture a sense of the mainstream *shōjo manga* world. Consequently, there are a variety of subgenres that are only touched on in this text, most notably *dojinshi, yaoi,* and *bishonen ai,* which have received a significant amount of scholarly interest in English publications, but for the most part these subgenres are not currently produced in the mainstream industry that this book covers.

13. Appendix A provides a list of the magazines covered in this book.

14. This story of *Shōnen jump*'s ascendancy was told to me on more than one occasion.

15. Appendix B provides an organizational chart representing the main contours of mainstream manga divisions.

16. See, for example, Allison 1994; Kondo 1990; Lutz and Collins 1993; Marcus 1983, 1998; Marcus and Myers 1995; Miller 1997; Moeran 1996.

17. This amorphous category of "free scholars" (*furi-kenkyūsha*) in Japan is comparatively large and is not limited to the study of manga. They are situated somewhere on the continuum from academics with university affiliation, to academics who left the academy, to freelance scholars, journalists, and manga enthusiasts.

18. I was fortunate to attend the first two meetings of the Manga Gakkai during my fieldwork. For more on the Nihon Manga Gakkai, see their Web page: http://wwwsoc.nii.ac.jp/jsscc/index.html. The Statement of Purpose in English (cited here) is available at http://wwwsoc.nii.ac.jp/jsscc/gaikoku/English .html.

### Chapter 2. Descent and Alliance in the *Shōjo Manga* Family Tree

1. This statement was translated from Shogakukan's Web page in the fall of 2002. The philosophy posted most recently (July 2006) has changed slightly (Shogakukan 2006).

2. This chapter would not have been possible without the knowledge and generosity of the members of the Mangashi Kenkyūkai, who let me join them to discuss manga history every month for my two years in Tokyo. In particular, Natsume Fusanosuke, Maruyama Akira, Yamamoto Junya, Miyamoto Hirohito, Yamada Tomoko, Hosogaya Atushi, Akita Takahira, and Saitō Nobuhiko were especially charitable and patient with me in discussing the illustrious history outlined in this chapter.

3. For a sampling of manga history in English, see Gravett 2004, Koyama-Richard 2007, Schodt 1983.

4. For more detailed accounts of the prewar publishing industry, see Kasza 1988, Sato 2003, Frederick 2006.

5. The history of the early years of publishing at Kodansha, Shogakukan, Shueisha, and Hakusensha was put together primarily from my interviews, as almost everyone told me a part of the history of manga. I also used the company history provided by each of the four publishing houses respectively, available at their Web pages (www.kodansha.co.jp/about/history.html; www .shogakukan.co.jp/company/history; www.shueisha.co.jp/history/index_f.html; www.hakusensha.co.jp/corporate/history.html).

6. Also called *rubi* text in the print and computer industry, *furigana* refers to characters written to the right of *kanji* to indicate pronunciation.

7. In her book on the development of women's magazines in the Meiji

period, Sarah Frederick outlines in more detail the confluence of events—technological, social, and political—that led to the flourishing of popular magazines in the Meiji and Taisho periods. Because children and women were both new audiences fueling the growth of the magazine industry in this period of early modernization, the children's magazines I am discussing here bear much resemblance to those Frederick analyzes (2006, 6–14).

8. Tezuka had two main theatrical influences that strongly shaped the innovations in his manga. He was born and raised in Takarazuka just outside of Osaka, known for the all-women's review theater of the same name located there (Maruyama 1999, 94; Phillips 2008). The glamour and sweeping breadth of Takarazuka's dramatic review-style performances added depth and a kind of grandiosity to Tezuka's imaginings of his manga stories. Likewise, Tezuka had always been intrigued by Disney animation he watched as a child and was inspired to use some of these techniques of film in the genre of manga. Most notably, his use of big, round eyes can be traced back to Disney. Babies' eyes are disproportionately large, and Disney mimicked this style in his creation of cute and lovable characters. Tezuka followed suit, adding his own flare, and one that would escalate in the pages of *shōjo manga* in the 1970s.

9. Tetsuwan Atomu is known in the West as Astro Boy. Ribon no Kishi is known as Princess Knight.

10. Countless books have been written about Tezuka Osamu, his life, and work in both Japanese (Maruyama 1999, Natsume 1992, Takahashi and Yonezawa 1997) and English (Gravett 2004; Schodt 1983, 2007).

11. Jacqueline Berndt argues that the first generation of manga scholars in Japan overemphasized the role Tezuka played in the development of modern manga in attempts to legitimate the genre (2008, 301–302).

12. This focus on story-manga is not to insinuate that all postwar manga is story-manga, although much of it would fit under this rubric. In the 1950s the older style of serial manga was still quite popular. This can be seen in quintessential early postwar *shōjo manga* titles like Ueda Toshiko's "Fuichin" (Fuichin is the protagonist's name) and Imamura Yōko's "Chakochan no nikki" (Chako's diary). Likewise, both then and now, gag manga (*gyagu manga*) and short four-panel manga (*yon-koma manga*) can be found both in the mainstream manga magazines and as recompiled books. As the name implies, gag manga are short slapstick episodes, usually running only a page or two and featuring characters with highly exaggerated features, even by manga standards. Similarly, *yon-koma manga* consist of only four frames and tend to be comical as well. Hasegawa Machiko's "Sazaesan" (Miss Sazae) is probably the most well known *yon-koma manga*.

13. While I trace this account through the manga world it is important to point out some similarities and differences from women's magazines in the prewar era. Sarah Frederick discusses the importance of readers submitting stories

for women's magazines in the Taisho period, which is a clear forerunner to the practice in the postwar manga world (2006, 119–121). This connection to readers and grooming of artists is an important feedback loop in manga production. However, in the postwar period it became the sole way to find artists, tightening the loop even further.

14. Thanks to Maruyama Akira, Natsume Fusanosuke, and Yonezawa Yoshihiro for helping reconstruct this sequence about how the new artists system got its start.

15. The Shogakukan *gakunenshi* are the exception. They have kept their general format and educational focus, although as they progress in age so too does the quantity of manga increase within their pages; in fact, in the earlier *gagkunenshi* children are literally taught how to read manga through numbered frames.

16. Kinsella's book, *Adult Manga,* provides a glimpse into the production of adult manga for men in the 1990s. She argues that this genre focused on the everyday life of an average company worker and serves to reinforce the ideology of hard work and success that pervaded both business culture and national culture more generally in Japan in the 1980s (2000, 163).

17. *Roricon,* short for "Lolita complex," is a genre that emerged in the late 1980s in the amateur manga world, bringing the cuteness of *shōjo manga* characters into the sexually explicit young men's manga (Kinsella 2000, 121–122; Shigematsu 1999). *Roricon manga,* anime, and software make up a substantial section of the Comic Market and spur an entire mini industry outside of the mainstream realm. In fact, in the late 1990s *roricon* images of sexy schoolgirls in their short uniforms are almost unavoidable in urban Japan.

18. Much has been written in English on *yaoi;* see, for example, Kinsella 2000, 112–121; McLelland 2000a, 49–55; Mizoguchi 2003; Nagaike 2003; Thorn 2004, 171–174.

19. Capitalizing on the new media-mix trend in the 1990s, another publishing house became a big player in the world of manga publishing—Kadokawa Shoten. While Kadokawa is an older publishing house (founded in 1945), it is a relative newcomer to the world of manga. Kadokawa launched its flagship magazine, *Asuka,* in 1985, promising to provide the "*shōjo manga* of the new century" (*shōjo manga shinseiki*) (Nagatani 1995, 160). Quickly, Kadokawa found its niche in the now-crowded manga world, working with well-known artists and focusing on titles outside of the mainstream love comedies, especially those that tie in with popular anime and video-game themes (Nagatani 1995, 160).

20. In Japanese there is a body of scholarship about *shōjo manga;* in particular there are two key texts that outline the history of the genre. For those interested in these histories I point you to Fujimoto 1998, Yonezawa 1980.

21. To be clear, there has always been crossover readership (although more

girls reading boys' titles than vice versa), but magazines are still organized and published along gendered lines, and the bulk of readership stays within those lines as well.

22. Kurakane Shōsuke's "Anmitsu Hime" (Sweet bean princess) was first published in 1948, Ueda Toshiko's "Fuichin" in 1958, and Hasegawa Machiko's "Sazaesan" in 1946.

23. Taking this gendered division of labor a step further, female artists have remained primarily ensconced within the gendered subgenre of *shōjo manga*. It wasn't until the 1980s that a few women began to write *shōnen manga*. Still today, popular female artists like Takahashi Rumiko and CLAMP are among the select few women writing manga for boys and men.

24. This group is a little amorphous as there are several artists included who were born in Shōwa 23 (1948) or Shōwa 25 (1950), but the general cohort remains relatively consistent.

25. "Japan as Number One" refers to Ezra Vogel's book by the same title on the Japanese economic and business success, which in some ways epitomizes the feeling of the time. That Japan had not only recovered from World War II, but could even teach the United States about successful business models and practices (Vogel 1979).

26. In making this point I am mindful of the tendency to read manga as a barometer for Japanese history itself, a mode that can reduce the genre to a social mirror, as pointed out by Berndt (2008, 296–297). However, without undermining specifics of *shōjo manga*'s development, this pattern of historical reflection seems apt.

27. The increasingly graphic content of manga for both men and women spurred legislation curtailing what could be shown. Most infamously, genitalia cannot be depicted, leading manga artists to be creative with substitute phallic objects. Both Anne Allison and Sharon Kinsella have excellent discussions of censorship in manga. See Allison 1996, 147–176; Kinsella 2000, 139–162. Because depictions of sex were already comparatively tame in *shōjo manga,* this legislation didn't severely affect this genre, and thus I have not addressed it in this chapter.

28. Fujimoto Yukari uses the term *beddo shin* (adapted from English) to distinguish scenes that represent sexual relations without graphic portrayal from sex scenes, and here I follow her lead (Fujimoto 1998).

29. There have been several insightful analyses of the *shōnen ai* trend in *shōjo manga*. See, especially, Matsui 1993, McLelland 2000a, Mizoguchi 2003, Ogi 2003, Orbaugh 2003a, Shamoon 2008a, Welker 2006.

30. In the past decade countless *shōjo manga* have been made into evening television drama known as *torendii dorama. Happy Mania, Hana yori dango* (Boys over flowers), *Wedding Planner,* and *Seiyou kottō yōgashiten* (Antique bakery, in English translation) are just a few examples.

### Chapter 3. Raising Readers, Rearing Artists

1. The *kure* in *sanka shite kure* indicates that the reader is doing the publishers a favor (or that the publisher is receiving the honor of the reader's participation), a sense that cannot easily be captured in English translation.

2. I have chosen to use the English equivalents of each of these features throughout this chapter in order to facilitate classroom use, even though the English equivalent loses some nuance in translation.

3. In particular, Sarah Frederick's research on prewar women's magazines discusses several similar features, most notably the readers' pages and submission contests (2006, 92–101).

4. This age segmentation reflects the readers to whom the publishers are pitching the stories and content. As most of my interviewees pointed out, girls prefer to read the magazine just above their own age and are interested in slightly older topics as a way of feeling more grown up. Furthermore, some of these magazines, especially *Ribon* and *Nakayoshi,* have readers who are much older and have simply been following the magazines their whole lives. Finally, while there are male crossover readers, they make up only about 10 percent of the readership of these main magazines.

5. Anne Allison provides an engaging account of the development of character marketing in postwar Japan in her book *Millennial Monsters* (2006).

6. Both boys' and girls' manga originally included supplements, but today the tradition lives on only within the covers of *shōjo manga.* Young boys' manga, as well as older manga for both genders, do occasionally include supplements for a special event or issue, but it is primarily the domain of the youngest girls' manga magazines.

7. Hakusensha's *Hana to yume* is the only magazine in this youngest set that does not usually include supplements. This is because Hakusensha's focus is a little less mainstream than Shueisha, Shogakukan, and Kodansha.

8. The mail order goods for older magazines tend to cost more because the readers can afford more and are less swayed by cheap character goods.

9. In the *imōto* magazines a six-page spread is typically devoted to readers' pages, but in the *oneesan* (older sister) magazines a two-page layout is common.

10. As I discuss at length in the next chapter, the gender dynamics in the manga industry are pronounced. Roughly 75 to 80 percent of *shōjo manga* editors are men, while 99 percent of the artists are women.

11. Daniel Pink found a similar disconnect between the amateur manga markets and the mainstream publishing industry, as discussed in chapter 2 (2007).

12. All of the *imōto* magazines in this chapter use the phrase "Manga School" except for *Hana to yume,* which refers to theirs as "HMC: *Hana to yume Manga* Course." I use the term "Manga School system" to refer to the system of rearing artists from readers through the Manga School pages in

magazines and individual magazine contests, as well as the bigger publishing-house prizes. This system varies somewhat from publisher to publisher, but I have tried to sketch the main parameters here.

13. With the exception of these big yearly contests, there is an elaborate process involved in debuting. Most artists debut with a manga short story in a magazine special edition (*zōkan*) that comes out several times a year for the express purpose of showcasing potential new artists. For example, *Ribon* has *Ribon bikkuri* (*Ribon* surprise), which comes out four times a year and runs one thousand pages. If an artist's work is popular she is allowed to run a short story in *Ribon original*. If that is popular she can try a serialized story in *Ribon original*, and if she is still very popular, finally she makes it to the main magazine (*honshi*), *Ribon* itself. The first appearance in *Ribon* is another short story, and if that is popular she creates a serialized manga. *Ribon*'s *zōkan* system is the most elaborate of the farm magazine systems, but all the other magazines have *zōkan*. Thus, according to one editor, "From the time an artist gets assigned an editor until they debut can take anywhere from a few months to several years, depending on how good the artist is and who else is in line to debut. Even so, many do not ever make it to the main magazines."

## Chapter 4. Affective Labor

1. Artists, editors, scholars, and acquaintances recounted this basic narrative to me time and again throughout my fieldwork.

2. Sharon Kinsella addresses the elite pedigree of most of the manga editors and its effect on their views on manga (2000, 167–169).

3. The breadth of this range reflects the size differential among the publishing houses I researched. Kodansha is the largest, hiring over twenty per year, and Hakusensha is the smallest, hiring closer to five to eight.

4. Appendix B provides an iconic representation of the general contours of the industry outlined below.

5. This discussion highlights the general contours of the corporate structure, much of which holds true for both *shōjo* and *shōnen manga* divisions. Hakusensha's overall organization is slightly different than outlined here in that it is a smaller publishing house that publishes primarily *shōjo manga*.

6. Here I follow Yuko Ogasawara's translation of *sōgōshoku* and *ippanshoku* (1998, 28), although Mary Brinton's designations, "career track" and "mommy track," are perhaps more telling of the realities of these two tracks (Brinton 2001, 31–32).

7. Mary Brinton has written extensively on the prevalence of part-time labor as a method for harnessing the labor power of women without disrupting the primacy of the male lifetime employment system. Heralding the turn to flexible labor, the *pāto* system primarily includes those who are contracted to work as

many hours as full-time workers but without the benefits of permanent full-time status (Brinton 1993, 135–139; 2001, 31–32).

8. These contracts are sometimes verbal, not always written and legally binding, which gives the company flexibility while the artist risks being blacklisted for breaking contract. Kinsella discusses artist contracts at length, noting that when she was conducting her research, only Shueisha required an exclusive contract (2000, 50–55). According to those I spoke with, due to economic conditions throughout the last decade, the other main publishers have turned towards a more exclusive system. Again, the flexibility lies in the hands of the publishing house, which may introduce its artists to other publishers from time to time, but few artists in the mainstream magazines today work for more than one publisher at a time.

9. Here I am focusing on editor-artist negotiations. In her second chapter Kinsella provides a step-by-step outline of the overall manga production process (2000, 162–201).

10. Kodansha is renowned for being more heavy-handed in its editorial and managerial processes. Rather than the one editor per artist system as explained above, Kodansha utilizes a committee system, where each artist works with three editors. The case of *Sailormoon* is a good example. Editor Irie Yoshio is credited with coming up with the idea for the blockbuster series and then seeking an artist to draw/write it. Kodansha's strict countenance explains some of the differences between Kinsella and my findings. While much of Kinsella's experience mirrors my own, her discussion of editors viewing artists as useless and talentless seems particular to Kodansha, where editors have a stronger role in determining what the story will be about (Kinsella 2000, 162–201).

11. Today these meetings are not always face to face; more frequently the business of editing manga is handled via phone and fax and, increasingly, e-mail.

12. Again, Hakusensha is the exception to this rule because it is a medium-sized company with a more specialized publishing focus. In fact, most of the editors I spoke with there highlighted the benefits of working in a smaller, more flexible company when discussing why they wanted to work at Hakusensha—although most had applied to other and larger publishing houses as well.

## Chapter 5. Material Gals

1. Fujimoto Yukari discusses this progression at greater length in her book, *Watashi no ibasyo wa doko ni aru no?* (1998).

2. Fujimoto uses this term, *beddo shin* (adapted from English), to distinguish scenes that represent sexual relations without graphic portrayal from sex scenes (1998, 45).

3. This age segmentation reflects to whom the publishers are pitching the stories and content. As most of my interviewees pointed out, girls prefer to read

the magazine just above their own age and are typically interested in slightly older topics as a way of feeling more grown up. In fact, *Ribon* and *Nakayoshi* have readers who are much older and have simply been following the magazines their whole lives.

4. These start dates mark their emergence as monthly magazines with their own themes. *Cheese!* existed before this as a special edition of *Shōjo comic*, which came out only two to four times a year. Such special editions tend to highlight new artists as a test market for ideas.

5. The term "H," pronounced "*etchi*," refers to the English letter and is shorthand for the Japanese word *hentai* (変体), which means "metamorphosis," "transformation," "abnormality," or "sexual perversion." Primarily referring to the latter, it has come to signify any kind of sexual content, e.g., *etchi manga, etchi* magazine, etc. In the 1990s H itself has come to signify sex, as "*H suru*" became slang for "to have sex."

6. "Ribon no kishi" was published by Tezuka Osamu (1953–1956) and "Fuichin" was published by Ueda Toshiko (1957–1963).

7. *Roricon,* short for Lolita complex, is a genre that developed in the amateur manga world, brining the innocent cuteness of *shōjo manga* characters into the sexually explicit young men's manga (Kinsella 2000, 121–139; Shigematsu 1999, 129–132).

8. Like *otenba, nekketsu* is an older word that has come to be strongly associated with early postwar manga. Meaning "hot-blooded," although with a slightly more positive tone to it, *nekketsu* is typically associated with boys' manga from the early postwar years. However, it has come to be used for the feisty girls that populate *shōjo manga* in the post-bubble years.

9. David Leheny's book, *Think Global, Fear Local,* provides an insightful and in-depth discussion of the moral panic surrounding youth culture violence and sexuality in the 1990s (2006).

10. Interestingly, by the turn of the twenty-first century social fears about youth had begun to realign around issues of labor, or working life epitomized by the discourses around *freetaa* (youth who chose work in service industry or short-term labor rather than corporate life) and parasite singles (young women who work and live at home, postponing marriage in order to retain their freedom).

11. For more on boys and violence in the 1990s, see Arai 2006, Leheny 2006.

12. Much of this fashion, particularly the blond hair, quickly trickled into wider society and other fashion genres. Likewise, there were several related fashions that could be seen at the time, most notably *ganguro* (black face). This was an offshoot of *kogyaru* that included similar fashions but added a dark tan-and-white makeup. For more on these styles, see Kinsella 2005; Miller 2004, 2006.

13. The similarities between the fears associated with new working women, most notably café girls and *moga* at the turn of the twentieth century and those associated with *kogyaru* at the end of the twentieth century, are particularly striking. Miriam Silverberg's analysis of the combination of production and consumption (working and spending) as well as sexuality that surfaced in discourse about these prewar women is an excellent parallel to this discussion. See 2006, 51–107.

14. Mobile phones as objects and enablers of transgression figured prominently in the discourse surrounding *enjo kōsai*. Girls' use of *keitai* has almost become synonymous with their sexuality or sexual activity (Ito, Okabe, and Matsuda 2005, 19–40, 165–182).

15. The roundtable participants are discussing a proposed juvenile welfare ordinance, which the Tokyo Metropolitan Government passed in 1997, that prohibits sexual activities with boys or girls under the age of eighteen (Shūkan Josei 1997). In concrete response to this phenomenon, many prefectures throughout Japan adopted similar ordinances to curb *enjo kōsai* activities. The debates surrounding these ordinances are interesting because they shift the issue from teens gone awry and teen responsibility to holding adults responsible. As a metropolitan government spokesman explained it, "Considering that restricting teenagers' sexual activity is a very sensitive and private issue that might violate their human rights, the ordinance aims to penalize adults who buy sexual relations" (*Japan Times* 1997). Since the original ordinances, there have been ongoing discussions on how to prohibit such behavior further, and all such discussions pivot on who precisely is responsible—youth or adults or society more generally.

16. Originally *oyaji* (親父) was an informal term for one's father, but it has taken on a more generalized usage in reference to a stereotypical *sarariiman* of one's father's generation, e.g., stubborn and stodgy middle-aged men. Because *oyaji* was the most common reference to men who partook of *enjo kōsai*, the term at times took on the connotation of a "sugar daddy" in this context in the late 1990s. *Ojisan* is the word for uncle and is used generally to talk about middle-aged men. Here the men may or may not be of avuncular age, but the usage symbolizes the distance between the ages of the girls and men.

17. This trend of *sarariiman* interest in schoolgirls can be understood as a contemporary extension of the hostess club. *Settei* (corporate outings), or required postwork bonding activities, most frequently in a hostess club, were fostered by the corporate system created in postwar Japan. In her ethnographic account of the after-work world of *sarariiman* in a "hostess club," Anne Allison argues that this system both enables and institutionalizes a particular kind of male dominance and male identity (1994). While companies certainly didn't pay for *enjo kōsai* directly, the pattern established by the hostess-club experience was mapped onto the bodies of schoolgirls in millennial Japan.

18. Again, David Leheny's book has a concise synthesis of the multiple perspectives involved in the media representations of this phenomenon, from social anxiety to social movement (2006, 49–82).

19. *Chō* was popularly recognized *kogyaru* slang for "super" or "great."

20. In the magazines there are frequently small ads for other manga or anime in the margins of the text. When the story is recompiled into a book, this blank space is filled in with little notes from the artist to the readers about the story, or in response to fan mail, etc. The left side of figure 5.5 is one such artist note in the form of a warning to accompany the text.

21. This rhetoric was common in discussions of *enjo kōsai,* as can be seen in the following survey conducted by *Non·no,* a leading women's fashion magazine. Readers were asked, "Do you think that to participate in *enjo kōsai* or not is an individual's freedom?" Seventy-four percent said yes, 26 percent no (Non·no 1998).

22. Fujii was in high school while writing "Gals!" and her mother was her main assistant.

23. This title is given in English in tiny letters on the cover of the book, so I have used their translation.

24. Like all surveys found in manga magazines, the respondents were eligible to win various goods advertised in the first color fold-out pages of the magazine. These surveys were a part of the *ankēto kenshō* system discussed in chapter 3.

25. This section is compiled from another book published by Kodansha, *Minna no H: Garuzuhen* (Everyone's sex: Girls' edition), written by Kawano Mika, the chief of obstetrics and gynecology at Tokushima Teishin Hospital, and manga artist Tsukamoto Tomoko, who writes for *BE LOVE* (2001).

### Epilogue: *Shōjo Manga* at Large

1. Interestingly, this use of survey prizes to learn "what girls want" is identical to the ways that survey prizes are used in *shōjo manga* magazines, as discussed in chapter 3.

2. The "Japanese schoolgirl watch" is typically culled from articles in the Japanese version of *Wired*.

3. This discussion focuses on the United States because during my fieldwork it was viewed as the new potential market, and I am an American, so almost all of my interviewees brought this up in some guise or another. Several authors provide more detailed discussions of Japanese popular culture in Asia (Craig and King 2002; Iwabuchi 2002, 2004b; Iwabuchi, Muecke, and Thomas 2004) as well as outside the United States (Johnson-Woods 2010).

4. In the late 1980s several of the big publishing houses brought anime closer to in-house by marketing their own series, rather than selling the rights for a story to an anime company. However, by the end of the 1990s this product line had fizzled out.

5. Interestingly, the manga creation process itself is still primarily manual. Artists, for the most part, don't draw/write their manga on computers. Manga drafts and final copies are hand drawn and put together with photocopiers. Similarly, manga drafts are not transmitted between artists and editors via e-mail, but by fax or mail. There are exceptions, Yazawa Ai being a particularly famous one, but for the most part the making of manga is not computerized yet. Manga, it seems, is now a traditional craft.

6. This nervousness is not particular to the manga industry. Print culture in general is threatened by the wealth of new media. In my time in Japan a mountain of books was published musing about the demise of the publishing industry (Kobayashi 1992, 2001; Sano 2001), and this conversation is not unfamiliar in the United States, either.

7. See, for example, http://ribon.shueisha.co.jp, http://www.nakayosi-net.com/, http://www.ciao.shogakukan.co.jp/, http://www.hanayume.com/.

8. In fact, Murakami's recent retrospective exhibit, © Murakami, produced by the Museum of Contemporary Art in Los Angeles, highlighted the links between manga, art, and commerce by featuring a Louis Vuitton store that sold special Murakami handbags in the middle of the exhibit itself.

9. It is important to point out that manga is not found in museums only in the West. There are several major museums in Japan that have focused one gallery on exhibiting manga, and the curators are frequently part of the *manga gakkai* discussed in chapter 1. The Kawasaki Shimin (Municipal) Museum is a leading example. In addition, the Kyoto International Manga Museum was opened in November 2006.

10. The brochure is available in PDF form from http://www.creativejapan.net.

11. I interviewed someone at each of the publishing houses about how international marketing and exports were handled, and it is from this set of interviews that the information for this section is derived.

12. One exception is Kodansha International (KI), which was founded in 1970. The goal of this offshoot of Kodansha was to introduce Japanese culture and literature to an English-speaking audience. However, KI has never made up a major profit share for Kodansha overall. Furthermore, while KI tried their hand at publishing manga in both Japanese and English through their Bilingual Manga series, as of 1999 they are available only in Japan. According to a KI editor in Japan, Japanese will read the bilingual comics as a way to learn English, but they didn't work with a Western audience. In fact, Kodansha publishes its manga in English through an American company, Del Rey, a subsidiary of Random House.

13. This observation comes from my own experience with anime and manga fans. For a more thorough treatment of fans in the United States and what drives them to manga, see Napier 2007, 2005.

14. This has not always been true, nor is it the market strategy of all Japanese popular culture. Several veteran editors I spoke with told me stories of trying to air or publish anime and manga in the United States before the 1990s, when all traces of Japanese culture had to be erased. Scholars working on Japanese popular culture and globalization all deal with this question of "Japaneseness" (Allison 2006; Iwabuchi 2002, 2004a; Napier 2005).

# WORKS CITED

Abu-Lughod, Lila. 1997. The interpretation of culture(s) after television. *Representations* 59 (Summer): 109–134.

———. 2000. Modern subjects: Egyptian melodrama and postcolonial difference. In *Questions of modernity*, edited by T. Mitchell. Minneapolis: University of Minnesota Press, 87–113.

Aguilar, Delia D., and Anne E. Lacsamana, eds. 2004. *Women and globalization*. Amherst, N.Y.: Humanity Books.

Allison, Anne. 1994. *Nightwork: Sexuality, pleasure, and corporate masculinity in a Tokyo hostess club*. Chicago: University of Chicago Press.

———. 1996. *Permitted and prohibited desires: Mothers, comics, and censorship in Japan*. Boulder, Colo.: Westview Press.

———. 2000. Sailor Moon: Japanese superheroes for global girls. In *Japan pop! Inside the world of Japanese popular culture*, edited by T. J. Craig. New York: M. E. Sharpe, 259–278.

———. 2006. *Millennial monsters: Japanese toys in the global imagination*. Berkeley: University of California Press.

Althusser, Louis. 1971. Ideology and ideological state apparatuses: Notes toward an investigation. In *Lenin and philosophy and other essays*. New York: Monthly Review, 127–186.

Amano, Masanao, and J. Wiedemann, eds. 2004. *Manga design*. Köln, Germany: Taschen.

Amano, Masanao, and Rika Sumiyama, eds. 2002. *Adidas manga fever*. Tokyo: Sutairu.

Anderson, Benedict. 1983. *Imagined communities: Reflections on the origin and spread of nationalism*. London: Verso

Arai, Andrea G. 2006. The "wild child" of 1990s Japan. In *Japan after Japan*, edited by T. Yoda and H. Harootunian. Durham, N.C.: Duke University Press, 216–238.

Ashcraft, Brian. 2005. Japanese schoolgirl watch. *Wired*, March, 54.

Askew, Kelly, and Richard R. Wilk. 2002. *The anthropology of media: A reader*. Malden, Mass.: Blackwell Publishing.

Behr, Maiko. 2003. Undefining gender in Shimizu Reiko's *Kaguyahime*. *U.S.-Japan Women's Journal* 25: 8–29.

Berndt, Jaqueline. 2008. Considering manga discourse: Location, ambiguity, historicity. In *Japanese visual culture: Explorations in the world of manga and anime*, edited by M. W. MacWilliams. Armonk, N.Y.: M. E. Sharpe, 295–310.

Brinton, Mary C. 1993. *Woman and the economic miracle: Gender and work in postwar Japan*. Berkley: University of California Press.

———. 2001. Married women's labor in East Asian economies. In *Women's Working Lives in East Asia*, edited by Mary C. Brinton. Stanford: Stanford University Press, 1–37.

Buckley, Sandra. 1991. "Penguin in bondage": A graphic tale of Japanese comic books. In *Technoculture*, edited by C. Penley and A. Ross. Minneapolis: University of Minnesota Press, 163–195.

Cassell, Justine, and Henry Jenkins. 1998. *From Barbie to Mortal Kombat: Gender and computer games*. Cambridge, Mass.: MIT Press.

*Ciao*. 2002a. *Ciao paradise*. July, 469.

———. 2002b. *Special W zenin service*. July, 7–8.

Condry, Ian. 2006. *Hip hop Japan: Rap and the paths of cultural globalization*. Durham, N.C.: Duke University Press.

Craig, Timothy J., ed. 2000. *Japan pop! Inside the world of Japanese popular culture*. New York: M. E. Sharpe.

Craig, Timothy J., and Richard King, eds. 2002. *Global goes local: Popular culture in Asia*. Honolulu: University of Hawai'i Press.

Currie, Dawn H. 1999. *Girl talk: Adolescent magazines and their readers*. Toronto: University of Toronto Press.

Das, Veena. 1995. On soap opera: What kind of anthropological object is it? In *Worlds apart*, edited by D. Miller. New York: Routledge, 169–189.

Davila, Arlene. 2002. Culture in the ad world: Producing the Latin look. In *Media worlds: Anthropology on new terrain*, edited by F. Ginsburg, L. Abu-Lughod, and B. Larkin. Berkeley: University of California Press, 264–280.

De Grazia, Victoria, and Ellen Furlough, eds. 1996. *The sex of things: Gender of consumption in historical perspective*. Berkeley: University of California Press.

Del Rey Manga. 2006. *Manga: About us*. Available from http://www.randomhouse.com/delrey/manga/about.html [cited August 8, 2006].

Denizet-Lewis, Benoit. 2004. Friends, friends with benefits and the benefits of the Local Mall. *New York Times Magazine*, May 30, 6–30.

Dessert Editorial Division. 2001. *10000 nin ni kiita onna-no-ko no etchi* (The questionnaire to 10,000 girls about their H [sex] experiences). Tokyo: Kodansha.

Douglas, Susan J. 1994. *Where the girls are: Growing up female with the mass media*. New York: Three Rivers Press.

Dower, John W. 1999. *Embracing defeat: Japan in the wake of World War II.* New York: W. W. Norton & Company.

Driscoll, Catherine. 2002. *Girls: Feminine adolescence in popular culture and cultural theory.* New York: Columbia University Press.

Ehrenreich, Barbara, and Arlie Russell Hochschild, eds. 2002. *Global woman: Nannies, maids, and sex workers in the new economy.* New York: Henry Holt and Company.

Eiri An. 1994. *Shōjo mangaka ashisutanto: Kindan no onna no sono no himitsu* (*Shōjo manga* artist's assistant: The secrets of the forbidden paradise of women). Tokyo: Data House.

Fishman, Charles. 2006. *The Wal-Mart effect: How the world's most powerful company really works—and how it's transforming the American economy.* New York: Penguin Press, HC.

Foucault, Michel. 1978. *The history of sexuality: An introduction.* Vol. 1. Translated by R. Hurley. New York: Vintage Books.

———. 1979. *Discipline and punish: The birth of the prison.* Translated by A. Sheridan. New York: Vintage Books.

———. 1980. *Power/knowledge: Selected interviews and other writings 1972–1977,* edited by C. Gordon. Brighton, U.K.: Harvester Press.

Frederick, Sarah. 2006. *Turning pages: Reading and writing women's magazines in interwar Japan.* Honolulu: University of Hawai'i Press.

Fujii Mihona. 1999. Gals! Vol. 1. Tokyo: Shueisha. [Original edition: *Ribon.*]

Fujimoto Yukari. 1998. *Watashi no ibasho wa doko ni aru no? Shōjo manga ga utsusu kokoro no katachi* (Where is my place? The shape of the heart reflected by *shōjo manga*). Tokyo: Gakuyō Shobō.

———. 2000. *Shōjo manga damashii* (The spirit of *shōjo manga*). Tokyo: Hakusensha.

———. 2002. Personal interview, May 28, Tokyo.

Ginsburg, Faye. 1991. Indigenous media: Faustian contract of global village? *Cultural Anthropology* 6(1): 92–112.

———. 2002. Screen memories: Resignifying the traditional in indigenous media. In *Media Worlds: Anthropology on new terrain,* edited by F. Ginsburg, L. Abu-Lughod, and B. Larkin. Berkeley: University of California Press, 39–57.

Ginsburg, Faye, Lila Abu-Lughod, and Brian Larkin, eds. 2002. *Media worlds: Anthropology on new terrain.* Berkeley: University of California Press.

Gobé, Marc. 2001. *Emotional branding: The new paradigm for connecting brands to people.* New York: Allworth Press.

Gordon, Andrew. 1998. *The wages of affluence: Labor and management in postwar Japan.* Cambridge, Mass.: Harvard University Press.

Gottlieb, Nanette, and Mark J. McLelland, eds. 2003. *Japanese cybercultures: Asia's transformations.* New York: Routledge.

Gravett, Paul. 2004. *Manga: Sixty years of Japanese comics*. London: Laurence King Publishing.

Gray, Ann. 1992. *Video playtime: The gendering of leisure technology*. New York: Routledge.

Grigsby, Mary. 1999. The social production of gender as reflected in two Japanese culture industry products: *Sailormoon* and *Crayon Shin-chan*. In *Themes and Issues in Asian Cartooning*, edited by J. A. Lent. Bowling Green, Ohio: Bowling Green State University Popular Press, 183–210.

Hagio Moto. 1972–1974. *Toma no shinzō* (Thomas' heart). 5 vols. Tokyo: Shogakukan. [Original edition: *Bessatsu shōjo comic*.]

Hamabata, Matthews Masayuki. 1990. *Crested kimono: Power and love in the Japanese business family*. Ithaca, N.Y.: Cornell University Press.

*Hana to yume*. 2001a. *Dai 39 kai big challenge shō* (The 39th big challenge award). December 5, 360–362.

———. 2001b. *Hanamushi* (Flower bugs). October 20, 450–454.

Hardt, Michael, and Antonio Negri. 2000. *Empire*. Cambridge, Mass.: Harvard University Press.

———. 2004. *Multitude: War and democracy in the age of empire*. New York: Penguin Press.

Hendry, Joy. 1987. *Understanding Japanese society*. New York: Routledge.

Hochschild, Arlie Russell. 2000. Global care chains and emotional surplus value. In *On the edge: Living with global capitalism*, edited by W. Hutton and A. Giddens. London: Cape, 130–146.

Horikiri Naoto. 1991. Onna wa dokyō, shōjo wa aikyō (Women have courage, *shōjo* have charm). In *Shōjoron* (Essays on *shōjo*), edited by M. Honda. Tokyo: Aoyumisha.

Horkheimer, Max, and Theodor W. Adorno. 1972. *Dialectic of enlightenment*. Translated by J. Cumming. New York: Herder and Herder.

Hosogaya Atsushi, ed. 2002. *Nihon manga wo shiru tameno bukku gaido* (A guide to books on Japanese manga) [Japanese/English], *Asian Manga Summit*. Yokohama: Kawasaki City Museum.

Ibata-Arens, Kathryn C. 2005. *Innovation and entrepreneurship in Japan: Politics, organizations, and high technology firms*. Cambridge: Cambridge University Press.

ICV2. 2009. Shueisha plans global digital comics. *IVC2: Inside pop culture*, http://www.icv2.com/articles/news/16280.html.

Ikeda Riyoko. 1972–1973. Berusaiyu no bara (The rose of Versailles). Tokyo: Shueisha. [Original edition: *Shūkan Magaretto*.]

———. 1994. *Berusaiyu no bara* (The rose of Versailles). Vol. 1. Tokyo: Shueisha.

Ito, Kinko. 2002. The world of Japanese ladies' comics: From romantic fantasy to lustful perversion. *Journal of Popular Culture* 36(1): 68–85.

————. 2003. Japanese ladies' comics as agents of socialization: The lessons they teach. *International Journal of Comic Art* 5(2): 425–436.

Ito, Mizuko, Daisuke Okabe, and Misa Matsuda, eds. 2005. *Personal, portable, pedestrian: Mobile phones in Japanese life*. Cambridge, Mass.: The MIT Press.

Ivy, Marilyn. 1993. Formations of mass culture. In *Postwar Japan as history*, edited by A. Gordon. Berkeley: University of California Press, 239–258.

————. 1995. *Discourses of the vanishing: Modernity, phantasm, Japan*. Chicago: University of Chicago Press.

Iwabuchi Koichi. 2001. *Toransunashonaru Japan: Ajia wo tsunagu popyurā bunka* (Transnational Japan: Connecting to Asia through popular culture). Tokyo: Iwanami Shoten.

————. 2002. *Recentering globalization: Popular culture and Japanese transnationalism*. Durham, N.C.: Duke University Press.

————. 2004a. How "Japanese" is Pokémon? In *Pikachu's global adventure: The rise and fall of Pokémon*, edited by J. Tobin. Durham, N.C.: Duke University Press, 53–79.

————, ed. 2004b. *Feeling Asian modernities: Transnational consumption of Japanese TV dramas*. Hong Kong: Hong Kong University Press.

Iwabuchi, Koichi, Stephen Muecke, and Mandy Thomas, eds. 2004. *Rogue flows: Trans-asian cultural traffic*. Hong Kong: University of Hong Kong Press.

Jackson, John L. 2001. *Harlem world: Doing race and class in contemporary Black America*. Chicago: University of Chicago Press.

*Japan Times*. 1997. Violators may be jailed. October 10.

Jenkins, Henry. 1992. *Textual poachers: Television fans & participatory culture*. New York: Routledge.

————. 2002. Interactive audiences? The "collective intelligence" of media fans. In *The new media book*, edited by D. Harries. London: British Film Institute, 69–81.

————. 2006. *Convergence culture: Where old and new media collide*. New York: New York University Press.

Johnson-Woods, Toni, ed. 2010. *Manga: An anthology of global and cultural perspectives*. New York: Continuum International Publishing Group Inc.

Jones, Gretchen I. 2002. "Ladies' comics": Japan's not-so-underground market in pornography for women. *U.S.-Japan Women's Journal* 22: 3–31.

————. 2005. Bad girls like to watch: Writing and reading ladies' comics. In *Bad girls of Japan*, edited by L. Miller and J. Bardsley. New York: Palgrave Macmillan, 97–109.

Kakinuma, Tsutomu, and Izumi Kobayashi, eds. 2001. *Asia in comics exhibit*. Tokyo: The Japan Foundation.

Kaminishikawara Jun. 2009. "Cute ambassadors" roam globe to promote

Japan's pop culture. *Japan Times,* June 17, online edition. http://search
.japantimes.co.jp/rss/nn20090617fl.html.

Kasza, Gregory J. 1988. *The state and the mass media in Japan 1918–1945.*
Berkeley: University of California Press.

Katō Ken'ichi. 1968. *Shōnen Kurabu jidai: Henshūcho no kaisō* (The *Shōnen
club* years: An editor's recollection). Tokyo: Kodansha.

Kawano Mika, and Tsukamoto Tomoko. 2001. *Minna no H: Gāruzuhen* (Everyone's sex: Girls' edition). *Kenkō raiburarī junia* (Junior health library).
Tokyo: Kodansha.

Kawashima, Yoko. 1995. Female workers: An overview of past and current
trends. In *Japanese women: New feminist perspectives on the past, present,
and future,* edited by K. Fujimura-Fanselow and A. Kameda. New York:
The Feminist Press, 271–293.

Kelly, William. 2004. *Fanning the flames: Fans and consumer culture in contemporary Japan.* Albany: State University of New York Press.

Kinsella, Sharon. 1998. Japanese subculture in the 1990s: *Otaku* and the amateur manga movement. *Journal of Japanese Studies* 24(2): 289–316.

———. 2000. *Adult manga: Culture and power in contemporary Japanese society.* Honolulu: University of Hawai'i Press.

———. 2002. What's behind the fetishism of Japanese school uniforms? *Fashion Theory* 6(2): 215–238.

———. 2005. Black faces, witches, and racism against girls. In *Bad girls of
Japan.* New York: Palgrave Macmillan.

Kirino Natsuo. 2005. *Out.* Translated by S. Snyder. New York: Vintage Books.

Kobayashi Kazuhiro. 1992. *Shuppan gyōkai* (The publishing business). Tokyo:
Kashiwa Shobō.

Kondo, Dorinne. 1990. *Crafting selves: Power, gender, and discourses of identity in a Japanese workplace.* Chicago: University of Chicago Press.

Koyama-Richard, Brigitte. 2007. *One thousand years of manga.* Paris: Flam-
marion.

Kyotani Shinichi. 1998. *Le otaku: Fransu otaku jijyō* (*Le otaku:* The situation
of the French *otaku*). Tokyo: KK Best Sellers.

Ledden, Sean, and Fred Fejes Ledden. 1987. Female gender role patterns in
Japanese comic magazines. *Journal of Popular Culture* 21(1): 155–176.

Leheny, David. 2006. *Think global, fear local: Sex, violence, and anxiety in
contemporary Japan.* Ithaca, N.Y.: Cornell University Press

Lehmann, Timothy R. 2005. *Manga: Masters of the art.* New York: Harper
Collins.

Lent, John A., ed. 1995. *Asian popular culture.* San Francisco: Westview Press.

———, ed. 1999. *Themes and issues in Asian cartooning.* Bowling Green, Ohio:
Bowling Green State University Popular Press.

Linhart, Sepp, and Sabine Fruhstuck, eds. 1998. *The culture of Japan as seen through its leisure.* Albany: State University of New York Press.

Lo, Jeannie. 1990. *Office ladies, factory women: Life and work at a Japanese company.* London: M. E. Sharpe, Inc.

Lunning, Frenchy, ed. 2006. *Mechademia 1: Emerging worlds of anime and manga,* edited by F. Lunning. Minneapolis: University of Minnesota Press.

———, ed. 2008. *Mechademia 2: Networks of desire,* edited by F. Lunning. Minneapolis: University of Minnesota Press.

Lutz, Catherine A., and Jane L. Collins. 1993. *Reading National Geographic.* Chicago: University of Chicago Press.

MacWilliams, Mark Wheeler, ed. 2008. *Japanese visual culture: Explorations in the world of manga and anime.* Armonk, N.Y.: M. E. Sharpe.

Mankekar, Purnima. 1999. *Screening culture, viewing politics: An ethnography of television, womanhood, and nation.* Durham, N.C.: Duke University Press.

Marcus, George E., ed. 1983. *Elites, ethnographic issues.* Albuquerque: University of New Mexico Press.

———, ed. 1998. *Corporate futures: The diffusion of the culturally sensitive corporate form.* Chicago: University of Chicago Press.

Marcus, George E., and Fred R. Myers, eds. 1995. *The traffic in culture: Refiguring art and anthropology.* Berkeley: University of California Press.

Martinez, D. P., ed. 1998. *The worlds of Japanese popular culture: Gender, shifting boundaries and global cultures* Cambridge: Cambridge University Press.

Maruyama Akira. 1999. *Tokiwasō jitsuroku: Tezuka Osamu to mangakatachi no seishun* (The real story of tokiwasō: The prime of Tezuka Osamu and manga artists). Tokyo: Shogakukan.

———. 2001. Personal interview, November 19, Tokyo.

Matsui, Midori. 1993. Little girls were little boys: Displaced femininity in the representation of homosexuality in Japanese girls' comics. In *Feminism and the politics of difference,* edited by S. Gunew and A. Yeatman. Boulder, Colo.: Westview, 177–196.

———. 2001. A gaze from outside: Merits of the minor in Yoshitomo Nara's Painting. In *I don't mind, if you forget me. Nara Yoshitomo,* edited by A. Taro. Yokohama: Tanbunsha, 168–175.

Matsuzawa Mitsuo. 1979. *Nihonjin no atama wo dame ni shita manga-gekiga* (The manga that have ruined Japanese minds). Tokyo: Yamate Shobō.

Mazzarella, Sharon R., and Norma Odom Pecora, eds. 1999. *Growing up girls: Popular culture and the construction of identity.* New York: Peter Lang.

McLelland, Mark J. 2000a. *Male homosexuality in modern Japan: Cultural myths and social realities.* Richmond, U.K.: Curzon.

————. 2000b. The love between "beautiful boys" in Japanese women's manga. *Journal of Gender Studies* 9(1): 13–25.

McRobbie, Angela. 1991. *Feminism and youth culture: From "Jackie" to "Just Seventeen."* London: Macmillan.

Miller, Daniel. 1995. *Acknowledging consumption: A review of new studies.* New York: Routledge.

————. 1997. *Capitalism: An ethnographic approach.* Oxford: Berg Press.

Miller, Laura. 2004. Those naughty teenage girls: Japanese *kogals*, slang, and media assessments. *Journal of Linguistic Anthropology* 14(2): 225–247.

————. 2006. *Beauty up: Exploring contemporary Japanese body aesthetics.* Berkeley: University of California Press.

Miller, Laura, and Jan Bardsley, eds. 2005. *Bad girls of Japan.* New York: Palgrave Macmillan.

Ministry of Foreign Affairs, Japanese embassy in the U.K. 2007. Creative Japan. Available from http://www.creativejapan.net/index.html.

Mitsui, Toru, and Shuhei Hosokawa, eds. 1998. *Karaoke around the world: Global technology, local singing.* London: Routledge.

Miyadai Shinji. 1994. *Seifuku shōjotachi no sentaku* (The choices of the girls in uniform). Tokyo: Kodansha.

————. 1998. *"Sei no jiko kettei" genron: Enjo kōsai, baibaishun, kodomo no sei* (A theory of sexual self-determination: *Enjo kōsai*, sex trade, children's sexuality). Tokyo: Kinokuniya Shoten.

Miyadai Shinji, Ishihara Hideki, and Ōtsuka Meiko. 1993. *Sabukaruchā shinwa kaitai: Shōjo, ongaku, manga, sei no sanjūnen to komyunikēshon no genzai* (Dismantling the subculture myth: Thirty years of girls, music, comics, and sexuality, and the current state of communication). Tokyo: Paruko Shuppan.

Miyahara Kojiro and Ogino Masahiro, eds. 2001. *Manga no shakaigaku* (The sociology of manga). Tokyo: Sekai Shisōsha.

Miyamoto Hirohito. 2001. *Manga no kigen: Fujun na ryōiki toshite no seiritsu* (The formation of an impure genre—The origins of manga ). *Shūkan asahi hyakka: Sekai no bungaku* (Weekly Asahi encyclopedia: World literature), *Tēmahen: Manga to bungaku* (Theme edition: Manga and literature) 110: 292–295.

———— 2002. The formation of an impure genre—The origins of manga. *Review of Japanese Culture and Society* 14: 39–48.

Mizoguchi, Akiko. 2003. Male-male romance by and for women in Japan: A history and the subgenres of yaoi fictions *U.S.-Japan Women's Journal* 25: 49–75.

Moeran, Brian. 1996. *A Japanese advertising agency: An anthropology of media and markets.* Honolulu: University of Hawai'i Press.

————, ed. 2001. *Asian media productions.* Honolulu: University of Hawai'i Press.

Morizona, Milk. 2002. Personal interview, June 4, Tokyo.

Murakami, Takashi. 2000. *Super flat.* Tokyo: MADRA Publishing Co.

————. 2001. *Summon monsters? Open the door? Heal? Or Die? (Shōkan suru ka doa wo akeru ka kaimono suru ka kaifuku suru ka zenmetsu suru ka).* Asaka, Japan: Kaikaikiki co.

Nader, Laura. 1972. Up the anthropologist: Perspectives gained from studying up. In *Reinventing Anthropology,* edited by D. Hymes. New York: Pantheon Books.

Nagaike, Kazumi. 2003. Perverse sexualities, perversive desires: Representations of female fantasies and *yaoi manga* as pornography directed at women. *U.S.-Japan Women's Journal* 25: 76–103.

Nagatani Kunio. 1995. *Nippon manga zasshi meikan* (Japanese manga magazine directory). Tokyo: Data Hausu.

Nakamura Keiko and Horie Akiko. 2001. *Sengo shōjo mangashi pāto 2, Kurakane Shōsuke, Ueda Toshiko, Imamura Yōko ten: Otenba shōjo no tōjō* (Postwar girls' manga history, part 2: Kurakane Shōsuke, Ueda Toshiko, Imamura Yōko: The debut of the otenba). Tokyo, Yayoi Bijutsukan, July 5–September 30.

Nakane, Chie. 1970. *Japanese society.* Berkeley: University of California Press.

*Nakayoshi.* 2002a. *Ankēto kenshō 500 nin ni purezento* (Survey prizes presents for 500 people). May, 17.

————. 2002b. *Furoku oshirase* (*Furoku* ad). May, 16.

Nanba Kōji. 2001. "Shōjo" to iu dokusha (Readers called *shōjo*). In *Manga no shakaigaku* (Sociology of manga), edited by K. Miyahara and M. Ogino. Tokyo: Sekai Shisōsha, 188–218.

Napier, Susan J. 1998. Vampires, psychic girls, fying women and sailor scouts. In *The worlds of Japanese popular culture: Gender, shifting boundaries and global culture,* edited by D. P. Martinez. Cambridge: Cambridge University Press, 91–109.

————. 2005. *Anime: From Akira to Howl's Moving Castle: Experiencing contemporary Japanese animation.* 2nd ed. New York: Palgrave.

————. 2007. *From Impressionism to anime: Japanese fantasy and fan culture in the mind of the West.* New York: Palgrave.

Nara, Yoshitomo. 2001. I don't mind, if you forget me, Nara Yoshitomo, edited by A. Taro. Catalog. Yokohama: Tanbunsha.

Nash, Ilana. 2006. *American sweethearts: Teenage girls in twentieth-century popular culture.* Bloomington: Indiana University Press.

Natsume Fusanosuke. 1992. *Tezuka Osamu wa doko ni iru* (Where is Tezuka Osamu?). Tokyo: Chikuma Shobō.

————, ed. 2001. *Manga sekai senryaku* (Manga's world strategy). Tokyo: Shogakukan.

Natsume Fusanosuke and Hosogaya Atsushi, eds. 2001. *Manga:* Short comics from modern Japan. Tokyo: The Japan Foundation.

Nihon Manga Gakkai. 2001. Japan Society for Studies in Cartoon and Comics statement of purpose for foundation, July 2001, at Kyoto Seika Daigaku. Available from http://wwwsoc.nii.ac.jp/jsscc/index.html.

Nimiya Kazuko. 1997. *Adaruto chirudoren to shōjo manga* (Adult children and *shōjo manga*). Tokyo: Kōsaidō Shuppan.

*Non·no.* 1998. *Enjo kōsai suru watashitachi no kimochi wa* (The feelings of those of us who do *enjo kōsai*). *Non·no,* October 20, 176.

Ogasawara, Yuko. 1998. *Office ladies and salaried men: Power, gender, and work in Japanese companies.* Berkley: University of California Press.

Ogi, Fusami. 2003. Female subjectivity and *shōjo* (girls') manga (Japanese comics): *Shōjo* in ladies' comics and young ladies' comics. *Journal of Popular Culture* 36(4): 780–803.

Okada Toshio. 1997. *Tōdai otakugaku kōza* (A chair of otakuology at University of Tokyo). Tokyo: Kodansha.

Ōmori Maki. 1993. Gender and the labor market. *Journal of Japanese Studies* 19(1): 79–103.

Orbaugh, Sharalyn. 2003a. Busty battlin' babes: The evolution of the *shōjo* in the 1990s visual culture. In *Gender and power in the Japanese visual field,* edited by J. S. Mostow, N. Bryson, and M. Graybill. Honolulu: University of Hawai'i Press, 200–228.

————. 2003b. Creativity and constraint in amateur manga production. *U.S.-Japan Women's Journal* 25: 104–124.

Ōtsuka Eiji. 1989a. *Emu no sedai: Bokura to miyazaki-kun* (The M-generation: Young Miyazaki and us). Tokyo: Ōta Shuppan.

————. 1989b. *Shōjo minzokugaku* (*Shōjo* ethnology). Tokyo: Kobunsha.

————. 1991a. "Kawaii" no tanjyō (The birth of cute). In *Shōjo zasshiron* (Theory of *shōjo* magazines), edited by Ōtsuka E. Tokyo: Tokyo Shoseki, 85–102.

————, ed. 1991b. *Shōjo zasshiron* (Theory of *shōjo* magazines). Tokyo: Tokyo Shoseki.

————. 1994. *Sengo manga no hyōgen kūkan* (The representational space of postwar manga). Kyoto: Hōzōkan.

————. 1995. *"Ribon" no furoku to otomechikku no jidai* (*"Ribon" furoku* and the virginesque period). Tokyo: Chikuma Shobō.

————. 1998. *Sekai ni kantaru "otakubunka"* (One of the greatest "*otaku* cultures" in the world). *Voice* (May): 174–183.

Partner, Simon. 1999. *Assembled in Japan: Electrical goods and the making of the Japanese consumer.* Berkley: University of California Press.

Patten, Fred. 2004. *Watching anime, reading manga: 25 years of essays and reviews*. Berkeley: Stone Bridge Press.

Phillips, Susanne. 2008. Characters, themes, and narrative patterns in the manga of Osamu Tezuka. In *Japanese visual culture: Explorations in the world of manga and anime*, edited by M. W. MacWilliams. Armonk, N.Y.: M. E. Sharpe, 68–90.

Pink, Daniel H. 2007. Japan, ink: Inside the manga industrial complex. *Wired*, November.

Pinsent, Pat, and Bridget Knight. 1998. *Teenage girls and their magazines*. London: Roehampton Institute London.

Plath, David W. 1964. *The after hours: Modern Japan and the search for enjoyment*. Berkeley: University of California Press.

Plath, David W., and Samuel Coleman. 1983. *Work and lifecourse in Japan*. Albany: State University of New York Press.

Rand, Erica. 1995. *Barbie's queer accessories*, edited by M. A. Barale, J. Goldberg, M. Moon, and E. Kosofsky Sedgwick. Durham, N.C.: Duke University Press.

Raz, Aviad. 1999. *Riding the black ship: Japan and Tokyo Disneyland*. Cambridge, Mass.: Harvard University Press.

*Ribon*. 2002a. *Mokuji* (Table of contents). May, 484.

———. 2002b. *Ribon manga sukūru 2002* (2002 *Ribon* manga school). April, 473–477.

Roberts, Glenda. 1994. *Staying on the line: Blue-collar women in contemporary Japan*. Honolulu: University of Hawai'i Press.

Robertson, Jennifer. 1998. *Takarazuka: Sexual politics and popular culture in modern Japan*. Berkeley: University of California Press.

Rofel, Lisa. 1994. Yearnings: Televisual love and melodramatic politics. *American Ethnologist* 21(4): 700–722.

Rothenbuhler, Eric, and Mihai Coman, eds. 2005. *Media anthropology*. London: Sage.

Sano Shin'ichi. 2001. *Dare ka "hon" wo korosu noka?* (Who killed the "book"?). Tokyo: Presidentsha.

Sato, Barbara. 2003. *The new Japanese woman: Modernity, media, and women in interwar Japan*. Durham, N.C.: Duke University Press.

Schodt, Frederik L. 1983. *Manga! Manga!: The world of Japanese comics*. Tokyo: Kodansha International Ltd.

———. 1996. *Dreamland Japan: Writings on modern manga*. Berkeley: Stone Bridge Press.

———. 2007. *The Astroboy essays: Osamu Tezuka, Mighty Atom, manga/anime revolution*. Berkeley: Stone Bridge Press.

Scholte, Jan Aart. 2005. *Globalization: A critical introduction*. 2nd ed. New York: Palgrave.

Seaman, Amanda C. 2004. *Bodies of evidence: Women, society, and detective fiction in 1990s Japan*. Honolulu: University of Hawai'i Press.

Shamoon, Deborah. 2004. Office sluts and rebel flowers: The pleasures of Japanese pornographic comics for women. In *Porn studies*, edited by L. Williams. Durham, N.C.: Duke University Press, 77–103.

———. 2008a. Revolutionary romance: *The Rose of Versailles* and the transformation of *shojo manga*. In *Mechademia 2: Networks of desire*, edited by F. Lunning. Minneapolis: University of Minnesota Press, 3–17.

———. 2008b. Situating the *shōjo* in *shōjo manga*: Teenage girls, romance comics, and contemporary Japanese culture. In *Japanese visual culture: Explorations in the world of manga and anime*, edited by M. W. MacWilliams. Armonk, N.Y.: M. E. Sharpe, 137–154.

Shigematsu, Setsu. 1999. Dimensions of desire: Sex, fantasy, and fetish in Japanese comics. In *Themes and issues in Asian cartooning*, edited by J. A. Lent. Bowling Green, Ohio: Bowling Green State University Popular Press, 127–164.

Shimizu Isao. 1991. *Manga no rekishi* (History of manga). Tokyo: Iwanami Shoten.

———. 1999. *Zusetsu manga no rekishi* (An illustrated history of manga). Tokyo: Kawade Shobō.

Shimotsuki Takanaka, ed. 1998. *Tanjō! "Tezuka Osamu": Manga no kamisama wo sodateta bakku guraundo* (Birth! "Tezuka Osamu": The background in which the god of manga was raised). Tokyo: Asahi Sonorama.

Shinmura Izuru. 1998. *Kōjien*. 5th edition. Tokyo: Iwanami Shoten.

Shiokawa, Kanako. 1999. Cute but deadly: Women and violence in Japanese comics. In *Themes and issues in Asian cartooning*, edited by J. A. Lent. Bowling Green, Ohio: Bowling Green State University Popular Press, 93–126.

Shiraishi, Saya S. 1997. Japan's soft power: Doraemon goes overseas. In *Network power: Japan and Asia*, edited by P. J. Katzenstein and T. Shiraishi. Ithaca, N.Y.: Cornell University Press, 234–274.

Shogakukan. 2006. *Kaisha no ayumi* (Our company's path). Available from http://www.shogakukan.co.jp/main/company/#ayumi [cited July 15, 2006].

Shūkan Josei. 1997. Tokyoto ni mo Inkō jōrei—kinkyū joshikōsei sā dōsuru? Zadankai (Ordinance for indecency, even in Tokyo—Emergency, what will high-school girls do? A roundtable discussion). *Shūkan josei*, March 25, 212–216.

Shuppan Nenpō, ed. 1996. *Shuppan shihyō nenpō: 1996-nenban* (Annual indices of publishing: The 1996 edition). Tokyo: Zenkoku Shuppan Kyōkai/ Shuppan Kagaku Kenkyūjo.

———, ed. 2001. *Shuppan shihyō nenpō: 2001-nenban* (Annual indices of publishing: The 2001 edition). Tokyo: Zenkoku Shuppan Kyōkai/Shuppan Kagaku Kenkyūjo.

————, ed. 2005. *Shuppan shihyō nenpō: 2005-nenban* (Annual indices of publishing: The 2005 edition). Tokyo: Zenkoku Shuppan Kyōkai/Shuppan Kagaku Kenkyūjo.

————, ed. 2007. *Shuppan shihyō nenpō: 2007*-nenban (Annual indices of publishing: The 2007 edition). Tokyo: Zenkoku Shuppan Kyōkai/Shuppan Kagaku Kenkyūjo.

Shuppan News Company, ed. 1997. *Shuppan data book* (Publishing data book). Tokyo: Shuppan Nūzusha.

Silverberg, Miriam. 2006. *Erotic grotesque nonsense: The mass culture of Japanese modern times.* Berkeley: University of California Press.

Skov, Lise, and Brian Moeran, eds. 1995. *Women, media and consumption in Japan.* Honolulu: University of Hawai'i Press.

Spielvogel, Laura. 2003. *Working out in Japan: Shaping the female body in Tokyo fitness clubs.* Durham, N.C.: Duke University Press.

Spies, Alwyn. 2003. Pink-ness. *U.S.-Japan Women's Journal* 25: 30–48.

Stevens, Carolyn S. 2008. *Japanese popular music: Culture, authenticity, and power.* New York: Routledge.

Sudō Hiroshi. 1999. Kodansha shōnenbu nitsuite: Kōennhyō (Concerning Kodansha's boys' division). *Nihon shuppanshika* (Japan publishing history materials) 4: 61–81.

Sugiyama Yumiko. 1998. *Mangaka Satonaka Machiko: Konna ikikata ga shitai* (Satonaka Machiko, the manga artist: I want this kind of life). Tokyo: Rironsha.

Takahashi, Mizuki. 2008. Opening the closed world of shōjo manga. In *Japanese visual culture: explorations in the world of manga and anime*, edited by M. W. MacWilliams. Armonk, N.Y.: M. E. Sharpe, 114–146.

Takahashi Yōji and Akiyama Masami, eds. 1986. *Kodomo no shōwashi, Shōwa 10–20* (Shōwa children's history, Shōwa 10–20), *Bessatsu taiyō* (Taiyō supplemental volumes). Tokyo: Heibonsha.

Takahashi Yōji and Yamamoto Akira, eds. 1987. *Kodomo no shōwashi, Shōwa 20–30* (Shōwa children's history, Shōwa 20–30), *Bessatsu taiyō* (Taiyō supplemental volumes). Tokyo: Heibonsha.

Takahashi Yōji and Yonezawa Yoshihiro, eds. 1991a. *Shōjo manga no sekai I, Kodomo no shōwashi, Shōwa 20–37* (The world of girls' manga part I, Shōwa children's history, Shōwa 20–37), *Bessatsu taiyō* (Taiyō supplemental volumes). Tokyo: Heibonsha.

————, eds. 1991b. *Shōjo manga no sekai II, Kodomo no shōwashi, Shōwa 38–64* (The world of girls' manga part II, Shōwa children's history, Shōwa 38–64), *Bessatsu taiyō* (Taiyō supplemental volumes). Tokyo: Heibonsha.

————, eds. 1996a. *Shōnen manga no sekai I, Kodomo no shōwashi, Shōwa*

*20–35* (The world of boys' manga part I, Shōwa children's history, Shōwa 20–35), *Bessatsu taiyō* (Taiyō supplemental volumes). Tokyo: Heibonsha.

————, eds. 1996b. *Shōnen manga no sekai II, Kodomo no shōwashi, Shōwa 35–64* (The world of boys' manga part II, Shōwa children's history, Shōwa 35–64), *Bessatsu taiyō* (Taiyō supplemental volumes). Tokyo: Heibonsha.

————, eds. 1997. *Tezuka Osamu manga taizen, kodomo no shōwashi* (The complete works of Tezuka Osamu, Shōwa children's history). *Bessatsu taiyō* (Taiyō supplemental volumes). Tokyo: Heibonsha.

Takemiya Keiko. 1976–1979. *Kaze to ki no uta* (Poetry of the wind and trees). Tokyo: Shogakukan. [Original edition: *Shūkan shōjo comic.*]

————. 2002. Shōjo manga no henka ni masa ni tachiatta mangaka no tachiba (The viewpoint of a manga artist who witnessed the changes in *shōjo manga*). *Manga kenkyuu* (Manga studies) 1: 126–129.

Tezuka, Osamu. 1953–1956. *Ribon no kishi* (Princess knight). Tokyo: Kodansha. [Original edition: *Shōjo club/Nakayoshi.*]

Thorn, Matt. 2004. Girls and women getting out of hand: The pleasure and politics of Japan's amateur comics community. In *Fanning the flames: Fans and consumer culture in contemporary Japan*, edited by W. Kelly. Albany: State University of New York Press, 169–187.

Tobin, Joseph, ed. 2004. *Pikachu's global adventure: The rise and fall of Pokémon*. Durham, N.C.: Duke University Press.

Toku, Masami. 2005. *Shōjo manga!* Girl power! Girls' comics from Japan. Chico: Flume Press at California State University.

————. 2008. *Shōjo manga!* Girls' comics! A mirror of girls' dreams. In *Mechademia 2: Networks of desire*, edited by F. Lunnin. Minneapolis: University of Minnesota Press, 19–32.

Treat, John Whittier. 1993. Yoshimoto Banana writes home: *Shōjo* culture and the nostalgic subject. *Journal of Japanese Studies* 19(2): 353–387.

————. 1995. Yoshimoto Banana's *Kitchen*, or the cultural logic of Japanese consumerism. In *Women, media and consumption in Japan*, edited by L. Skov and B. Moeran. Honolulu: University of Hawai'i Press, 274–298.

————. 1996a. Yoshimoto Banana writes home: The *shōjo* in Japanese popular culture. In *Contemporary Japan and popular culture*, edited by J. W. Treat. Honolulu: University of Hawai'i Press, 275–308.

————, ed. 1996b. *Contemporary Japan and popular culture*. Honolulu: University of Hawai'i Press.

Tsurumi, Maia. 1997. Gender and girls' comics in Japan. *Bulletin of Concerned Asian Scholars* 29(2): 46–55.

Turner, Terence. 2002. Representation, politics, and cultural imagination in indigenous video: General points and Kayapo examples. In *Media worlds: Anthropology on new terrain*, edited by F. Ginsburg, L. Abu-Lughod, and B. Larkin. Berkeley: University of California Press, 75–89.

Ueda Toshiko. 2001. Conversation over tea at the Yayoi Bijutsukan (Yayoi Art Museum), September 16.

Vardigan, Benj. 2006. Traditional Japanese foods for all occasions. *Shōjo beat,* August, 12.

VIZ Media, LLC. 2005. *Announcing VIZ Media!* Available from http://www .viz.com/news/newsroom/2005/04_vizmedia.php [cited June 25, 2006].

Vogel, Ezra. 1963. *Japan's new middle class: The salary man and his family in a Tokyo suburb.* 2nd ed. Berkeley: University of California Press.

———. 1979. *Japan as number one.* Cambridge, Mass.: Harvard University Press.

Welker, James. 2006. Beautiful, borrowed, and bent: "Boys' love" as girls' love in *shōjo manga. Signs* 31(3): 841–870.

White, Merry. 1993. *The material child: Coming of age in Japan and America.* New York: The Free Press.

Yamada Masahiro. 1999. *Parasaito shinguru no jidai* (The age of parasite singles). Tokyo: Chikuma Shobō.

Yamada Tomoko. 1998. Shuppan shiryō ni miru shōjo manga (A look at girls' manga through publishing materials). Paper read at Shuppan Shiryō Ni Miru Shōjo Manga Ten (A look at girls' manga through publishing materials Exhibition), Kawasaki Public Museum, July–September.

Yano, Christine. 2002. *Tears of longing: Nostalgia and the nation in Japanese popular song.* Cambridge, Mass.: Harvard University Press.

Yokomori Rika. 1999. *Ren'ai wa shōjo manga de osowatta* (I learned love from girls' manga). Tokyo: Shueisha.

Yonezawa Yoshihiro, ed. 1980. *Sengo shōjo mangashi* (A postwar history of *shōjo manga*). Tokyo: Shinbyosha.

———. 2002. Personal interview, June 28, Tokyo.

# INDEX

Page numbers in *boldface italic* refer to illustrations.

## About the Author

Jennifer Prough received her Ph.D. in Cultural Anthropology from Duke University and is assistant professor of Humanities and East Asian Studies at Christ College at Valparaiso University. This is her first book.